Melancholy Politics

JEAN-PHILIPPE MATHY

Melancholy Politics

*Loss, Mourning, and Memory
in Late Modern France*

THE PENNSYLVANIA STATE UNIVERSITY PRESS
UNIVERSITY PARK, PENNSYLVANIA

Library of Congress Cataloging-in-Publication Data
Mathy, Jean-Philippe.
Melancholy politics : loss, mourning, and memory in late modern France / Jean-Philippe Mathy.
p. cm.
Summary: "A study of the cultural politics of loss and mourning in France from 1978 to the present. Focuses on national identity, secularism, Jacobin republicanism, and political-cultural exceptionalism"—Provided by publisher.
Includes bibliographical references and index.
ISBN 978-0-271-03783-7 (cloth : alk. paper)
ISBN 978-0-271-03784-4 (pbk : alk. paper)
1. France—Politics and government—1958– .
2. Politics and culture—France.
3. Loss (Psychology)—Political aspects—France.
4. Grief—Political aspects—France.
5. Collective memory—Political aspects—France.
6. Nationalism—France.
7. Secularism—France.
8. Republicanism—France.
9. Jacobins—France.
10. Exceptionalism—France.
I. Title.

DC417.M387   2011
306.20944—dc22
2010039065

Copyright © 2011
The Pennsylvania State University
All rights reserved
Printed in the United States of America
Published by The Pennsylvania State University Press,
University Park, PA 16802-1003

The Pennsylvania State University Press is a member of the Association of American University Presses.

It is the policy of The Pennsylvania State University Press to use acid-free paper. Publications on uncoated stock satisfy the minimum requirements of American National Standard for Information Sciences—Permanence of Paper for Printed Library Material, ANSI Z39.48-1992.

For my parents

Contents

ACKNOWLEDGMENTS ix

Introduction: Loss, Mourning, Memory 1

1
Specters of the Sixties 21

2
French Postmodern 49

3
Le Débat, Year One: The Generation of 1980 71

4
The Return of the Prophet: Bourdieu, Zola, and the Dreyfusist Legacy 96

5
Desperately Seeking Marianne: The Uses of the Republic 127

6
Memory Wars 143

7
Old Wine, New Skins: Race, *Laïcité,* Frenchness 180

Conclusion 216

BIBLIOGRAPHY 227

INDEX 235

Acknowledgments

Several colleagues gave me an opportunity to share some of the views expressed in this book in written and oral form, whether in journals, colloquia, conference panels, or invited lectures. Special thanks to Gilles Bousquet, Roger Célestin, Kimberlé Crenshaw, Eliane DalMolin, Joe Golsan, Luke Harris, Leah Hewitt, Marie-Pierre Le Hir, and Larry Schehr.

The following journals and publications have kindly granted me permission to use earlier, shorter versions of some of the chapters in this book: *Contemporary French and Francophone Studies*, *Contemporary French Civilization*, *Journal of European Studies*, *L'Esprit Créateur*, and the Occasional Paper Series of the Department of Modern and Classical Languages, Texas A&M University.

INTRODUCTION
Loss, Mourning, Melancholy

In his study of nationalism in Renaissance England, Andrew Escobedo remarks on the sense of belatedness that comes with the emergence of national consciousness. Moments of significant historical change generate an ambiguous, tense relation to the past. On the one hand, there is the pride of the path-breakers as they stand on the threshold of a new era, a sense of accomplishment that comes from the making of new laws, the testing of new beliefs, the invention of a bright future, emancipation from the fetters of tradition. On the other hand, we have the fear of the unknown and the guilt born of the painful break with the world of the fathers. Examples abound in western European history alone: 1688 in England, 1789 in France, 1871 in Germany. The birth of a new social and cultural order leads to estrangement from history, the sense of an unbridgeable gap between past and present. The trauma of revolution—after the exhilaration stemming from the destruction of the old order and the immediate redress of the most glaring injustices and inequities—leaves many with a feeling of emptiness, a mood of bereavement and mourning, a painful yearning for the good old days of cultural certainty. Here lies the source of all restorations, of the reactive affect and tone of all romanticisms. "English nationhood in the Renaissance," Escobedo writes, "was linked to a perception of historical loss, the sense that the past was incommensurate with and possibly lost to the present."[1] The

---

1. Escobedo, *Nationalism*, 3.

rhetoric of rebirth was a compensation for a missing history, never to be recovered.

This book argues that contemporary France in some ways resembles the sixteenth-century England evoked by Escobedo. In both cases the unsettling novelty of the times and the acceleration of history led to various, and often contradictory, attempts to come to terms with the passing of what once was a fairly stable, meaningful cultural formation. But the British in the days of Spenser and Milton saw their nation, and the cultural agenda that came with it, as lying *ahead* of them, while to many French people today the national grandeur has been left behind. Those who have been mourning the demise of la République, of socialism, and of the great legacy of the Enlightenment often view themselves, in the words of Nietzsche describing his German contemporaries, as latecomers, "faded last shoots of mighty and cheerful generations, to whom Hesiod's prophecy applies that men would one day be born with grey hair."[2] The break with Catholicism forced the English to reconcile their past to their present; the advent of postmodernity, or late modernity, or hypermodernity, has the French desperately trying to reconcile their present to a fast disappearing past.

This mood of disenchantment and loss is not peculiar to the French, of course; it pervades all western European democracies, affecting the elites and ordinary citizens alike, fueling the return of tribal identities, traditionalisms, and fundamentalisms and turning the practice of bittersweet commemoration into an ever-growing industry. The haunting, powerful figure of Walter Benjamin's "angel of history" is the obligatory reference, it seems, of many studies of the national sentiment in a transnational age. The angel's face, like that of many of our contemporaries, is turned backward. The angel "would like to stay," Benjamin writes, "awaken the dead, and make whole what has been smashed." But the "storm . . . from Paradise," "piling wreckage upon wreckage" and hurling it at the angel's feet, "irresistibly propels him into the future to which his back is turned, while the pile of debris before him grows skyward. This storm is what we call progress."[3]

If anything, the storm has been blowing stronger, and the refuse of history piling higher, since Benjamin's days. Strewn all over the European landscape are torn-off bits and pieces from what were once established, respected, self-assured, and freestanding nations, welfare states, colonial empires, parliaments, churches, public schools, family structures, sexual mores and taboos,

---

2. Nietzsche, *On the Advantage and Disadvantage of History for Life*, cited in Escobedo, *Nationalism*, 2.

3. Benjamin, *Illuminations*, 257–58.

philosophical canons, principles of aesthetic valuation, revolutionary creeds, redistributive economies, and foundationalist regimes of truth. The chapters collected in this volume forage through what is left standing in the wake of the hurricane of progress as it has ripped through French society and culture over the past thirty years. No wonder the current mood in France (but, again, this is true of other countries as well) has been described as one of *déclinisme* or *sinistrose*, pessimism about the future and a sinister sense of an irreversible decline unfolding in the present.

Pierre Bourdieu once remarked that "literary history well shows how very often what is common to the intellectual life of an era is not the content of books but rather their titles."[4] In 1990, Pascal Bruckner, one of the most visible of France's public intellectuals, wrote an influential book called *La mélancolie démocratique* (Democratic melancholia), in which he argued that the end of the cold war had deprived France of an enemy, thereby weakening national identity; in his view, conflict opens up a future, fosters a sense of cohesion, and gives both individual and collective life its meaning.[5] More recently, best sellers bearing titles such as *La France qui tombe: Un constat clinique du déclin français* (France in free fall: A clinical assessment of the French decline, 2003) and *Adieu à la France qui s'en va* (Farewell to a France gone by, 2005) leave no doubt as to some of the most pervasive trends in the current French life of the mind. The first book is a devastating survey of the country's economic woes by a leading economist. The second text is a collection of nostalgic vignettes in which the celebrated novelist, and member of the Académie française, Jean-Marie Rouart looks back at the intimate connections between his own past and that of his country; he evokes the latter's glorious cultural and military history while he spends a lot of time, it seems, attending funerals, visiting cemeteries, and reminiscing about lost loves and friendships.

Even the economic elites, presumably upbeat and forward-looking, and invigorated not so long ago by the triumph of the market economy over the sins and illusions of socialism, are giving in to a kind of historical-philosophical pessimism. The major French business organization, the MEDEF (Mouvement des entreprises de France, or Movement of the French Enterprises) organized in August 2005 a symposium called "The Re-enchantment of the World." Managers, politicians, intellectuals, and leaders of civic associations debated "a society in quest of meaning" in panels with such titles as "Nostalgia, Fears, and Chimeras: Has Our Imagination Grown Narrower" and "Has

4. Bourdieu, *Political Interventions*, 51.
5. Bruckner, *La mélancolie démocratique*.

France Dropped the Ball?" Although it is quite ironic to see the practitioners of global capitalism deplore, with a reference to Max Weber, the erosion of ideals and values that the fall of the Berlin Wall was supposed to have revived all over the world, one can appreciate the extent to which the eclipse of politics and the uncertainty of the future has affected a large part of the ruling elites as well. The recent collapse of the financial markets worldwide and the ensuing economic crisis are not likely to reverse this trend.

The mood of the 2005 colloquium was encapsulated in the following questions, proposed as a framework for a discussion on "Overcoming Despair": "Are the French morose? If one is to believe the observers of French society, our country is going through a serious crisis of confidence, marked by the hopelessness of a large part of the population, a fear of the future, and an anxiety in the face of the immediate present. If so, what can we do? Such is the question asked every day by social entrepreneurs, associations, and even some industry representatives." The various participants in the panel painted a bleak picture of a "situation that has become unbearable," with "legions of excluded individuals," "unfortunately untapped potentials," and the absence of "diversity in the various social bodies." Azouz Begag, then minister for the promotion and equality of opportunity, and himself the son of illiterate immigrants from North Africa, drew up the now familiar list of all the ailments of French society: "Insecurity, acts of racism, bankruptcies, poverty, unemployment fill media reports and daily accentuate the somber views the French have of their situation. . . . Because so many French people today feel excluded and do not see any future for themselves, the whole of society must react and reinvent itself to prevent the rise of hopelessness and its consequences."[6]

Both the national conversation and academic historiography are related responses to a heightened sense of social and cultural disruption. It is as true today as it was five centuries ago, when European modernity emerged from the ruins of the feudal order. In the words of Andrew Escobedo, "Nations have often emerged as figures of mediation between a community's need for historical origins and its anticipations of social change" (15). Because the nation creates representations that in turn help further create the nation, the writing of history plays a similar role in mediating between the duty to remember and the need to forget. The tense relation between these two terms is, as Ernest Renan pointed out over a century ago, central to the

---

6. A summary of the panels can be found on the MEDEF website, http://archive.medef.com/main/core.php?pag_id=39112.

invention of national narratives. Michel de Certeau highlighted the paradoxical combination of loss and recovery that complicates all fundamentalist attempts to (re)invent a tradition by (re)writing a history. This is quite obvious in contemporary culture, obsessed as it is with the threat of amnesia and the necessary cultivation of "sites of memory." For de Certeau, "The 'return to origins' always states the contrary of what it believes, at least in the sense that it presupposes a *distancing* in respect to a past . . . and a will to *recover* what, in one fashion or another, seems lost in a received language. In this way, 'the return to origins' is always a modernism as well."[7]

The writing of history is a way of salvaging the relics of the dead, those pieces of the deceased person's body that stand for the whole and participate, in the words of Eric Toubiana, "in the illusion of [that person's] presence despite the acknowledgment of her absence."[8] The nation as fetish is a compromise formation between the denial of absence and its inescapable recognition. Moreover, the conversation of historians, professional or amateur, over time is very much like a collective wake: everyone has something to say about the dead, and "as the narratives go on, death seems to be denied and the person of the deceased takes shape again."[9] This paradoxical attempt to represent an absence, to recoup one's losses and fill out a body with words, echoes de Certeau's meditation on the historian's enterprise: "It is an odd procedure that posits death, a breakage everywhere reiterated in discourse, and that yet denies loss by appropriating to the present the privilege of recapitulating the past as a form of knowledge" (5). Historical discourse, then, is "incessantly articulated over the death that it presupposes, but that the very practice of history contradicts. For to speak of the dead means to deny death and almost to defy it. Therefore speech is said to 'resuscitate' them. Here the word is literally a lure: history does not resuscitate anything" (47).

As we shall see, the nation as fetishistic relic suffuses contemporary French discourse: multiple processes of identification crystallize around the idea, since it is through the appropriation or incorporation of an object, attribute, or property belonging to the dead (whether individual or collective, real or imaginary, personal or national) that a subject attempts to deal with what no longer exists. Andrew Escobedo identifies the three main strategies of English national writers as they confronted the disappearance, or at least recession, of their immediate past in the wake of the Reformation: "(1) they must link

---

7. De Certeau, Writing, 136.
8. Toubiana, L'héritage et sa psychopathologie, 126. Unless otherwise cited, the translations from French texts are my own.
9. Ibid., 115.

the past to the present; (2) they must lament the gap between past and present; (3) they must forget the (alien) past to make sure it does not infect the present" (9).

In many ways, mutatis mutandis, the participants in the French debates discussed in this book have drawn similar conclusions from their predicament. The first task, traditionally left to the historical profession, has of late been taken over by activists who—dissatisfied with the distanced gaze of the academic professionals and the interested, consensus-seeking rhetoric of the politicians—have sought to collapse the past into the present, or to infuse the present with the passions of the past, as in the paradigmatic case of the controversies surrounding Vichy France (see chap. 6). More generally, the current obsession for museums, commemorations, and historical narratives, learned or popular, is a glaring testimony to the power of the first imperative, that of linking the past to the present. The national-republican, *souverainiste* camp has resisted change and taken the path of nostalgia, lamenting the passing of the glorious days of the early Third Republic and of the Gaullist era, while urging the citizenry to ignore the fateful sirens of neoliberalism. Finally, postmodernists and multiculturalists opted for active forgetting and the joyful smashing of idols. They have welcomed the storm of history and the new France it carried in its wake, and rejoiced in the iconoclastic project to "mourn all the refusals to mourn," as Eric Santner has put it.[10]

In his *Mourning and Modernity*, Isaac Balbus deplores that the current political choice seems to be between obliterating the past and idealizing it. Liberal postmodernists want to move past the "archaic" project of socialism, laden as it is with remnants of nineteenth-century statism and positivism, while nationalists yearn to resurrect the golden days of an imagined organic community, each position reinforcing the other, locking the present in an endless, nightmarish cycle of violence and counterviolence. "At unspeakable cost," Balbus writes, "we have finally learned that the modernist murder of the past only feeds the fundamentalist fantasy of resurrecting it." Balbus sees the need to "counter the modern assault on memory without mobilizing the noxious weapons of nostalgia" as "one of the central political tasks of our time" (71).

Many of the texts discussed in the following chapters were attempts to come to terms with the passing of an old France and the dawn of a new one, and with the need for the citizens of a reconfigured polity to find new descriptions of emerging practices, feelings, and expectations that no longer fit with previous imaginings of the nation. But the consensus over the diagnosis of what ailed the country does not translate into a commonality of views

---

10. Santner, *Stranded Objects*, 9.

as to what constitutes the best possible cure for the disease. Loss implies recovery, but the term itself is highly ambiguous: to recover means both to retrieve and to heal, and the semantic hesitation points to the heart of the work of mourning, which, as Melanie Klein argued, involves both anamnesis and integration. The word "remembrance," of course, shares a similar equivocity. To re-member is to recall the past *and* to put together again (to recollect) what has been violently disrupted by the storm of history.

Within today's debate over the future of late modernity, there are pessimists and optimists, iconoclastic postmodernists and reactive fundamentalists, as well as people inhabiting various niches within the vast space in between. Was the advent of a "cool," individualistic, consumerist, antiauthoritarian society in the years following May '68 worth the jettisoning—sometimes willed, sometimes forced—of so many elements of the modernist project, from republican secularism and the steadfast cultivation of a public sphere to aesthetic distinction and the once enduring faith in a socialist revolution? The events, texts, and intellectual figures examined in this study, as far as they reflect or illustrate the various ideological positions that make up the field of French public debates on the contemporary, all constitute significant attempts to answer this very question.

Writing in the thick of the postmodernism dispute, some twenty years ago, Eric Santner documented in his book *Stranded Objects* the "rhetoric of mourning which has come to occupy the semantic field of so much critical theory in recent years, . . . the recurrence, in so many postmodern discourses, of a metaphorics of loss and impoverishment" (7). Both deconstruction and Lacanian psychoanalysis insisted on the elegiac nature of all symbolic processes. The linguistic predicament in post-structuralist theory is such that the speaking subject is, as Santner put it, "perpetually in mourning: for the referent, for beauty, for meaning, for home, for stable terms of orientation, because these losses are always already there as soon as one uses languages" (15). The postmodernist stance has been to exult amid this bereavement, to turn the "symbolic castration" performed by the play of the signifier into a source of jouissance. In this view, the constitutive dispossession and the deep narcissistic wound that lie at the core of human subjectivity must be affirmed rather than deplored. The relentless, radical critique of all forms of nostalgia that underscores these interpretive strategies is ultimately of a political nature, since all forms of fascism, authoritarian nationalism, and patriarchal fundamentalism are seen as inherently regressive and narcissistic.[11]

11. In the words of Alice Jardine, referring to the American context, "Our epoch of impossibility . . . is an epoch of extreme difficulty, a configuration of knowledge which causes some to long for the good ol' days when art was art, politics was politics, men were men, women were women,

Jean-François Lyotard, echoing Freud's well-known essay on "Mourning and Melancholia," once claimed that his contemporaries failed to accomplish the necessary process of working through the abominations of their century: fascism, Stalinism, colonialism, and imperialism. As a result, they remained trapped within the nets of depression, the psychic price to be paid for the denial of a traumatic past that is part and parcel of what the philosopher calls the modern project. "Under the pretense of safeguarding that project," Lyotard argued, "the men and women of my generation in Germany imposed on their children a forty-year silence about the 'Nazi interlude.' This interdiction against anamnesis stands as a symbol for the entire Western world. Can there be progress without anamnesis? Anamnesis constitutes a painful process of working through, a work of mourning for the attachments and conflicting emotions, loves and terrors, associated with those names. . . . We have only gotten as far as a vague, apparently inexplicable, end-of-century melancholy."[12]

Lyotard's remarks suggest that if depression is the result of an inability to bury the dead a second time through successful mourning, late modern subjects have a duty to remember, lest they fall prey to the politically dangerous spectral spell of the deceased's absence, followed by the desperate attempt to become one with the lost object of collective identification. In *Memory, History, Forgetting*, Paul Ricoeur also underscored the dialectics of remembrance and bereavement, and the difference between mourning and melancholia:

> But why then is mourning not melancholia? And what is it that makes mourning tend toward melancholia? What makes morning a normal, albeit painful, phenomenon is that [according to Freud] "when the work of mourning is completed the ego becomes free and uninhibited again." . . . It is as a work of remembering that the work of mourning proves to be liberating, although at a certain cost, and . . . this relation is reciprocal. The work of mourning is the cost of the work of remembering, but the work of remembering is the benefit of the work of mourning. (72)

Freud's essay identified two major ways of dealing with the loss of the loved object. The successful *Trauerarbeit*, or work of mourning, implies a

---

and Americans were Real Americans. . . . These individuals opt for the 'nostos,' the desire to return, and a general climate of nostalgia prevails for them within a larger postmodern logic of simulation." Introductory remarks in *Copyright* (Fall 1987), cited in Santner, *Stranded Objects*, 165n14.

12. Lyotard, "Ticket to a New Decor," cited in Santner, *Stranded Objects*, 8.

painful, sometimes prolonged process of libidinal disinvestment from the lost object, which can be "a loved person or . . . some abstraction which has taken the place of one, such as one's country, liberty, an ideal, and so on."[13] The reality principle commands the whole development, since the final overcoming of grief alone signals the successful completion of the *Trauerarbeit*. In Freud's own words,

> Reality-testing has shown that the loved object no longer exists, and it proceeds to demand that all libido shall be withdrawn from its attachments to that object. . . . Normally, respect for reality gains the day. Nevertheless, its orders cannot be obeyed at once. They are carried out bit by bit, at great expense of time and cathectic energy, and in the meantime the existence of the lost object is psychically prolonged. Each single one of the memories and expectations in which the libido is bound to the object is brought up and hyper-cathected, and detachment of the libido is accomplished in respect of it. (244–45)

Should the test of reality fail to carry the day, however, and the psyche prove unable to free itself from the prolonged existence of the lost object, a dysfunctional process, described by Freud as melancholia, starts to take place. Immersed in an interminable labor of mourning, the melancholic subject is unable to "get over" her loss; she cannot "move on" with her life and let go of the deceased in order to invest in the new. It is as though, as Freud put it, "the shadow of the object has fallen upon the ego." Because of a strong narcissistic identification with the lost object, the ego is no longer grieving another, but rather a vital part of itself: "In mourning it is the world which has become poor and empty, in melancholia it is the ego itself" (246).

Freud legitimized the transfer of individual categories of interpretation to the sociocultural analysis of collective, intersubjective behaviors when he suggested that ideological objects ("metaphysical abstractions" such as one's country, liberty, or other ideals) could be substituted for a loved person in the process of grieving. Following his lead regarding the work of mourning, many interpretations of the contemporary have applied the dynamics of dealing with loss from individual pathology to historical condition.

Adrian Stokes and Hannah Segal, for example, have used Melanie Klein's views on object relations and manic-depressive states to propose an aesthetic theory that likens artistic creation to a successful act of mourning, implying

---

13. Freud, "Mourning and Melancholia," 243.

destruction, loss, and restoration.[14] Frankfurt School theorists, especially Herbert Marcuse, relied on Freudian categories to explore the cultural consequences of the deployment of the dialectics of instrumental reason, and Slavoj Žižek's influence on contemporary theory is based on his application of Lacanian notions to the study of political ideology and popular culture. In the same vein, Julia Kristeva spoke a decade ago of a French "national depression" brought about by "migratory flows," an acute sense of the decline of the country's influence in the world, and "social distress" caused by unemployment, humiliation at work, poverty, and the lack of "ideals and perspectives": "In addition to individuals, France is living today through a national depression, similar to that of private persons. . . . The country does not react in any other way than a depressed patient."[15]

One way of complicating the contemporary politics of loss is to distinguish between the two separate modalities of the melancholic and the nostalgic. The latter, as Charity Scribner has remarked, "refuses to kill the lost object; he steels himself against the work of mourning."[16] Unreconstructed Stalinists in the former East Germany or national-republicans in France today provide examples of such a strategy. "The nostalgic's refusal of mourning," Scribner goes on, "metastasizes into funerary excess and artifice. If the nostalgic affixes himself to the object's loss, then the melancholic, in contradistinction, focuses on the lack that always inhered in the primordial lost object" (308). Scribner refers to Lacan's "objet petit a," which "is not simply the lost object, but rather one that comes into being only through its loss, that is to say, an object that merely gives body to the loss" (318n20). In this Lacanian reading, the melancholic has "got it right" concerning the fundamental structure of the human subject, forever deprived by the advent of the Symbolic of a symbiotic union with the Real, while the nostalgic is deluded into thinking that he ever possessed anything. In Scribner's words, "The nostalgic confounds loss and lack: he interprets the original lack as the loss of something that he previously possessed" (308).

In *Black Sun*, her study of clinical and literary depression, Julia Kristeva relied both on Kant and Freud to describe nostalgia less as a relation to a lost object than as a fixation on a *temps perdu*, an absent past in dire need of quest and recovery. According to Kristeva, "Concerning the specific variant of depression constituted by nostalgia, Kant asserted that nostalgic persons did

---

14. See Alford, *Melanie Klein*, chap. 4.
15. Kristeva, *Dépression nationale*, 67.
16. Scribner, "Left Melancholy," 308. On the distinction between the melancholic and the nostalgic, see also Balbure, "La mélancolie."

not desire the place of their youth but their youth itself; their desire is a search for the *time* and not for the *thing* to be recovered" (60). Similarly, the psychic object for Freud is "a memory event, it belongs to lost time, in the manner of Proust. It is a subjective construct, located not within a physical space but within the imaginary and symbolic space of the psychic system" (61). This suggests that the ideal institutional and cultural regime eulogized by *les nostalgiques de la République*, who have defined a good part of the discursive space within which current ideological debates have been deployed for the past three decades, is a psychic object reconstructed from memory that exists not in *the* past, but in *their* past—that is, in their youth, the golden age of the immediate postwar period, before everything went to pot in the sixties and seventies.

The use of Freudian, Kleinian, or Lacanian approaches to explore intersubjective dynamics of mourning is not limited to French literary theory or Anglo-American cultural studies. The recent historiography on the politics of commemoration, in addition to reviving Maurice Halbwachs's notion of collective memory, has often couched, so to speak, its interpretations in psychological and psychoanalytical language. Henri Rousso, for example, used a Freudian vocabulary to describe the existence of what he famously named the "Vichy syndrome" in French contemporary culture.[17] The historian's periodization of the contested memory of the Pétain regime during the postwar years is clearly inspired by psychoanalysis. In Rousso's narrative, the initial "unfinished mourning phase" (1944–54) is followed by a "repressive stage" (1954–71), the short period of the "return of the repressed" (1971–74), and finally, an acute "obsessive" stage marked by the "awakening of Jewish memory" after 1974. "Rather like the unconscious in Freudian theory," Rousso writes, "what is known as collective memory exists first of all in its *manifestations*, in the various ways by which it reveals its presence. The Vichy syndrome consists of a diverse set of symptoms whereby the trauma of the Occupation, and particularly the trauma resulting from internal divisions within France, reveals itself in political, social, and cultural life. Since the end of the war, moreover, that trauma has been perpetuated and at times exacerbated" (10).

Although he was careful to caution his readers (and his fellow historians) that "what is borrowed from psychoanalysis is simply a metaphor, not an explanatory schema" (23), Rousso was roundly chastised for his uncontrolled use of Freudian concepts outside their original field of applicability. He nevertheless defended his interpretive framework in the foreword of the second

17. Rousso, *Vichy Syndrome*.

French edition of his book, claiming that words such as repression, mourning, forgetting, and trauma had now acquired a common meaning independent of their original association with clinical psychiatry.[18] "I do not repudiate in any way this interpretative grid," he persisted, "however empirical it might be" (24). Undeterred, Rousso persisted in using Freudian "metaphors" to make sense of cultural-political developments in the book's sequel, cowritten with Eric Conan.[19] Remarking on the evolution of the Vichy syndrome since the late 1980s, the authors remained squarely within a psychological register. They uncovered "the phony taboos and historical fantasies" (11) involved in the duty to remember at all costs, explored how "the present obsession is being fed by a two-fold feeling of guilt" (3), and diagnosed "a denial of the legitimacy of the 'right to forget,'" and its "paralytic effects" on politicians who "have gotten caught up with slips of the tongue" (5).

The methodological questions raised by Rousso's books prompted Paul Ricoeur to wonder whether the transposition of psychological categories from the individual to the collective was legitimate.[20] As explored in *Memory, History, Forgetting*, Ricoeur found ample justification for such an interpretive move both in Freud's own work and in what he called the phenomenology of wounded memory. Freud himself did not hesitate to extrapolate beyond the original scene of psychoanalytic treatment to considerations on culture, the psychosocial order, and historical situations in *Totem and Taboo*, *Moses and Monotheism*, *The Future of an Illusion*, and *Civilization and Its Discontents*. For Ricoeur, the pathological situations psychoanalysis is concerned with can be found in the traumas of collective identity, even "in the absence of recognized therapists in interhuman relations." "The notion of the lost object," he goes on, "finds a direct application in the 'losses' that affect the power, territory, and populations that constitute the substance of a state" (78). Going beyond Rousso's prudent use of psychological labels as "metaphors," Ricoeur argued that "we can speak not only in an analogical sense but in terms of a direct analysis of collective traumatisms, of wounds to collective memory." The great funeral celebrations where an entire nation is assembled "constitute a privileged example of the intersecting relations between private and public expression. It is in this way that our concept of a sick historical memory finds justification a posteriori in this bipolar [i.e., personal and communal] structure

---

18. Rousso, *Le syndrome de Vichy*.
19. Conan and Rousso, *Vichy*.
20. For a discussion of the legitimate use of psychoanalytical concepts derived from the analysis of individual fantasies for the interpretation of collective practices, see Stavrakakis, *Lacan and the Political*, 1–9; and Alford, *Melanie Klein*, 1–22.

of mourning behaviors" (78–79). The public space of collective debate becomes the equivalent of the intermediary domain between the therapist and the analysand in the individual setting of the cure.

National contexts produce specific manifestations of the collective management of a traumatic past. The Vichy trials and their impact on the public conversation in France are reminiscent of the German situation examined by Santner in *Stranded Objects*, from Alexander and Margarete Mitscherlich's "inability to mourn" thesis to the related *Historikerstreit* (historians' debate) over the revisionist interpretations of the Third Reich. In contrast, France and Britain differ markedly in the way they have been dealing with the shadows of the past, as Perry Anderson pointed out in a recent essay. On the one hand, Britain's world-historical decline since the war has been a drawn-out process: "Little alteration of political arrangements; moderate growth but still low productivity, pinched universities and crumbling railways, . . . an underling diplomacy. The British way of coming down in the world might itself be termed a mediocre affair."[21] France, on the other hand, has told quite another story, in large part because of the political and cultural brilliance of the country during the Gaullist era: "The arrival of the Fifth Republic coincided with the full flowering of the intellectual energies that set France apart for two generations after the war" (5).

This blooming of the French mind (from "theory" and experimental literature to cinema and historiography), coupled with assertive, principled Gaullist foreign policy, enabled the country to regain an enviable position in the world. This underscores, by contrast, the depression of the current scene, where, according to Anderson, "*le déclinisme* burst into full flow with the publication of *La France qui tombe*, a spirited denunciation of national default" (3). France's reckoning with its own cultural-historical diminution since 1980 has led, on the one hand, to a "working through" of the legacies of an unpalatable past and, on the other hand, to the cultivation of interminable grief reflected in the current mood of resigned despondency among many in the cultural elites, especially on the Left.

21. Anderson, "Dégringolade," 3. A French version of Anderson's essay, "La pensée tiède" (Lukewarm thought), appeared in the spring of 2005, with a response by Pierre Nora titled "La pensée réchauffée" (Warmed-over thought). Anderson's book caused quite a stir in French intellectual circles. His position is symptomatic of the Anglo-American Left's lament that France, the former purveyor of both theoretical and practical examples of revolutionary politics (as distinct from the congenital consensual liberalism of the United States and the United Kingdom), has now betrayed its critical tradition, leaving the world deprived of one of its most progressive laboratories of ideas.

Anderson deplored the passing of the great French revolutionary tradition, repeating the metaphor of the fall: "The feeling is widespread that the Fifth Republic, as it approaches its half-century, presents a fallen landscape" (6). Thereafter follows a long list of the devastations wrought on the Republic by Benjamin's storm of history: an ailing economy, crawling forward at 1 percent a year through the 1990s; unemployment at 9 percent (two-fifths of black and Arab youths are unemployed); one of the lowlier rates of reading in the Organisation for Economic Co-operation and Development; a political system riddled with corruption and increasingly held in public contempt; a foreign policy reduced to "a mottled parody of Gaullism"; and, last but not least, a widespread tumble in cultural matters (6). Death has picked off all the great names of France's sixties Renaissance, from Barthes in 1980 to Derrida in 2004, leaving the field wide open for Bernard-Henri Lévy, whom Anderson summarily dismisses as the "crass booby of France's public sphere," to step forward as the country's leading public intellectual in the eyes of the world (7).

The figures and moments in recent French intellectual and cultural history discussed in the following chapters all address, in various and conflicting ways, the predicament of the democratic individual, deprived of the ideological certainties of yesteryear and condemned to face the anxieties of an open-ended, undetermined historical condition. In the spirit of this dramatic change in contemporary societies' relationship to historical teleology, the periods corresponding to each chapter should not be taken simply as uniquely defining moments, pivotal points in a one-directional chronological development, but also as symptomatic events, signs of effects rather than temporal markers of sequential causality. Each of these moments (March 19, 1978 for chap. 2, April 1980 for chap. 3, July 14, 1989 for chap. 6, December 1995 for chap. 4, April 21, 2002 for chap. 5, and March 2004 and September–October 2005 for chap. 7), are not turning points or starting points, but crystallization points of processes that overlap and intersect one another, contributions to the story of this "new France" that is perplexing so many domestic and foreign observers today. As illustrated in Anderson's own nostalgic account, the birth pangs of the new France include the cooling of revolutionary passions, the displacement of politics by humanitarian rhetoric, the painful, nostalgic rapport to an increasingly distant cultural eminence, and the growing inability of the republican framework to address the challenges of social exclusion, economic marginalization, and racial discrimination.

Chapter 1 starts with a retrospective survey of the commemoration of May '68 in the media in 1978, 1988, and 1998, and ends with a reading of

Jacques Derrida's *Specters of Marx*, providing various angles from which to approach the fate of the revolutionary imagination in "post-political" France. Chapter 2 looks at the failure of the Socialist-Communist coalition to come to power in March 1978 as an illustration of what Marcel Gauchet later called the eclipse of the political, and provides an opportunity to reevaluate the French postmodern debate (launched the following year by the publication of Jean-François Lyotard's *The Postmodern Condition*).[22]

Chapter 3 is a close reading of the first three issues of the influential journal *Le Débat*, which was an attempt to set a new intellectual agenda for the postrevolutionary era. The publication of the first issue in April 1980 coincided with Sartre's death, and both events were markers of a significant shift in French cultural politics. Under the leadership of the historians Pierre Nora and Marcel Gauchet, the new publication, soon to be a must-read among the intelligentsia, proved to be extremely successful in establishing the preeminence of the social sciences over literature and philosophy, opening French academic interests to the rest of the world, and ushering in a new generation of scholars and public intellectuals. These newcomers, born during the decade following World War II, and whose coming of age had coincided with the turbulent late sixties and early seventies, would transform the ideological landscape of the country, replacing Marxism and structuralism with a pluralistic, more pragmatic conception of the role of cultural producers in a liberal-democratic environment. The original enthusiasm generated by what was perceived by many as the end of theory-driven dogmatism soon gave way to disenchantment with the excesses of liberal individualism, as initial hopes in the return of participatory democracy and the "modernization" of French political culture failed to materialize.

Chapter 4 places Pierre Bourdieu's political evolution in the last decade of his life in the context of the strikes of December 1995, the most extensive social movement in France since May 1968. I suggest that the usual comparison between Sartre and Bourdieu as the latest avatar of the traditional figure of the committed intellectual misses the mark. In his defense against the threat of neoliberal globalization—of what he called a civilization "associated with the existence of a public service, the civilization of republican equality of rights, rights to education, to health, culture, research, art, and, above all, work"—Bourdieu was much closer to Zola than to Sartre.[23] The evolution of Bourdieu's conception of the state, from the institutional site of the reproduction of economic and cultural inequality to the guarantor of collective

---

22. On the notion of the eclipse of the political, see Gauchet, *Condition historique*.
23. Bourdieu, *Acts of Resistance*, 24.

social rights, paralleled the sociologist's growing concern with safeguarding the best of the republican tradition as the last line of defense against free-market ideologies. Both his militant and journalistic interventions and the theoretical texts of the 1990s showed his unwillingness to jettison Enlightenment models of commitment and rationality while refusing to embrace the narrow nationalism of the neo-Jacobins. In his later years, Bourdieu attempted to recover the threatened legacy of both the Third Republic, illustrated by Zola's struggle for justice and democracy, and the Fourth Republic, during which the main tenets of the Conseil national de la Résistance's program became reality, laying the groundwork for what Bourdieu saw as a "civilization" associated with the social state. The institutionalization of the postwar welfare state and the figure of the public intellectual speaking truth to power were associated in Bourdieu's writing as an expression of what would be lost with the triumph of neoliberalism.

Chapter 5 centers on one of the most traumatic moments in recent French political history, the presidential election of April 2002. During the first run of the election, Jean-Marie Le Pen, the nationalist and xenophobic candidate, edged the Socialist candidate, Lionel Jospin, for second place behind Jacques Chirac, the incumbent. Chirac eventually won with 80 percent of the vote, as the Left had no choice but to support "a crook rather than a fascist." The two-week period between the first and second runs of the election saw a flourishing of references to the national "republican compact" in politicians' speeches, media reports, and public intellectuals' contributions to op-ed columns. These political uses of the republican legacy revealed the semantic vagueness of the word, which serves as an equivalent to democracy, cultural exceptionalism, or simply "Frenchness." The Republic has become a floating signifier that can attach to a variety of referents according to the whim of its user or the specific context of its utterance. This polysemic uncertainty shows to what extent public discourse on the current national predicament in France is at a loss for words. "Republican" has become a catchword for what the culture has to come to terms with, in an as-yet unarticulated way, in the wake of tremendous social change: individualism, the weakening of patriarchal authority, the retreat of the nation-state, and ethnic and religious diversity. The national conversation, groping for words, is finding in the semantic constellation associated with the republican reference, in its all-encompassing vagueness, the least inadequate carrier for meanings that have yet to become fully comprehended.

Chapter 6 takes the year 1989 as its starting point: the collapse of the Berlin wall, the bicentennial of the French Revolution, and the controversy over the right of Muslim students to wear a veil in public schools all happened within a few weeks. These three events illustrate the role of memory in current reformulations of the republican and revolutionary legacy. The subsequent memory wars over Vichy and the Algerian War, and the professional historians' growing discontent with the interested appropriation of the national past by politicians and militant cultural organizations (what the French call the "instrumentalization of history"), form the background of a study of three books published a decade ago by Editions du Seuil. In these short volumes aimed at a general public, prominent intellectuals or historical figures attempt to educate the youth about values and events threatened by oblivion: patriotism, the republican tradition, and the French Resistance during World War II.

Chapter 7 ends this survey of recent ideological disruptions with comments on the 2004 law on *laïcité*, which banned large religious emblems and articles of clothing from public schools. The interminable debate on the veil (which has recently resurfaced as a controversy about the burqa, a garment that covers the whole body rather than just the head, increasingly visible in French streets and taken to signal a step-up in female subjugation) points to the loss of a long-standing fiction of the national community as culturally homogenous. What is mourned through the veil is more than a threatened form of political institutions (the Republic) or historical legacy (the revolutionary tradition, secularism); it is the notion of a *people* conceived through the prevalence of uniformity over difference.

Rather than examining the array of positions that have been staked time and again since 1989, I chose to approach the law on *laïcité* and its consequences from the side, as it were, as a symptom of a larger problem. In the same way that la République functions as a code word for a democracy in trouble, the much-debated notion of *laïcité* as another marker of the French difference serves to displace, and obfuscate, some of the salient issues linked to ethnic diversity. The uprisings in predominantly black and Arab working-class neighborhoods of major French cities a year after the law was passed were in many ways the return of the repressed of a decision that targeted teenage girls as metonymies of the entire French Muslim population; the *laïcité* law framed their lives through the prism of Enlightenment rationalism and the history of the separation of church and state, ignoring their concrete, ordinary, everyday "immigrant" or "minority" experience of confrontation with chronic unemployment, job discrimination, and spatial segregation. The chapter ends with considerations on the related recent debate on affirmative action—or "positive discrimination," as the French prefer to call it—as another attempt to deal with the dismembering of the body politic.

This book is not an intellectual or cultural history of post-1968 France (many such studies have been written in the past two decades).[24] A contribution to the understanding of the present, it is rather a collection of soundings into what remains largely a complex, murky, ongoing *process*. I have been fascinated by these developments since I left France twenty-five years ago, as it became clear that a significant change was underway, even though its precise contours remain difficult to delineate, precisely because it is in process. Many of the changes were already happening in the late sixties and early seventies, but, as one colleague once remarked to me two decades later, "we did not know then that it was going on." From one visit to the next, I witnessed behaviors, heard comments, saw images, and read arguments that could not easily be reconciled with what I thought it meant to be French.

Born in the old, Fourth Republic France of gray-smocked public school teachers, tree-lined two-lane highways, the comedies of Bourvil and Fernandel, and politicians whose worldview and rhetorical flourish had been shaped by World War I, the Great Depression, the Popular Front, and the Nazi Occupation, the postwar generation came of age in a new France of personal computers, nongovernmental media, wide-ranging multicultural claims, and the collapse of communism. Baby boomers are said to be arrogant and self-indulgent; many of the books they wrote about the transition to the new times may well reflect these unsavory traits, as they often equated the fate of their generation to that of 1789, arguing that the "second French Revolution" that took place between 1965 and 1985 rivaled the first in terms of the magnitude of cognitive and material disruptions involved.

The controversies addressed in this book display a wide range of affects, from despair, anger, and resignation to claims that the way things used to be will not do any longer, that the republican framework is in serious need of overhauling if the political disenchantment, cultural malaise, economic woes, and social and racial tensions currently facing the country are to be addressed and, hopefully, redressed. Even the direst accounts of the "new France" written in the eighties and early nineties often ended on an optimistic note. It is as though their authors were reluctant to follow the logic of their argument to its most depressive end, perhaps comforted by the thought that the country had been there before (in 1598, 1793, 1871, and 1940), mired in chaos, bled

---

24. See, for example, Dosse, *History of Structuralism*, vol. 2; Ory and Sirinelli, *Les intellectuels en France*; Christofferson, *French Intellectuals Against the Left*; Mongin, *Face au scepticisme*; and Starr, *Logic of Failed Revolt*.

by civil or foreign war, threatened with dissolution, and yet always rising, phoenixlike, from the dead.

Emmanuel Todd concluded his study of the disruptive effects of technological change and cultural liberalization on political and electoral processes with a belief in the capacity of the nation's time-tested ideological values to survive the challenge: "Today France suffers from . . . an absence of ideological identification [that] has everywhere produced a feeling of unrest, and the impression that the system does not work, even when there is no threat of a serious crisis. The disappearance of the Right-Left dualism is the most obvious aspect of the disintegration of the old system."[25]

Marcel Gauchet has repeatedly argued that the gradual erasure of the idea of collective power, almost entirely replaced by the notion of individual freedom, is a threat to contemporary democracies: "This broadening of the dimension of individual independence at the expense of the dimension of a common government upsets the balance" of democratic institutions.[26] And yet he refers to himself as "pessimistic in the short term, but optimistic in the long run," finding solace in the fact that "farmers, teachers, middle-level managers, railroad workers, and small business owners" often seem more capable than professional politicians and public intellectuals to engage in open-minded dialogue and to try to find workable solutions to their problems (346).

Cornelius Castoriadis, who has condemned in no uncertain terms the complete atrophy of political imagination in contemporary social formations, shared a similar confidence in the ability of ordinary citizens to reinvigorate the dynamics of autonomous self-creation that stand at the core of the Western democratic project.[27] According to Castoriadis, "One cannot

---

25. Todd, *Making of Modern France*, 204.
26. Gauchet, *Condition historique*, 332.
27. The self-institution of society as the creation of a human, historical world out of the meaninglessness of the natural order is at the center of Castoriadis's political philosophy. In his view, the problem with late modern liberal societies is that they lack self-transcendence. See, for example, "The Greek *Polis* and the Creation of Democracy": "History is creation: the creation of total forms of human life. Social-historical forms are not 'determined' by natural or historical 'laws.' Society is self-creation. 'That which' creates society and history is the instituting society, as opposed to the instituted society. The instituting society is the social imaginary in the radical sense" (84). Democratic political activity (as the questioning of instituted society) is inseparable from philosophical self-reflection, as first conceived by the ancient Greeks: "Greece is the first society where we find the explicit questioning of the instituted collective representation of the world—that is, where we find philosophy" (102). On the contrary, nondemocratic societies are regimes of instituted heteronomy, in which the source and foundation of laws, norms, values, and meanings are transcendent. All societies, for Castoriadis, are self-instituted, but only democratic formations do so explicitly and reflectively. See also *The Imaginary Institution of Society*.

say that Western societies are dead, simply writing them off from history. We are not yet living in fourth-century Rome or Constantinople.... There are signs of resistance, people who are struggling here and there.... Important books that appear. In the letters to the editor columns of *Le Monde*, for example, one often finds letters expressing entirely healthy and critical points of view."[28] Far from being an epochal catastrophe, the effacement of the belief in a "guaranteed historical progress" was for Castoriadis an opportunity to free up "our creative social imaginary" and to make contact with the living past: "It is only by coming out of... the fantasy of immortality... that one can establish a genuine relationship to time,... it is only then that we will be able to be truly present to the present, by being open to the future and by having a relationship with the past that is neither a repetition nor a rejection" (73).[29]

In his monumental *Memory, History, Forgetting*, Paul Ricoeur suggested that Freud might have missed the affirmative, joyful side of sublimated melancholia. Sublimation as "the missing piece in the panoply of Freud's metapsychology might perhaps have provided him with the secret of the reversal from the complaisance toward sadness to sadness sublimated—into joy. Yes, grief is that sadness that has not completed the work of mourning. Yes, joy is the reward for giving up the lost object and a token of the reconciliation with its internalized object" (77). From this perspective, melancholy politics in late modern France could be described as a process of "new mourning," the double entendre suggesting that historical loss is not only a tragedy, but that it can also open up a space for new mornings, for the task of hopeful politics, and, who knows, for the gift of what Ricoeur called *la mémoire heureuse*, a happy memory, reconciliation through remembrance.

---

28. See Castoriadis, *Rising Tide of Insignificancy*, 153.

29. See also the cautiously hopeful conclusion of Castoriadis, "Culture in a Democratic Society": "Thus, just as the current evolution of culture is not wholly unrelated to the inertia and the social and political passivity characteristic of our world today, so a renaissance of its vitality, should it take place, will be indissociable from a great new social-historical movement which will reactivate democracy and will give it at once the form and the contents the project of autonomy requires" (347).

Chapter One

SPECTERS OF THE SIXTIES

> We are still haunted by the ghost of the Sixties. For thirty long years we have not ceased either to lament or celebrate the death of this singular decade. The remarkable longevity of this death of the Sixties story unwittingly testifies to the survival of its subject. For many of us who cut our political teeth on the civil rights, antiwar and student movements, the Sixties live on as a longing for a golden age that has been lost to a permanently pallid present. But nostalgia for the Sixties is only the most obvious sign of their ghostly presence. Other progressives are still so spooked by them that they cannot refrain from periodically presiding over their burial. The intensity of these efforts to exorcise the Sixties, I would suggest, only serves to confirm the survival of their spirit.
>
> —Balbus, *Mourning and Modernity*

Toward a Political Theory of Mourning

These remarks from Isaac D. Balbus's *Mourning and Modernity*, although written with the American context in mind, apply just as well to the "mourning of the movement" in contemporary France. Half the country's current population was born after 1968, and yet the memories of May still play a major symbolic role in political conflicts, haunting, as it were, the French imagination. One of Nicolas Sarkozy's recurrent themes during the 2007 presidential campaign was the need to do away once and for all with the deleterious legacy of the sixties. Former oppositional icons such as Daniel Cohn-Bendit or José Bové, still active in Green Party and antiglobalization politics, are a constant reminder that the radical ferment associated with the decade continues to inform the present, even though the generation that brought this radicalism to the fore (Balbus's "many of us") is passing the baton. In this chapter, the enduring, ghostly presence of the turbulent decade will serve as the leading metaphor to interpret the intricate correlations between death, mourning,

---

An earlier version of this chapter appeared as "Les mémoires de Mai, ou la politique éclipsée," *L'Esprit Créateur* 41, no. 1 (2001): 9–19.

and memory that make up what Julia Kristeva has called France's "national depression." Unsurprisingly, Kristeva's analysis of the nostalgic mood of the late nineties was made in explicit reference to May 1968. Her conversations with Philippe Petit were published in April 1998, as part of the thirtieth anniversary of the events. The first part of the interview was titled "What Is Left of May 1968?" and was devoted to a critical assessment of what the author called "the double face of 'the spirit of 68'—both as a liberation of subjective desires and a concern for the dignity of the most miserable among the people" (*Dépression nationale*, 17).

Balbus argues for his part that the profound political pessimism associated with the current wave of "left-wing melancholy" is a direct consequence of the inability of the children of '68 to mourn the movement in a significant way. "The atrophy of our imagination," he writes, "is a symptom of our *political depression*. Political depression is every bit as much the result of unmourned intersubjective losses as individual depression is the result of unmourned personal losses. In either case, hope is crushed under the accumulated weight of unexpressed grief. Thus the renewal of political hope—the resuscitation of our currently moribund political imagination—requires that we summon up the strength for our simultaneously emotional and political task of giving in to our grief" (81). The current inability of the French Left, whether moderate or extreme, to articulate a political and cultural alternative to the right-wing coalition in power is ample evidence that the diagnostic is valid, mutatis mutandis, beyond the American context of Balbus's remarks.

In his view, the only way to exorcise the ghost of the sixties is for the survivors to face the magnitude of their loss and to confront the profound ambivalence of the feelings occasioned by such a loss: anger and hatred directed at the reproduction of domination within a movement that was supposed to end all domination; guilt at having contributed to the demise of their own dreams; and sorrow from being deprived of the hopes invested in the brief, "enchanted" encounter with "the time of the now," a magical reversal of the homogeneous, empty time of the continuum of history denounced by Water Benjamin in his "Theses on the Philosophy of History." The necessary labor of remembrance called for by such a need to sort out the loved and hated aspects of the sixties' legacy implies the rescuing of the latter from the various official versions it has been subject to over the past decades. The combined idealization and denigration of the movement during the decades that followed are for Balbus both "a sign and a defense against a profound political-cultural loss from which we have yet to recover" (80), the unexpressed mixture of guilt and grief associated with the failure of the radical political imagination of sixties progressivism.

In the course of his argument, Balbus underscores the limits of Benjamin's "anamnestic solidarity" and its value for the 1968 generation, and turns to Kleinian categories to construct "a more adequate theory of political mourning" (79). Benjamin's clear-cut separation between a pure tradition of the oppressed and the tainted official past of the oppressive order leaves little room for the ambivalence of the relation between the orphaned offspring of the sixties and their own past. Benjamin's idealization of the oppressed (and demonization of the oppressor) cannot account for the fact that the militants of May repeatedly betrayed in practice their egalitarian, anti-power rhetoric. In addition, while Benjamin exhorted the masses of his days to remember the oppressed past of their predecessors, the class of 1968 is called to perform the demanding labor of remembering its own past.

Like many advocates of the legitimacy of a psychoanalytic theory of intersubjective mourning, Balbus relies on Freud's definition of mourning as "the reaction to the loss of a loved person, or to the loss of some abstraction which has taken the place of one, such as one's country, and ideal, and so on," as a warrant for such a transfer from the individual to the collective. The displacement of the libido from a "real" person to a cultural abstraction, and the fact that our ideals can serve as substitutes for the people we love, implies that "the mourning of cultural or political losses may be as necessary to our emotional well-being as the mourning of individual losses" (81).

Balbus goes on to argue that Melanie Klein's elaborate descriptions of mourning work, object relations, and the depressive position are more useful than Freud's, since the latter confined "the ambivalence toward, guilt over, and identification with the lost object to the pathological" (82). Kleinian theory also underscores for Balbus the profound ambivalence of the relationship of the mourner to the lost object, and describes the successful work of mourning as one of selective identification with the positive attributes of that object (the "good" internal mother), whether an individual or an abstraction. Balbus proposes that the only way for the orphans of the sixties to come to terms with their grief is to come to understand that the movement was not all good or all bad. In order to do so, they need "to own the anger" they felt against a form of political activism that not only failed to deliver on its promises but had entailed significant personal sacrifices, leading to a painful break with family, social class, and a motherland suddenly perceived as oppressive, patriarchal, racist, and fascist.

Balbus concludes that the loss of political imagination that followed the counterrevolution against the counterculture (the "backlash"), from the mid-seventies onward, "is the result of a collective failure to mourn a Movement that gave birth to a profound and pervasive sense of social solidarity and collective agency. All the individual grief-work in the world will not help us to work through the terrible loss of that sense of solidarity and collective agency we have suffered and for which we are, in part, responsible. Social losses—intersubjectively shared losses—can only be properly mourned in a proper social setting" (90).

Balbus, like many members of his generation, is seeking a way out of the seemingly endless haunting of the present by the ghosts of the decade, a compulsion to repeat that has its source in his fellow former radicals' inability to rescue from the past what has been lost to the present. What was true of the moribund working-class movement in Hitler's Germany is true of the political impotence of the sixties generation (then and now), since "the ghost of domination haunts the Benjaminian project of overcoming it" (72). Balbus describes the current political predicament as one of opposition between two dominant forces: those of modernism, that want to get rid of the past, and those of fundamentalism, that wish to bring it back to life. "At unspeakable cost," he writes, "we have finally learned that the modernist murder of the past only feeds the fundamentalist fantasy of resurrecting it" (71).

As a consequence, one of the central political tasks of our time is to "arrest this deadly dialectic—to counter the modern assault on memory without mobilizing the noxious weapons of nostalgia" (71). A similar task confronts those in France who refuse to choose between the modernist obliteration of the past and the fundamentalist resuscitation of it, between turning the country into another liberal democracy and returning it to the phantasmic golden age of the Republic. The intersubjective grieving of the "May revolution" that took place in the following decades fell short of those expectations, oscillating between the manic denial of the sixties ("we never really loved them") and their depressive idealization ("how can we stop loving them?").

Memories of May

As shown by many narratives of late modern France, whether explicitly or implicitly, the student movement and the general strike that followed during the spring of 1968 remain a turning point in the nation's collective imagination. Many of the intellectual and cultural developments discussed in this book all stem from "the events" (as they're known), the forces they set in motion, the changes they reflected or brought about, and the subsequent debates they generated, all the way to the present. The pre-1968 era stands in stark contrast to subsequent years in the narrative proposed by most histories of the present. Before the sixties, the patriarchal, disciplinary society, the world of *lycées-casernes* (high schools built in the late nineteenth century that looked, and often felt, like prisons and military barracks); after the sixties, the media explosion, electronic networks, the cool and tolerant culture of narcissism. Before, the story goes, people believed in revolution and national identity; after, amid the crisis of the future, the era of emptiness opens up, and we have the empire of the ephemeral, hybrid identities, and multiculturalism. Before, reason and the written word rule supreme in the educational institutions of the Republic; after, the world of the simulacrum replaces the Enlightenment's symbolic order, splitting up the unitary subject of Western metaphysics.

The events of May have become, together with other privileged moments of French national history, a site of recollection that the press, television, and intellectuals go and visit at the end of each decade to revive the memories of a temporal rupture suffused with nostalgia. Even though the form of the commemorative ritual often remains the same, its content changes over the years, as repeated commentaries seek the elusive meaning of an event that keeps receding further into the past. Every ten years, the labor of remembrance starts again, a seemingly paradoxical and derisory task, since we inhabit a world of instant information and fading historical consciousness. The celebrations of the tenth, twentieth, and thirtieth anniversaries attempted to counter this erasure of the past, to keep alive in the national consciousness the event that opened up the time of oblivion, since the French, and especially the younger generations, are now said to have forgotten about national grandeur, the colonial empire, the politics of the French Revolution, the canon of classical humanities, and so on and so forth.

When reading some of the press articles and essays published in 1978, 1988, and 1998, one witnesses both the evolution of French society *and* the continual assessment of those very changes. The discourse on 1968 is far from univocal, of course, but the contest of interpretations striving to penetrate the "mystery of May" stands out against a common zeitgeist, a perception of the state of the country at a particular juncture shared by many journalists and essayists. One of the characteristic features of our contemporary culture is the constant need to take the pulse of society, through repeated health reports that often appear to have been, with hindsight, hasty and inaccurate.

Ritualized commemorations provide opinion makers with another opportunity to come up with the medical checkup of a nation that periodically remembers, with a mixture of regret, remorse, and relief, what it once passionately believed in, or was passionately opposed to.

May 1968, born under the auspices of free speech, was from the start a loquacious affair, a talkative revolt that provided its own running commentary, each practical initiative being immediately discussed, dissected, justified, or condemned in the name of one or the other of the many theories that competed for the militants' minds and informed their various agendas. The student rebellion, the workers' general strike, and the crisis of the Gaullist regime gave rise after the fact to a surfeit of readings, a glut of analyses that each new book on the subject felt a duty to examine and cross-examine, in order to confirm or invalidate the long list of preceding interpretations.

As early as 1969, Philippe Bénéton and Jean Touchard took stock of the competing versions of May, grouping them in eight different categories. Fifteen years later, Luc Ferry and Alain Renault went back to Bénéton and Touchard's typology, reorganizing it according to a different set of classificatory principles. Prominent among the narratives written "from the point of view of the actors" was the contribution Cornelius Castoriadis and Edgar Morin published immediately after the fact. The opposite, objectivist approach, based on the perverse logic of the "ruse of reason," informed the readings by Régis Debray and Gilles Lipovetsky; the former, following Marx, and the latter, Tocqueville, both claimed that May 1968 was a pseudo revolution. As a necessary moment of the evolution of capitalism or democratic individualism, the sixties had completed the shift from modernism to postmodernism (Lipovetsky), or furthered the expansion of commodity production to the whole of the social field, illustrating "the French route to America" (Debray).[1] Both approaches, whether neoliberal or post-Marxist, argue that the student rebels, who claimed they were toppling the "Old World," in fact had unwittingly hastened its modernization.[2] Ferry and

---

1. Quoted in Ferry and Renault, *French Philosophy of the Sixties*, 64.
2. One of the most famous slogans of May '68 was "Cours, camarade, le vieux monde est derrière toi" (Run, comrade, the Old World is behind you). See Lipovetsky, *L'ère du vide*; and Debray, *Modeste contribution*. On the historical function performed by May '68 of adapting French society to the requirements of cultural and economic modernization, see the "roundtable" on "The Mystery of 1968" organized twenty years after the fact by *Le Débat* 50 (May–August 1988), notably Pierre Nora's remarks on the contradictions of the postwar period and the "frustration of history" (69), as well as the demographer Hervé Le Bras's comments on the seventies (70). Daniel Cohn-Bendit offered similar views in the next issue of the journal: "Gaullism wanted to carry out industrial modernization without cultural modernization. It created an economically new society while pretending to maintain traditional lifestyles. Its authoritarian style was the target of the student revolt" (161).

Renault added another kind of reading to the list. Inspired by Heidegger's phenomenology, this approach described the event as unheard-of and unclassifiable, as a sudden opening, the irruption of a transcendent freedom from elsewhere. Henri Weber's *Que reste-t-il de Mai 68?* (What is left of May '68?), published in 1988 and reprinted ten years later with a preface looking back at yet another decade of contradictory approaches, also reviewed the whole corpus of previous accounts to criticize them and substitute its own set of interpretations.[3]

This variety of readings does not only reflect the commentators' ideological diversity, from the most favorable (Castoriadis and Morin) to the most critical (Raymond Aron on the Right[4] or Debray on the Left); it also stems from the heterogeneity of the movement itself, the contradictions within the programs and practices of groups and individuals mobilized by a seemingly unifying political crisis. The highly disciplined militants of Trotskyist and Maoist groups, who shared a Leninist conception of the seizure of state power by a determined, highly trained revolutionary vanguard, took to the streets alongside the great mass of unorganized high school and college students, for whom protest was first and foremost an opportunity to reject the alienating everyday life of the postwar urban-industrial society, as expressed in the well-known slogans "métro, boulot, dodo" (subway, work, and sleep) and "changer la vie" (change life), the latter borrowed from one of Rimbaud's poems.

It is precisely because some aspects of the events were, as one observer put it, equally "ill-assorted and contradictory"[5]—and, as such, difficult to integrate into an all-encompassing analysis—that the numerous posthumous readings raise more vexing questions than provide satisfying responses, thereby adding to the aura of mystery, opacity, and resistance to interpretation that still surrounds the "enigma of May." Was it a Leninist revolution or an anarchist revolt rejecting the Gaullist state together with the Stalinist model? Was it the ultimate breakthrough of Western Marxism or the decisive surge of anticommunism amid an increasingly prosperous economy? A failed socialist uprising or the growing pains of a new kind of capitalism? The triumph of hedonistic individualism or a communitarian rejection of the consumerist anomie? A "liberal revolution" (as Michel Crozier called it) or a

---

3. Weber, a student leader of the Trotskyist Ligue communiste révolutionnaire in the sixties, later became a Socialist senator from Normandy, a social and political trajectory emblematic of many of the leaders of the student uprising.

4. See Aron, *Elusive Revolution*.

5. Narot, "Mai '68," 186.

movement that was more liberational than liberal (in Edgar Morin's opinion)?[6] Was it informed by Sartre's humanism or Foucault's antihumanism? To each his own: the complexity of the occurrence itself has allowed every observer to project on it her own interpretive desire, acting as a kind of political Rorschach test.

The array of possible readings provided each commemoration with its volume, structure, and emotional intensity. Is there anything more media-friendly than this possibility of revisiting the debate every ten years, of giving former "actors" (in the sociological as well as theatrical senses of the word) and younger commentators the opportunity to confront once again their competing views about what made May 1968 such a defining moment? The ideological charge invested at first in the object of the debate lives on in the debate itself, albeit in different forms, since with every new decade the political and social issues confronting French society have changed. In other words, the changing memories of May are inserted every ten years in a new ideological framework, in a complex of discourses and representations increasingly distant from the original scene, ranging from the rejection of the "excesses of May" and the nostalgia for the "blessings of May" to the messianic expectation of "another May."

The fascination with May 1968 and its aftermath shows no sign of dying down, both in France and abroad. The fortieth anniversary was another opportunity for special editions, documentaries based on film archives, prime-time television debates, and new publications of old classics of the decade. In the academic field, recent studies in English include books by Kristin Ross and Julian Bourg. Bourg argues that most readings of the event fall within an inverted mirror structure of oppositions—Left versus Right, May as failed revolution versus May as delusional farce—and that recent interpretations are no exception to the rule. Comparing Ross's account with Tony Judt's indictment of the irresponsibility of postwar French intellectuals in their support of communism presented in *Past Imperfect* and *The Burden of Responsibility*, Bourg writes that "Kristin Ross's analysis of the May events, their prelude, and their inheritance shares a curious parallel with Judt's neo-liberal critique. At first glance the parallel seems surprising; if Judt is dismissive, Ross is wistful" (12). Bourg presents his own account as breaking away from the traditional left-right dichotomy. May 1968 "was more than a dismissible anachronism but less than an authentic, defeated revolution," since the "liberational *épanouissement*" it advocated proved to be "not incompatible with liberalism, but neither could it be reduced to it" (13).

6. See Crozier, "Révolution libérale."

On the French side, the book by François Cusset (who was born one year after the events), *Contre-discours de Mai*, published in time for the fortieth anniversary, is a recent attempt to rescue the authenticity of the movement and its disruptive force from the coalition of "embalmers and grave diggers" who agree on making it a thing of the past (whether through sacralizing or demonizing it), thereby denying its transformative relevance to the present. Cusset's rehabilitation of the theoretical and militant sixties (both in *Contre-discours* and in his earlier *La décennie*) goes hand in hand with his contempt for the 1980s as the anti-sixties, the reactionary decade par excellence.

François Furet famously argued in 1978 that it took the French almost two hundred years to end the 1789 revolution. The last two decades of the twentieth century were spent drawing the lessons of this consummation, and the anniversaries of May 1968 played a central role in this collective work of mourning. For some, keeping alive the flame of the student revolt meant that the passing of its older model, the grand lady of revolutions, might not be irremediable after all. While the official, solemn, state-sponsored celebration of the bicentennial of 1789 sealed the coffin of the first modern uprising, its memory no longer a threat to national concord, the images and testimonies of May remained controversial, as if something of the unpredictable restlessness of French politics kept smoldering under the ashes of history. Hence the paradoxical nature of all these commemorations, as they are both repetitive and novel. The same people are on TV decade after decade, their familiar faces showing the passage of time, from the youthful fervor visible on film archives to the sententious stiffness of established, middle-aged celebrities. Yet the revolutionary epiphany is subjected each time to the rereading imposed by the flow of history, from Salvador Allende's death (1973) to the Socialists' espousal of the market economy (1981). The commemoration of 1978 put "Mai" on trial; 1988 drew up the balance sheet, from the sentencing of the culprit to her execution and burial; 1998 would exhume the corpse to see whether it was still moving, as if the hopes raised by the victory of the Left in the presidential and legislative elections of 1981, the student demonstrations of 1986, and the state workers' strikes of 1995 were signs of a promising, or threatening, afterlife.

It has been said that the seventies were the "exorcism of May 68."[7] A wide section of the aging radical intelligentsia loudly indulged in the public confession of their youthful erring ways. The ubiquitous rhetoric of self-criticism proclaimed that the revolutionary idea was inherently "totalitarian,"

---

7. Jean-François Narot, "Mai '68: Les années d'imposture," *Le Monde*, May 17, 1988.

and the word became the master signifier of the decade. Jean-Claude Guillebaud wrote one of the defining books of the 1970s, tellingly called *Les années orphelines* (The orphaned years). The book's value lies less in its account of all the lost illusions of the revolutionary Left, a somewhat banal diagnosis after 1975, than in its conclusion. The author refused to give in to the blasé pessimism of those repentant former *gauchistes* who were busy reinventing themselves as scourges of Marxism, and whose scathing attacks against the Hegelian legacy made the covers of newsmagazines and provided the subject matter for televised literary salons.

"The days of suspicion," Guillebaud wrote, "are for now coming to an end. We will never again be reduced to a 'mechanism,' to our 'objective' interests or to a class . . . but this vanishing burdensome suspicion *also* revives in us a kind of 'convivial' warmth formerly prevented by the hatred among splinter groups. . . . Ten years ago, we kept talking about bringing imagination to power. Is it now time to whine because in front of us—at last—a blank page is open?" (108–9). And yet Guillebaud put the illusions of the sixties generation, including himself, in the dock. Solzhenitsyn and Pol Pot; the failure of the Bolivian guerrillas; the war between China and Vietnam that signed the death warrant of "proletarian internationalism"; the crushing of the Palestinian resistance by the unnatural alliance of the Syrian Army and the Lebanese Christian Phalanx; Greece, Spain, and Portugal, just freed from fascism and falling into the camp of bourgeois democracies: these were only a few among the many returns of the Real that, short of fulfilling the latent desire of the rebels, now filled their manifest discourse.

Guillebaud's book testifies to the fact that the jury was still out by the close of the first decade. The erring ways of the past, he argued, far from ruining the progressive agenda, required that it be both more cautious and more demanding. By contrast, the defeat of the parliamentary Left in the elections of March 1978 could only strengthen the emancipatory mythology that stood at the heart of the revolutionary nostalgia. The group of intellectuals invited in May 1978 to share their recollections in *Le Nouvel Observateur* agreed that an unusually disruptive power had been unleashed in French society a decade earlier: *something* had really happened, they said, but what? Gone from the intellectuals' commemorative accounts were the Matignon labor agreements, the missed opportunities of the parliamentary Left, the awakening of the silent majority, and the conservative backlash of the June elections—that is, the depressing, prosaic reality of backroom deals and compromises the French call *la politique politicienne* (the politics of politicians).

The selective reconstruction at work in the remembering process seems to have left those who refused to take part in "May's funeral," as Bernard-Henri Lévy had put it, with the cherished memory of a youthful, energetic, exhilarating outburst of freedom, as intense as it was short-lived. From the impression of having been in "communication with something essential" (D. Mascolo) to the sentiment of "a violent break, [the] power of this break, [the] loss of an numbed body and 'self' that congeals [people] in their persona" (J. Duvignaud), the descriptions of the event all shared a lyrical, hyperbolic quality: "mixture of density and weightlessness" (P. Nora); "tremor, landslide, shift, faults, or lapses in behavior, beginnings of drift and ungluing, tiny earthquakes . . . no split rock can reveal" (M. Clavel); "tear in the weft of the world, break in the business of things, transparency of souls, instants of fire, madness, flash from another world" (M. Le Bris). May 1968 had been a dream, a collective slip of the tongue, a miracle, an apparition, and a poem—unreal, fleeting, wonderful.[8]

Very little of this ethereal vision, at least in public discourse, would survive the onslaught of the neoliberal eighties. In 1978, as evidenced in the conclusion of *Les années orphelines*, the ambiguity remained, and the playful, hysterical, libertarian side of May could still be cherished, kept apart from its paranoid, authoritarian, Leninist side. The Stalinist version of Marxism had failed, but there remained the hope of another history, convivial and congenial, in the image of the "socialism with a human face" of the 1968 Prague uprising, the eastern European companion piece to the French events. Rather than the last hurrah of communism, as its critics claimed it to be, was not the rebellious spirit of May, on both sides of the Iron Curtain, the most blatant refutation of authoritarianism?

May at Twenty

The commemoration of the twentieth anniversary, on the eve of the bicentennial of the French Revolution, was the outcome of the long process of deinvestment from the revolutionary idea that had started after World War II. In the seventies, both social democrats and radicals had completed the postwar critique of communism, denouncing the camps and renouncing the dictatorship of the proletariat. But the new intellectual generation that stepped on the stage after 1978 went further, denying even the possibility of a democratic socialist alternative to capitalism. Paradoxically, the "anti-totalitarian

---

8. "A la recherche du Mai perdu," *Le Nouvel Observateur*, May 8, 1978.

movement" used the anti-power thrust and anti-institutional individualism of the sixties counterculture to discredit any form of social engineering and deal the final blow to the activism of the previous decade.

In other words, the return of liberalism and human rights implied a rejection of all the radical components of the events, from the most authoritarian to the most utopian. The only thing still standing, once the dust had settled, was May 1968's connection to a long process of democratization and individualism going back to the Enlightenment, or even before. *Longue durée* had replaced epistemological breaks as the dominant interpretive paradigm. The new, liberal-Tocquevillian interpretation of May (as articulated, for example, by Gilles Lipovetsky) was that its true meaning was not to be found in the convulsions and ruptures of an elusive, enigmatic event, or in the dream of a students' and workers' commune, but in the imagination of acquisitive consumers, in the narcissistic obsession with self-expression and self-fulfillment, in the hedonistic propensity to have more and more fun, all of which defined the 1980s.

The social energy born of the hopes of May '68 would flare up again, briefly, at the beginning of the decade, as evidenced by the support of the Solidarność movement in Poland. Historical momentum carried the Left to power in 1981, despite the Communists' suspicion of their Socialist allies. But the popular euphoria was short-lived (the intellectuals, for their part, had long before renounced all their illusions). The eighties saw the triumph of *radios libres* (i.e., commercial broadcasting) and *écoles libres* (i.e., private and Catholic schools), confirming one of the predictions of May: the extension of the market to the entirety of social existence and the innermost recesses of the individual psyche. If in 1978 France had already entered the "era of post-politics," few people seemed to have been aware of it. By 1988, everyone knew.

The celebration of the twentieth anniversary was a publishing bonanza: no fewer that nineteen books on the "events" came out that spring. The auctioneers at the Hôtel Drouot put up for sale, to phenomenal bids, the inventive, often humorous posters that had adorned the walls of universities and factories. In the ultimate irony, the remains of the creative revolt against consumer society, often hastily cranked out on low-tech mimeos, in the heat of the action, had become highly priced commodities, forever divorced from the social context of their production. The electronic media were quick to ride the wave of commemoration. The industry of historical nostalgia offered the French public four special broadcasts between May 15 and June 2, including a television show in which May was put on trial in front of an audience of young people, some of them born after the events.

The major media happening of 1988 was undoubtedly the broadcast of *Génération*, a fifteen-episode series inspired by the best-selling book by Hervé Hamon and Patrick Rotman. The TV show, like the book itself, featured most of the stars of May '68, former student leaders and radical militants who had since assumed positions of prominence in the worlds of publishing, academia, journalism, and politics, from Serge July, editor of *Libération*, to the Socialist senator Henri Weber. The paradoxical personalization of a collective movement that had glorified anonymity, questioned the master thinkers (from Sartre to Lacan), and denounced the Stalinist cult of the leader was a product of the structural constraints of electronic communication. A decade later, Pierre Bourdieu, among others, would analyze the media's perverse effects on democracy and the production of knowledge.

The rare commentators who tried to remain faithful to the "spirit of May" blamed the press for offering the public a distorted narrative reconstruction based on images and commentaries that gave the last word to Cusset's grave diggers and embalmers. Legitimized in the eyes of the media by their former participation in highly visible extremist groups and their current membership in the cultural elites of *le tout-Paris*, the so-called representatives of the movement embodied, their critics argued, all that the anonymous actors of May '68 had hoped to eliminate. By privileging the Parisian glitterati over the obscure, forgotten militants from the provinces, the media performed an ideological recoding of the past, turning the events into a kind of playful revolution, a youthful happening that had opened the way to the much-needed cultural liberalization of the country. Was there a better proof of the success of this modernization than the brilliant careers of former student radicals who had become over time the self-appointed guardians of its official memory?

This "normalization" of May '68, the dissolution of the enigma in the act of its rewriting, has made it into a bizarre "historical curiosum" combining the picturesque and the archaic, as Jean-François Narot put it at the time. By inscribing the event in a seamless, totalizing narrative frame, its proponents were able to exonerate themselves for having fallen prey to the fascination of revolutionary violence in a momentary fit of adolescent distraction ("how could we have been so naive?"), and to congratulate themselves for having so quickly snapped out of it ("thank God it was only child's play"). While many of the actors of May had tried in 1978 to preserve its mystery, the 1988 television interpreters did everything they could to clear it up. The tenth anniversary had taken to task the imaginary component of the student movement; the twentieth went after its symbolic content, and the political project it carried along with it.

Post-Marxist Philosophy and the Legacies of May '68

What was left of May 1968 in the last decade of the twentieth century can be found in the symbolic domain, precisely, in the question of the difference between politics (*la politique*) and the political (*le politique*). The spirit of the events survived the "cryogenization" of the eighties in a subterranean way, and many continuators of May '68, both in spirit and in practice, rarely made explicit reference to the legacy. The thirtieth anniversary did not receive the media exposure and did not display the nostalgic intensity of the '78 and '88 commemorations. The passing of time had banked the fires of a thirty-year-old passion. Ironically enough, the thirtieth anniversary happened amid the unexpected revival of a social and political movement that the baffled media, looking for a proper peg on which to hang this new coat, called "radical Left," "third Left," and even, in a more ominous manner, "red Left." When asked for the roots of their radicalism, the youthful supporters of this new antiestablishment constellation, the future *altermondialistes*, were more likely to cite as inspiration the strikes of December 1995, the threats of globalization, and the rise of neoliberalism rather than the utopian legacy of the sixties. The lessons of recent history had lowered expectations, limited objectives, and increased the pragmatism of the new militants. But the coalition of Trotskyist splinter groups that garnered a surprising 5 percent of the vote in the elections of spring 1998 did send to the National Assembly a handful of former 1968 leaders, including Alain Krivine and Arlette Laguiller.

The social movement that made up this new new Left brought together organizations reflective of the evolution of French society and culture since the seventies, such as the gay rights group ACT UP and the antiglobalization movement Attac, with long-established groups whose objectives harked back to the *autogestionnaire* component of May '68, such as tenants' unions. Following the publication of his best-selling book *La misère du monde* (*The Weight of the World*), Pierre Bourdieu became one of the most influential voices of the new radicalism. His contribution to the tradition of intellectual engagement was a characteristic mix of theoretical reflections on the mutation of capitalism and the ideological justifications that went with it, on the one hand, and pointed, targeted interventions in local, national, and international struggles (for more on Bourdieu, see chap. 4).

In addition to the persistence of grassroots social movements and the reinvention of the traditional style of engagé intellectual politics, some of the legacy of 1968 lived on throughout the eighties and nineties in the more rarefied domain of political philosophy. The Heideggerian, metaphysical reading of May 1968, discussed above, contributed in two related ways to the increasingly popular notion of "post-politics." The description of the revolutionary event as an Advent—a breakthrough, a gap in the order of Being, the sign of an irruption in the banality of everyday life of a force from elsewhere, or nowhere (i.e., properly u-topian)—legitimized the resistance to those reductive, positivistic interpretations of May 1968 that attempted to think the unthinkable, and reinscribed the experience of the wholly, and holy, other within a continuous, objectivist explanatory framework. Moreover, this metaphysical view bestowed on May the characteristic of genuine revolutions: their radical novelty, their *emergent* nature, the fact that they elude, at least in part, the structural conditions of their occurrence, the fact that they cannot be entirely explained or produced by the situation that preceded them. The work of several contemporary French philosophers are grounded in this interpretation of May 1968 as the sudden occurrence of "the Real" of psychoanalytic discourse, the unpredictable appearance of a "Thing" that consciousness could not anticipate and inscribe within its symbolic, representational framework.

Although there are few explicit references to May 1968 in the post-seventies works of Alain Badiou, Etienne Balibar, and Jacques Rancière (all three were actively involved in sixties radicalism), the breach opened up in the social fabric that year lives on in the way they write about the strange destiny of politics in years since.[9] If the three of them do not make up some kind of "school of thought," as Nick Hewlett has remarked, they share a similar conception of postrevolutionary politics based on the opposition between two kinds of processes, one social, the other ontological. Rancière contrasts *la police* (policing) and *la politique* (politics), while Badiou pits *l'être* (being) against *l'événement* (the event). In addition, both Rancière and Balibar place the call for equality at the center of all emancipatory political activity, with Balibar joining the two revolutionary principles of liberty and equality in the concept of *l'égaliberté*. Equaliberty is what disrupts the order of Rancière's *police*, that is, the "configuration of the sensible" through which individuals as bodies are assigned to such and such place in the social structure.

In Rancière's words, the policed order of things "is an order of the visible and the sayable that sees that a particular activity is visible and another is not, that this speech is understood as discourse and another as noise."[10] The

---

9. For recent studies of the resistance to the liberal turn in French thought, see Hewlett, *Badiou, Balibar, Rancière*.
10. Rancière, *Dis-agreement*, 29.

meeting of the two heterogeneous processes—equality and police—is what opens up the possibility of politics, conceived as the interruption of the domination of those who institute the arbitrary order of bodies and discourses over those who are subject to it. In Balibar's rendering of the same basic opposition, the history of contemporary societies implies an "indefinite oscillation and a structural ambiguity between two obviously antinomic kinds of politics: a politics of insurrection and a politics of constitution. Or, if one prefers, a politics of permanent, uninterrupted revolution, and a politics of the State as institutional order."[11] Balibar's formulation is reminiscent of the student movement's opposition to the Gaullist and the Stalinist states alike, as well as the sixties radicals' penchant for a permanent "revolution in the revolution," to borrow from the title of Régis Debray's first book.

Alain Badiou provides Balibar's historical-empirical distinction between the politics of insurrection and the politics of constitution with an ontological framing, based on the tension between event and being. Democracy and totalitarianism are for Badiou the two major versions of the deployment of the political (*le politique*) as an ontological order based on reified social relations and the notion of representation (the political is thus on the side of Rancière's *police*). Like Balibar, Badiou conceives of the state as the most widespread form of the political, and like many 1968 radicals, he views Stalinism as the most accomplished version of the institutionalization of the state. He wrote in *Peut-on penser la politique?* (How to think about politics) that "there is no question that, at the core of the [twentieth] century, in its Soviet paradigm, the political has unfurled as the universal pretension of the State" (17). The point is to free *la politique* (politics) from the social order from which it is always an exception, to restore its mobility, its inability to be represented: "One must deliver politics from the tyranny of history, in order to return it to the event" (18).

Badiou patterns his notion of "the event" after Lacan's "the Real," as what escapes the order of the symbolic. The event disrupts the field of positive knowledge as an occurrence that consciousness (in this case political discourse) cannot anticipate, represent, or comprehend. Lacan famously described May 1968 as a hysterical symptom, the expression of the rebellious students' desire to find a master.[12] Politics in Badiou's sense is also a symptom, although one with opposite, emancipatory consequences. As the neurotic symptom dislocates the discourse of the subject, politics as event slips

11. Balibar, *Frontières*, 130.
12. "What you are aspiring to, as revolutionaries, is to have a master. You will get one." Roudinesco, *Jacques Lacan*, 446.

out of the masterly embrace of state and history and dismantles the social relations that form the basis of the fiction of the political. In this sense also, May 1968 remains a mystery, a fascinating enigma whose meaning cannot be exhausted by the sum of its interpretations.

The absolute exteriority of politics is described in terms of excess and exception, of inconsistency and unpredictability, of lack and the impossible. In Badiou's words, "Excess designates the difference between being and the event."[13] The event is the Real's irruption in the fictive reality of the political, the "singular inscription" from which politics proceeds, interrupting "the law." "The political," Badiou writes in *Peut-on penser la politique?* "has never been anything but the fiction where politics cuts the hole of the event" (12). One is reminded here of the metaphor of the "breach" used by Morin and Castoriadis, and of all those witnesses for whom May 1968 was first and foremost the flash of another world.

Rancière, for his part, views the contemporary as the collapse of politics in the order of the political. He argued in *Dis-agreement* that "how some new politics could break the circle of cheerful consensuality and denial of humanity is scarcely foreseeable or decidable right now" (139–40). Our present is post-political insofar as there is no end to the mourning of politics as insurrection against the order of the police. Postrevolutionary philosophy occurs in the wake of May 1968 (in both senses of the word, the visible track of a moving object and the watch over the deceased's body before burial), but without always acknowledging so. It assumes the event's legacy, but modestly, with detachment, almost stealthily, as though the passage of time had turned the burning nostalgia of the orphaned generation into a kind of disenchanted melancholy, one that pop psychology best sellers depict as the most common form of the contemporary malaise. Those who remain stubbornly faithful to the promises of May are reduced to watching in wait, like so many sentinels in the dark, for the return of the event.

Revenants: Specters of Derrida

The uneasy tension between the open-endedness of politics, the closure of the political, and the event as the sign of the unpredictability of historical becoming also informs Jacques Derrida's *Specters of Marx*, published in 1993. Derrida's argument, a critical response to the then-ubiquitous theme of the "triumph of neoliberalism," owes a lot to the widespread debate on the "end

---

13. Badiou, *Being and Event*, 507.

of history" started by the publication in 1992 of Francis Fukuyama's book bearing the same title. An expanded version of a lecture given by Derrida at a conference on the topic of "Whither Marxism?" *Specters of Marx* was written in the immediate aftermath of the collapse of Soviet communism. The philosopher's meditation on spectrality engages the depressive ideological climate that prevailed among left-wing intellectual circles at the time.

The book's subtitle, *The State of the Debt, the Work of Mourning, and the New International*, says it all. It is about historical grief, the symbolic debt owed to the dead by the living, and the messianic hope of a new emancipatory movement. But it is also about melancholy, and the exemplary figure of Hamlet, whose sullen relationship to the spirit of the father triggers Derrida's exposition. As already mentioned, Freud described the work of mourning as "the reaction to the loss of a loved person, or to the loss of some abstraction which has taken the place of one, such as one's country, liberty, an ideal, and so on" (243). The post-sixties melancholy Derrida indirectly addresses in the book mourns the loss of a plurality of abstractions put in the place of the object of desire: the nation, the Republic, the Enlightenment, the public school, culture, the great narratives of collective identification, and the like.

As is always the case with Derrida's texts, the argument is cautious, circumspect, ambiguous, carefully guarded against hasty and deceptively obvious readings. The specter of Marx, whom so many would like to see buried once and for all, never stops coming back, haunting contemporary consciousness, preventing the closure of economic liberalism as the end of history, which would make any surprise, any revolt, any event, impossible. "After the end of history," Derrida writes, "the spirit comes by *coming back* [revenant], it figures *both* a dead man who comes back and a ghost whose expected return repeats itself, again and again" (10).

Derrida names as "hauntology" his meditation on the spectral, on that which is never present as such, but lies in between—that is, between life and death, or between two deaths (10). There are lots of *revenants* in Derrida's text (the French word for ghost, *revenant*, literally means "the one who returns"), from Shakespeare and Marx to Blanchot, Benjamin, and Levinas, and since there are always "more than one" of these ghosts, the text keeps repeating. On the French ideological scene, the demise of one or another of these spectral signifiers has been ceaselessly proclaimed for the past fifty years—not only the end of history, but also the death of the author, of the intellectual, of the discourses of modernity, of the colonial empire, and of a certain idea of what France ought to be.

What is a specter, then, for Derrida? It is an embodied spirit, but incarnated in "a proper body without flesh" (7), able, consequently, to pass through walls. "As soon as one no longer distinguishes spirit from specter, the former assumes a body, it incarnates itself, as spirit, in the specter" (6). The ghost is a paradoxical incorporation, a hybrid, equivocal Thing "that remains difficult to name: neither soul nor body, and both one and the other" (6). The genesis of this phantom thing, "the production of the ghost, the constitution of the *ghost* effect is not simply a spiritualization or even an autonomization of spirit, idea, or thought. . . . For there to be ghost, there must be a return to the body, but to a body that is more abstract than ever. . . . Once ideas or thoughts (*Gedanke*) are detached from their substratum, one engenders some ghost *by giving them a body*" (126). Through the process of idealization, of ideological formation, thoughts acquire a consistency of their own, become so many objects, exist in the strange, eerie space between the mind that conceived them and the reality they are supposed to inform and illuminate.

The paradoxical body of the specter is another instance of Derrida's supplement, a prosthesis that comes to duplicate, to redouble the spirit, the idea, the Freudian "abstraction," and this disturbing double is what refuses to go away when the spirit dies, when an idea has finally run its course. The spectral Thing of ideology lives on as belief, as creed, long after the thoughts it has come to embody have lost any relevance, any adequacy to reality. Melancholia's distinctive feature is that in it the work of mourning never ends. The melancholic subject refuses to "kill the dead" a second time, to transfer her desire onto another object, a living one, another being, or an idea still pregnant with meaning. All along the process of mourning, according to Freud, "the existence of the lost object is psychically prolonged," sometimes in the form of a "hallucinatory psychosis." The lost object keeps on living, then, but as a vision, a ghost, a shadow haunting the psyche. In melancholia, as Freud famously put it, it is as though "the shadow of the object has fallen upon the ego."[14]

Specters of Marx is traversed by the interminable and inconclusive work of mourning by Marx's opponents, who keep rejoicing over his demise, claiming in a loud voice that he will never return: "Marx is dead, long live the market!" The rhetoric of the victorious Right, in Derrida's words, is "a dominant discourse [that] often has the maniacal, jubilatory, and incantatory form that Freud assigned to the so-called triumphant phase of mourning work" (52).

---

14. Freud, "Mourning and Melancholia," 246.

Derrida returns to the manic character of right-wing melancholy later in the book, in order to argue that the success of Fukuyama's thesis is a symptom of the West's anxiety, an effort to conceal the historical failure of the neoliberal orthodoxy. The so-called victory of liberal democracy has never been "so critical, fragile, threatened, even in certain regards catastrophic, and in sum bereaved. Bereaved by what the specter of Marx still represents today and which it would be a matter of conjuring away one more time in a jubilatory and manic fashion (a necessary phase of unsuccessful mourning work, according to Freud), but also virtually bereaved for itself" (68). Right-wing melancholy manifests itself as nostalgia for the good old days when capitalism still had an identifiable opponent. The seemingly endless struggle between labor and capital opened up a future for history and gave it a meaning. The failed process of mourning turns into an obsessive, haunting need, or regret (*hantise* in French), that shadows economic liberalism wherever it goes.

But in addition to the interminable, dispossessed grief of the Right, don't we encounter also in *Specters of Marx* another kind of mourning—the kind Walter Benjamin called "left-wing melancholy" in the context of the interwar period, which was another elegiac moment haunted by the ghosts of enlightened, modern reason, of democracy in agony, and by the triumph of the enemies of the Left? Thus enters the specter of Benjamin, then, who denounced in an essay titled "Left-Wing Melancholy" the revolutionary intellectuals who put more value in the dogmas of the past than in a changing reality. For Benjamin, "This left-wing radicalism is precisely the attitude to which there is no longer, in general, any corresponding political action. . . . All it has in mind is to enjoy itself in a negativistic quiet."[15] The melancholic gets invested in things, Benjamin argued in *The Origin of German Tragic Drama*, imbuing knowledge itself with a thing-like quality: "In its tenacious self-absorption [melancholy] embraces dead objects in its contemplation" (156–57). Wendy Brown has remarked that Benjamin's melancholy suggests "a certain logic of fetishism—with all the conservatism and withdrawal from human relations that fetishistic desire implies—contained in the melancholic logic."[16]

One is reminded here of this "something" that the spirit becomes, according to Derrida, when it enters the spectral body of ideology. Benjamin's melancholic subject fetishizes beliefs and structures of feeling, transferring her loyalty to the "world of objects" rather than to the movement of history.

15. Benjamin, "Left-Wing Melancholy," 425.
16. Brown, "Resisting Left Melancholia," 459.

Refusing to embrace the flow of the Real, and to adapt his theory and his practice to the new forms emerging from the transformation of the world, the melancholic leftist nurtures a dogmatic fixation, a sacralization of doctrine, a narcissistic identification with past orthodoxy. In Brown's words, "Left melancholia is Benjamin's name for a mournful, conservative, backward-looking attachment to a feeling, analysis, or relationship that had been rendered thing-like and frozen in the heart of the putative leftist. If Freud is helpful here, then this condition presumably issues from some unaccountable loss, some unavowably crushed ideal, contemporarily signified by the terms *Left, Socialism, Marx,* or *the Movement*" (460).

Echoing Benjamin's critique of ideological closure, Derrida recalls in *Specters of Marx* the "dogma machines and the 'Marxist' ideological apparatuses (States, parties, cells, unions, and other places of doctrinal production) . . . in the process of disappearing" (13), and "the Marxist dogmatics linked to the apparatuses of orthodoxy" of recent memory (64). In relation to the "becoming-god of gold" in Marx's text, he further qualifies the process of ideology as idolatry, via "the theological fetishization" that "always links ideology irreducibly to religion (to the idol or the fetish) as its principal figure, a species of 'invisible god' to which adoration, prayer, and invocation are addressed" (42). In a striking statement about religion, quoted by Derrida from *Capital*, Marx described the reification and autonomization of thought associated with ideology: "There [in the religious world], the products of the human brain . . . appear as autonomous figures endowed with a life of their own, which enter into relations both with each other and with the human race" (166).

Benjamin's left-wing melancholy is a fitting term for what holds many of our contemporaries in its grip, frozen as they are in the sullen contemplation of the lost objects of modernity. In the French context, doesn't the theological fetishization described by Derrida apply as well to those unconditional supporters of *laïcité*, the Enlightenment, and the republican legacy, who rely on a largely reified, mythified, and mystifying past, the golden age of the early Third Republic and the 1905 separation of church and state? Today's debates often resemble a shadow theater, the staging of a dubious battle where the living and grief-stricken confront the memories of the dead, from the paternal specters of Gambetta and Jaurès to the great Jacobin generals, de Gaulle and Bonaparte? The spectral nation of *radical-socialisme* or of the First Republic of 1793 haunts the liberal paean to globalization, while the secular party is obsessed with the veiled faces of Muslim teenagers, spectral figures par excellence, who seem to be returning from a fanatical pre-modernity everyone thought had been buried for good.

In a highly controversial book, *Le rappel à l'ordre* (2002), Daniel Lindenberg likened the intellectual climate in turn-of-the-century France to "a wintry wind" blowing across the nation, "a desire for reaction" shared by disappointed former sixties radicals that "now spills out in the open through various 'trials': of May 1968, of mass culture, of human rights, of antiracism, [and] more recently of Islam" (11). The new reactionary politics have something spectral about them as well. "At the bottom of this new thought," Lindenberg writes, "floats the ghost of a heroic politics, weighed down with the history of nations and mesmerized by the representation of a people one and indivisible, a democracy perhaps, but that never appeared on earth. To invoke the shadows of Robespierre or General de Gaulle won't change anything: this recurring fantasy condemns its partisans, as in the past, either to frustration or to a drifting toward more uncertain shores" (14).

Leaving behind the ghosts of the great Jacobin generals, let us return to the specters of Marx, and of Maurice Blanchot. The essay Blanchot wrote on the "end of philosophy" in the late fifties allows Derrida to remind his readers that the end of history was already on the intellectual agenda half a century before Fukuyama.[17] Calling to mind the crepuscular mood of his own generation, Derrida lists the "classics of the end," "the canon of the modern apocalypse" that was the "daily bread" of his student days: "the eschatological themes of the 'end of history,' of the 'end of Marxism,' of the 'end of philosophy,' of the 'ends of man,' of the 'last man' and so forth . . . Hegel, Marx, Nietzsche, Heidegger, with their Kojevian codicil and the codicils of Kojève himself" (14, 15). At the crossroads of thought and politics, the intellectual staple of the future philosophers of suspicion was *"on the other hand and indissociably*, what we had known or what some of us for quite some time no longer hid from concerning totalitarian terror in all of the Eastern countries, all the socio-economic disasters of Soviet bureaucracy, the Stalinism of the past and the neo-Stalinism in process. . . . Such was no doubt the element in which what is called deconstruction developed—and one can understand nothing of this period of deconstruction, notably in France, unless one takes this historical entanglement into account" (15).

There is indeed a nostalgic tone in this reminiscing about bygone college days, about the "we" of this emerging interpretive community, an entire generation that was to leave such a deep imprint on its time, indeed change the way of doing philosophy. There is also a tinge of nostalgia in the regret, noted in passing, that "many young people today (of the type 'readers-consumers of Fukuyama' or of the type 'Fukuyama himself')" are unaware of

---

17. Blanchot, "La fin de la philosophie," 293.

the headiness and excitement of that nearly forgotten intellectual odyssey (14). But Derrida's commemoration of the great philosophical fathers and his invocation of the ghosts of Kojève and Stalin never slide into the full-bloom left-wing melancholia that was then fueling acrimonious debates on the postmodern defeat of the mind.

Maurice Blanchot provides Derrida with the key to avoiding melancholy and turning it into its opposite, the successful completion of the work of mourning, the rebirth of desire. The twilight glow, the funereal, elegiac tone pervading Blanchot's piece on the end of philosophy, is overturned in the course of his essay, becoming "resurrectional" and "re-insurrectional" (as Derrida puts it)—hope for the rising of the dead, the sign of a renaissance and a *revenance*. Out of the dead, something new emerges, out of the twilight, a new dawn, and out of being, an event. Derrida quotes Blanchot as saying, in "La fin de la philosophie," "This then is the sunset that from now on accompanies every thinker, a strange *funereal* moment which the philosophical spirit celebrates in an exaltation that is, moreover, often joyful, leading its slow funeral procession during which it expects, in one way or another, to obtain its *resurrection*" (Derrida's emphasis, 36). At the outset of "this wake, this joyous death watch, this promotion in death," as Derrida puts it, philosophy becomes its own specter, haunting its own premises, and opening up not simply a future, but an *avenir* (literally, that which is to come).

Blanchot's description of the completion of metaphysics as the "precursor sign of another possibility that does not yet have a name" serves as a reference point for several passages in *Specters of Marx*, devoted to what Derrida calls the "messianic without messianism" that says "'come' to the future that cannot be anticipated" (168). Derrida shared with Badiou, Balibar, and Rancière the strategy of hope against all hope that keeps open the possibility of an emancipatory desire, "the condition of a re-politicization, perhaps of another concept of the political" (75). The goal is to convince the reader that this is not wishful thinking on the part of those whom the failed revolution has left bereaved, but simply the lesson of "hauntology," the necessary outcome of the movement of *différance* and spectrality, of the fact that (historical) time is always, as in *Hamlet*, "out of joint." The end of history is nothing but the end of a particular history, born with the Enlightenment and predicated on the idea of the state as the engine of social and economic progress. Derrida's way out of left-wing melancholy implies the successful completion of the mourning of the Jacobin-Marxist tradition. It calls for the imagining of new forms of democracy, new forms of relationship between the state and civil society, new forms of cosmopolitanism, in part because the new media ("the techno-tele-mediatic apparatuses") have profoundly transformed the very idea of public space and the function and functioning of government.

The opposition of being and event, or police and politics, takes here the form of the distinction between the good news of democracy and the inadequate structures in which it is always already inscribed: "The idea of democracy to come . . . is the opening of this gap between an infinite promise . . . and the determined, necessary, but also necessarily inadequate forms of what has to be measured against this promise" (65). The death of Marxism as historical determinism opens up a space for a critique without end, since the gap between democratic ideals and their implementation will never be fully closed. The death of the philosophy of history does not sound the knell of the critical stance, but rather ensures its rebirth as an insurgency without end. Beyond the liberal Right's desire for the death of Marx and the end of history, on the one hand, and the melancholy of the Left, gazing wistfully at the mausoleums and the funereal masks of the past, spectral politics resonates as a call to move on and let the dead bury the dead (Nietzsche's active forgetting), since, after all, politics cannot end or vanish in the reconciliation of society with itself. The reconciliation of society with itself, the closure of the social, is precisely the totalitarian utopia.

What will happen, then, after the eclipse of politics? More politics, of course, since in the space of modernity politics cannot end. More politics then, but in what form? No one knows, and that is a good thing, for if what is to come (*l'avenir*) was contained in some form of knowledge, it would be nothing but the future, the endless repetition of a living present. Such a future would no longer contain the emancipatory promise that is free of messianism; it would not have any room for the event; it would renounce the idea of justice itself: "If one could *count* on what is coming, hope would be but the calculation of a program" (169). Loss, then, is the condition of possibility of recovery.

Melancholy: Left, Right, and Center

Wendy Brown has remarked that what Walter Benjamin diagnosed half a century ago as left-wing melancholia continues to affect many progressive intellectuals, "an unambivalent epithet for the revolutionary hack who is, finally, more attached to a particular political analysis or ideal—even to the failure of that ideal than to seizing possibilities for radical change in the present."[18] As a "structure of desire," Left melancholia contains a healthy dose of narcissism concerning one's past political investments, as well as an "unavowed loss—the promise that Left analysis and Left commitment would supply its adherents a clear and certain path toward the good, the right, and the true" (460).

Freud, followed by Karl Abraham and Melanie Klein, insisted on the self-destructive elements inherent in the transition from love to melancholy. Someone, or something, has to be blamed for the loss of the object of desire, or rather, for the loss of desire itself, since the melancholic, unlike the nostalgic, acknowledges the loss of the object, but cannot accept the loss of the libidinal charge that was invested in it. "If the love for the object—a love that cannot be given up though the object itself is given up—takes refuge in narcissistic identification," Freud claimed in "Mourning and Melancholia," "then the hate comes into operation on this substitutive object, abusing it, debasing it, making it suffer and deriving sadistic satisfaction from its suffering" (251).

Brown provides us with a useful framework for interpreting debates on culture and society in France since the early 1980s when she suggests that the substitutive object of the modernist Left is the postmodernist, multiculturalist worldview, accused of having betrayed the revolution by abandoning the classical critique of capitalism and the notion of a unified front against the bourgeois state. The charge is well known: instead of adhering to an analysis of society in terms of class and economic relations, the proponents of "identity and cultural politics" have mistakenly indulged in the nominalist formalism of language games theory. They are also faulted for having adopted a relativistic, constructivist view of meaning creation, social practice, and identity formation, turning a blind eye to the hard, material "reality" of oppression, profit making, and political hegemony.[19] Brown has little sympathy for

---

18. See, for example, Cornelius Castoriadis's ambivalent 1982 evaluation of the consequences of "the great movements that shook Western societies for twenty years—youth, women, ethnic and cultural minorities, ecologists." While they "have certainly had (and potentially retain) considerable importance from all standpoints . . . their present ebb leaves them in the state of groups that are not just minoritarian, but fragmented and sectoral, and incapable of articulating their goals and their means in universal terms that would be both objectively relevant and mobilizing. These movements shook the Western world, they even changed it—but at the same time they rendered it even less viable. This is a striking but ultimately not a surprising phenomenon, for if these movements have been able to contest powerfully the established order, they have been neither able nor willing to assume a positive political project." "Crisis of Western Societies," 258.

19. In the conclusion to *The Hard Road to Renewal*, Stuart Hall writes that the sectarianism of the defensive Left, in the British context, was "due to a certain notion of politics, inhabited not so much as a theory, more as a habit of mind. We go on thinking a unilinear and irreversible political logic, driven by some abstract entity we call 'the economic' or 'capital,' unfolding to its preordained end" (273).

what she calls the narcissistic orthodoxy of the traditional Left, "caught as it is in a structure of melancholic attachment to a certain strain of its own dead past, whose spirit is ghostly, whose structure of desire is backward looking and punishing."[20]

And yet melancholy is not only the structure of desire of the traditionalist Left, whether Marxist, social-democratic, or national-republican. One of the most telling developments in this respect took place in the 1980s, when those who had heeded the postmodernists' call to move on and let go of the love objects of modernity (from the Enlightenment to Stalinism) found themselves disenchanted, unexpectedly orphaned by the sudden cooling of the revolutionary passions. Ironically enough, while the neo-Jacobins can be described as *nostalgic* for the good old days of the Third Republic (in the sense that they can't quite reconcile themselves with the fact that it might be gone forever), their reformist, centrist, neoliberal opponents (many of them former communists and Maoists) turned out to be the truly *melancholic* ones, for they lost both the object and the desire for it, having made sure the revolution would no longer be possible, both in theory and practice. All that was left was the empty place of an absence.

François Furet's reading of the disenchanting politics of post-1968 France is a case in point. No one did more than the author of *Interpreting the French Revolution* to liquidate what remained of the illusions of the Left. While his historical writings were meant to provide evidence that "the French Revolution was over," his political essays on the contemporary situation argued for "the end of French exceptionalism." He wrote extensively about "the great hurly-burly born of the urban and industrial modernization of the country" since World War II, and the "landslide" that carried away the once-stable landmarks of French political life.[21] "Let us dare walk through the field of ruins in all its dimensions: the idea of the Left, the idea of socialism, the idea of the Republic have declined together," he told his readers in *La République du centre*. "The classical Left, embodied in François Mitterrand, entrusted to no one else the task of finishing off the illusions it had created. In order for the irony of history to be complete, [Socialist Prime Minister] Michel Rocard was left to bury the idea of civil society. . . . What gives French politics this look of scorched earth is less the change in the landscape we were used to than the brutality of this change, which happened so quickly" (10, 65).

The Right was not doing any better in Furet's opinion, sharply divided as it was between its democratic wing, which was weakened by the twilight of

---

20. Brown, "Resisting Left Melancholia," 464.
21. Furet, Julliard, and Rosanvallon, *République du centre*, 25.

Gaullism, and the National Front, whose emergence the historian diagnosed as "the pathology of the new France" rather than some belated resurgence of old-style *pétainisme* (26). "The irony of the first ten or fifteen years of the Fifth Republic during which General de Gaulle and his supporters governed the country," Furet argued, "lies in the fact that they superimposed a traditional idea of the nation, as the revolution and the monarchy put together, upon what is in the process of subverting it, the enrichment of the country, the hedonism of mores, the birth of a European economy and consciousness. . . . Our times provide yet another proof of the anachronism of French politics in relation to what it is experiencing" (20).

Furet's writings shared some of the euphoric mood of neoliberalism in that one finds in them a controlled, yet unmistakable, sense of exhilaration in helping to dismantle the last bastions of Jacobinism. And yet his latest books are also suffused with a profound melancholy, as if the antitotalitarian movement he helped lead to victory with the support of key institutions such as *Le Nouvel Observateur*, l'Ecole des hautes études en sciences sociales, and the Saint-Simon Foundation had not kept all its promises. His last major book, *The Passing of an Illusion*, devoted to the fate of the "communist idea" throughout the twentieth century, ended with a funeral oration for what had been the messianic hope of millions: "The Soviet Union left the scene of history before exhausting the patience of its foreign partisans. It left many orphans throughout the world."[22]

The death of communism does not only affect bereaved family members and fellow travelers: even their opponents feel the loss. According to Furet, "Once again, history has become a tunnel that we enter in darkness, not knowing where our actions will lead, uncertain of our destiny, stripped of the illusory security of a science of what we do" (502). This "we" encompasses the whole political spectrum, totalitarians and liberals and democrats alike, since the passing of communism is a symptom of a larger epochal shift: the end of the historical consciousness constitutive of the modern outlook, the belief that human praxis can determine the future by shaping present society. "Deprived of God," Furet continues, "at century's end, the democratic individual has seen the foundations of deified history crumbling—an anxiety that she will somehow need to ward off. . . . The idea of *another* society has become almost impossible to conceive of, and no one in the world today is offering any advice on the subject or even trying to formulate a new

22. Furet, *Passing of an Illusion*, 501.

concept. Here we are, condemned to live in the world as it is" (502).[23] Furet's melancholy conclusion to his epic narrative of the life and death of the communist idea was also a fitting epitaph to a debate that had polarized the French intellectual field for almost two decades, following the publication of Jean-François Lyotard's *The Postmodern Condition* in 1979. The following chapter examines that postmodern debate as a turning point in the politics of loss.

---

23. I have slightly modified Deborah Furet's published translation to bring it closer to the original text in French.

Chapter Two

FRENCH POSTMODERN

The spring of 1978 tinged the tenth anniversary of May 1968 with irony. Ten years after the largest social and cultural movement since the Popular Front failed to bring the Left to power, the electoral alliance of Communists, Socialists, and Radicaux de gauche—united around the painstakingly cobbled-together Programme commun de gouvernement—proved unable, once again, to rally the votes of a majority. One interpretation of the failure was that the tireless campaign of the antitotalitarian "new philosophers" and their supporters in the media had succeeded in discrediting the political Left by assimilating its program to Stalinism, preventing once again the PCF (Parti communiste français) and its allies from gaining power. Others, especially on the Left, claimed that the Communists had shied away from the challenge, as they had in 1968. They had deliberately sabotaged the elections, making last-minute unacceptable demands of their partners, scaring the moderates, and casting doubts on the Left's ability to govern. In this view, the Communists had acted out of fear that the changing balance of power in favor of the Socialists would confine them to a minority status.

The electoral defeat opened up a period of soul-searching among rank-and-file militants and intellectuals alike, marking the end of what would be known as *les années '68*, a decade during which post-Marxist leftists and anti-Marxist *nouveaux philosophes* debated whether the revolution was already dead or whether it was still a threat needing to be put to rest. By 1978, it looked as if the corpse was no longer moving, and that even mainstream electoral politics were doomed to fail as far as the Left was concerned. The Socialist-Communist alliance would never come to power, and all hopes for reform, let alone revolution, were lost. Even though the Left came to power three years later, following the 1981 election of François Mitterrand to the presidency, by then the confidence of the critical intellectuals in the new government was severely eroded, leading to the 1983 debate over the "silence of the intellectuals." Max Gallo and a number of prominent members of the Socialist Party (Parti socialiste, or PS) blamed the intelligentsia for their lack of support for the new administration. Several intellectuals responded in kind, and the controversy raged on throughout the summer and the fall of that year.[1]

Genealogies of Postmodernity

Fittingly, the following year saw the publication of Jean-François Lyotard's *The Postmodern Condition: A Report on Knowledge*, which provided the mourning of the revolution with a world-historical rationale. Originally written at the request of the president of the Quebec government's Council of Universities, the study soon became one of the defining books of the decade, "a kind of crossroads in which a number of different themes intersect and problematize each other," as Fredric Jameson would put it in the preface to the English edition (vii). Going beyond its original concern with the development of sciences in the contemporary context, Lyotard's central thesis ("I define the postmodern as incredulity toward metanarratives") would have a lasting impact on the intellectual conversation in sociology, philosophy, literature, the arts, the media, and popular culture. The term "postmodernism," until then limited to academic discussions of postwar innovative styles in architecture and literature, became the new buzzword, and so did its correlate, "postmodernity," the historical and sociological conditions that had given rise to postmodernism.

Lyotard's argument presented several features that would be recycled throughout the subsequent debates on the postmodern: the question of chronology (when does the postmodern era begin?), the significant connection between postmodernity and technology, and the tension between philosophical and sociological genealogies of the postmodern condition (was it the result of a mutation in aesthetic categories and historical narratives, or was it the

---

1. See Baudrillard, *Gauche divine*; and Lyotard, *Tombeau pour l'intellectuel*.

result of "objective" changes in economic and social structures?). Although historical materialism would prove to be one of the most prominent victims of the postmodern redescription, a large part of the discussion still mirrored the traditional opposition between infrastructure and superstructure in classical Marxist thought. Definitions of the postmodern throughout the eighties ran the whole gamut, from metaphysical system to interpretive discourse, and from new structure of feeling to empirically documented socioeconomic transformation.

The opening paragraph of *The Postmodern Condition* pointed to a rather wide range of periodicity, tracing postmodern developments back to the nineteenth century: "The object of this study is the condition of knowledge in the most highly developed societies. I have decided to use the term "postmodern" to describe that condition. The word is in current use on the American continent among sociologists and critics; it designates the state of our culture following the transformations that, since the end of the nineteenth century, have altered the game rules for science, literature, and the arts. The present study will place these transformations in the context of the crisis of narratives" (xxiii). While acknowledging that he was borrowing the key notion of his argument from American sociologists, Lyotard anchored his interpretation squarely within the realm of ideational and representational practices (science, literature, and the arts). Making sense of cultural change remained the task of philosophical inquiry, redefined as the study of language games. This giving of the last word to the discipline of philosophy was reminiscent of the classic Kantian move that had established philosophy as the foundation and arbitrator of all other disciplines of knowledge, but this was done in a new context and with unprecedented consequences.

Although it originally came from American art criticism and architecture circles, the notion of postmodernism acquired in France a stridency and a momentum of its own, in large part because Enlightenment metanarratives, whose loss defined for Lyotard the essence of the postmodern attitude, had been so central to French conceptions of culture, state, and society, framing a host of political ideologies, from republican universalism to nationalism to revolutionary utopianism. Among these now largely discredited narratives of legitimation, Lyotard gave prominence to "the educational policy of the Third Republic," based as it was on a conception of humanity as the "hero of liberty" (31). In this now-outdated worldview, "all people have a right to science. If the social subject is not already the subject of scientific knowledge, it is because it has been forbidden by priests and tyrants. The right to science must be reconquered" (31). Given the French contribution to the discourses of modernity from the sixteenth century on, is it surprising that a French philosopher would ponder the end of that legacy, and that so many of his compatriots would enter the fray and offer their contribution to what soon became a worldwide intellectual debate?[2]

France, as Max Silverman has argued, "was the quintessential modern nation-state. Nowhere else did the star of equality, freedom and solidarity burn so bright. Yet nowhere else was that brightness deemed to be under such threat of eclipse by visions of disharmony and backwardness. France epitomized the essential Janus-face of modernity."[3] In *Facing Postmodernity*, Silverman wrote that "the level of 'malaise' experienced in France was in direct proportion to the idealized perception of the French Enlightenment tradition." The mythology surrounding the French republican model of the nation and culture was simply not matched anywhere else: "The sense of crisis in France today therefore frequently appears sharper than in other countries because of the widely held perception in France that that model—founded on universalism, progress, the political nation, republicanism, the word, Culture—is being resolutely effaced by contemporary trends" (5–6). If Silverman is right, then French intellectuals reacted so strongly to the postmodern "malaise" because they felt they had so much to lose in the process, their national culture having been more thoroughly modernized, universalized, and secularized than that of any other country.

France also figures prominently in the genealogy of the modern proposed by Zygmunt Bauman, a major influence on Silverman's view of contemporary French thought. In his book *Intimations of Postmodernity*, Bauman described the shift from the modern to the postmodern in terms of the replacement of one style of intellectual engagement by another. The *legislators* of old, who had a lofty conception of their world-historical role as professionals of the word, have given way to today's more modest, and self-deprecating, *interpreters*. According to Bauman, the advent of modernity is

2. In my own discussion of the French postmodern debate, I will focus on authors who described or opposed postmodernism from a modernist, mostly Tocquevillian, perspective (e.g., Furet, Gauchet, and Lipovetsky). Approaches informed by semiotics, such as those of Baudrillard and Virilio, are better known in the English-speaking world. See, for example, Baudrillard's *Antiaesthetic*; *Seduction*; *Simulacra and Simulations*; and *Fatal Strategies*. See also Virilio's *Speed and Politics* and *Aesthetics of Disappearance*.

For a comparative, transnational perspective, see Vattimo, *End of Modernity*; Huyssen, *After the Great Divide*; and Fredric Jameson's seminal *Postmodernism, or the Cultural Logic of Late Capitalism*. In many ways, the postmodern debate reactivated most of the discussions, and replicated most of the positions, surrounding the legacy of May 1968 during the preceding decade. As I argued in the previous chapter, the events of May could be seen either as the withering away of the modernist era or the flowering of the postmodern one.

3. Silverman, *Facing Postmodernity*, 1.

inseparable from the "cultural crusade" of the intelligentsia in the wake of the early modern crisis of self-confidence. Armed with a new certainty based on the emancipatory use of philosophical reason, the legislators, who found in the French philosophes their most radical, and most accomplished, expression, came to see forms of life as culturally produced objects of practice; they also came to see the state as the proper tool to enlighten both the rural and urban masses and free them from the premodern, traditional ways of life that hindered their humanization. In the eyes of the new intellectual elites, the rational state was no longer only a collective ruler, it was to become a collective teacher as well. The civilizing task of the legislators became "the essence of the thoroughly modern idea of 'hegemony': the role of the 'superior' way of life and their carriers as the moral mentor, missionary and pattern to be followed by all others" (7).

For Bauman, *les sociétés de pensée*, those old-regime associations ranging from provincial academies to Masonic lodges and intellectual clubs, were the exemplary institutions of the modern legislative spirit (their seminal role in the genealogy of the French Revolution was first brought to the fore by Augustin Cochin and later revisited by François Furet). The republic of letters was the social manifestation of the new ideology of culture that called for the regulation of human life through the cultivation of reason: "Culture, civilizing, refining were so many names given to the crusade proclaimed against the 'vulgar,' 'beastly,' 'superstitious' habits and customs and the forces allegedly presiding over their perpetuation. The givers of names were the first modern intellectuals of *la république des lettres*, of *sociétés de pensée*, men free of all institutional dependences and loyalties, united solely by their voluntary participation in a discussion of issues that, thanks to the public nature of the discussion, came to be defined as 'public'" (9). Bauman's description of the ideology of the modernist intellectuals, in which they appear as "the organic intellectuals of themselves," echoes Lyotard's reflections on the educational policies of the Third Republic in *The Postmodern Condition*. "This unique ideology," Bauman writes, "is one of culture: that narrative representing the world as man-made, guided by man-made values and norms and reproduced through the ongoing process of learning and teaching" (2).

The second half of Bauman's account, the emergence of the postmodern, tells of the growing divorce between the intellectuals and the state as the main agency of civilization. As its power, reach, and efficiency increased, the state apparatus no longer needed the philosophers' legitimation: it could afford to be free from ideology, and as a consequence, free from the ideologists. Paradoxically, postmodern intellectuals, who come at the end of the delegitimation process, enjoy "freedom of thought and expression they could not dream of at the time that words mattered politically" (16). Divested of their role as legislators of culture, they are now content with being its interpreters. But their newfound freedom to explore the multiplicity of language games that inform the ideological conversation in a pluralistic liberal society does not always compensate for their nostalgia for the good old days when philosophical treatises mattered to the Leviathan. Postmodern relativists and pragmatists, as Bauman puts it, are left with the "melancholic admission of Wittgenstein: philosophy leaves everything as it is" (19).

The political nature of the modernist crusade (the fact that it relied on the state and its institutions, from the schools to Parliament) has given way to a market-driven society. Whereas politics was at the heart of the project of modernity, economics is the driving force behind the postmodern universe. Culture has escaped the state, only to fall to the market, further dispossessing the intellectuals: "As the interest of the state in culture faded (i.e. the relevance of culture to the reproduction of political power diminished), culture was coming within the orbit of another power the intellectuals could not measure up to—the market. . . . More and more the culture of consumer society was subordinated to the function of producing and reproducing skilful and eager consumers, rather than obedient and willing subjects of the state; in its new role, it had to conform to needs and rules as defined, in practice if not in theory, by the consumer market" (17). It is not that postmodernism has effectively abolished the old Marxist distinction between the infrastructure and the superstructure. Rather, culture itself has migrated down from the realm of ideas and the management of knowledge and behavior through law and politics to the economic base itself.

Bauman argued that many intellectuals on the Left cannot resign themselves to the irrelevance of the legislative ideology, instead mounting against postmodernism the rearguard resistance Silverman amply documents in his own study. "Post-Marxian socialists and post-Enlightenment intellectuals alike," Bauman wrote, "are still reeling in the face of the world reluctant to conform to the model in terms of which they originally defined their role and function. Rather than admit their error, they would explain away the gap pointing to the world betraying its promise, taking a wrong turn or otherwise failing to live up to its potential" (14). In other words, the pessimism of the modernist intellectuals had its roots not in the denial that the object had been lost, for the loss had largely been acknowledged, but in the refusal to let go of their libidinal investment in the object, in defiance of the reality principle.

The triumph of a market-driven culture of consumption is a profoundly ambiguous event for its interpreters: to some it is good tidings, to others very bad news indeed, and to the rest a mixture of both. During the opening skirmishes of the postmodernism war, the pessimism of Bauman's "post-Enlightenment intellectuals," from Habermas to Finkielkraut, was matched only by the initial exhilaration of the *libertaires*, who celebrated freedom from all norms and limitations (freedom from the state as teacher), and the liberals, who welcomed the end of holistic, totalitarian models of political action (freedom from the state as ruler). The rejoicing would be short-lived, however, as we shall see in the following chapter, in view of the thoroughly immanent, unsophisticated, and conformist nature of postmodern culture. The *libertaires* (Baudrillard is a prime example) would soon point to the alienating character of the ubiquitous simulacra, while the neoliberals (the intellectual constellation surrounding the review *Le Débat*) acknowledged that the market had not only dissolved the totalitarian state and its revolutionary tradition, but had incapacitated civil society and impoverished the public sphere as well, undermining the very idea of a participatory democracy. The combined forces of consumerism and information technology were throwing the liberal-democratic baby out with the bathwater of state-sponsored nation building. The initial neoliberal celebratory phase (1979–89) was followed by a collective mood of lamentation, marked by anxieties of decomposition, and the concomitant return of radical politics (antiglobalization *altermondialistes* and an increasingly conservative worldview bent on salvaging what Silverman calls in *Facing Postmodernity* "the profoundly entrenched narratives of republican ideology" (153).

The resistance to the dissolution of the philosophical project of modernity and its consequences for French exceptionalism was very different from that of the immediate postwar years. Throughout the fifties and sixties, France had marshaled its high cultural tradition and the worldwide influence of its intellectuals (from the existentialists to the structuralists) against the growing threat of the society of spectacle. These were the days when de Gaulle, in a letter to Sartre, addressed him as *cher maître* (my dear master). France may no longer have been a major economic and military power, and it may have lost its colonial empire, but it still held the keys to the intellectual subversion of the new philistine order. As *les trente glorieuses*, the unprecedented thirty-year period of economic growth and national self-confidence that started in 1945, was coming to an end in the wake of the first "oil crisis" of 1973, an advertising slogan proclaimed, "In France, we might not have any oil, but we have ideas."

The mood in the eighties was profoundly different: it was clear now that the battle had been lost, that the Trojan horse of consumerism had camped inside the walls of the republic of virtue for quite some time now. Scores of essayists and media pundits had gone over to the enemy (represented more often than not by the United States, as the embodiment of the new order). As a matter of fact, intellectual stars such as Bernard-Henri Lévy had long ago turned themselves into market forces and their image and writings into commodities. The intrinsic superiority of the French national model meant that the contamination could only come from outside, with the complicity of useful idiots and other willing stooges of global capitalism inside the country. While reserving some of their most violent attacks for postmodern relativism, the neo-republicans had in fact resigned themselves to the demise of French universalism, but only as a model for the rest of the world—it still works for *us*, they argued. Within the borders of the besieged citadel of legislative reason, France remained the eldest daughter, if no longer of the Church, at least of the Enlightenment.

The last modernists settled for a paradoxical, local form of universality, a universalism of the parochial. In Zygmunt Bauman's words—not specifically written about the French neo-republicans, but fittingly applicable to them—the last legislators had accepted the fact "that the massive conversion of the world to our standards is not on." Accordingly, Bauman continues,

> We can better concentrate on the task at hand, . . . to keep the unique values of western civilization alive, if only as the content and the pragmatics of philosophical discourse; to continue a cultural tradition out of conviction of its intrinsic worth, all the more zealously for the realization that it is indeed a "local" tradition and in all probability would at best remain so. Insiders as we are, we need not wax humble or cynical as we admit the "locality" of tradition we guard: it is not just a local tradition, it is our local tradition, and we would go on praising its virtues even if the rest of the world refuses to join in the accolade.[4]

Chronologies of Postmodernity

While it is relatively easy to mark the temporal limits of the postmodernism debate, the periodization of its object—that is, the determination of the beginnings of postmodernity—is a more complex affair. Lyotard famously

---

4. Bauman, *Intimations*, 21.

argued that the *post* in postmodernism was not a marker of temporal succession, since postmodernism was always already present as a subversive principle at the heart of modernity. In this view, Montaigne was already postmodern, while Descartes, who came after him, was one of the great modernists. But what about the *post* in postmodernity? Socioeconomic processes lack the plasticity and reversibility of cultural constructs; surely the new era had to start at some point. A number of French historians and sociologists suggested possible dates to mark the birth of the postmodern. Unsurprisingly, May 1968 came up quite frequently. There resides perhaps the last hurrah of French universalism: the epoch-making emergence of the new times had to coincide with the most significant event in recent national history. Just as the French Revolution had introduced the world to democratic politics as the materialization of Enlightenment ideas, May 1968 is often said to have revealed, albeit in a masked, unself-conscious way, the profound mutation undergone by contemporary societies. May 1968 closed the historical parenthesis opened by July 1789.

Going back a little further in time, Cornelius Castoriadis, author of an influential interpretation of May 1968, proposed to set the beginning of the crisis of Western societies around 1950. He argued in an essay called "Culture in a Democratic Society" that 1950 is "the approximate date starting from which I believe one can discern the onset of a new situation" marked by a "covering back over [*recouvrement*]" of the modern project of political autonomy associated with "the great revolutions at the end of the eighteenth century, which were democratic and in fact de-Christianizing" (346, 345). While the 1950s had witnessed a gradual decrease in social, political, and ideological conflicts, 1968 confirmed the eclipse of the project of autonomy, a complete atrophy of political imagination, the waning of a genuine critical spirit, and the intellectual impoverishment of the Left and the Right.[5] Castoriadis noted that the most pessimistic prophecies, from Tocqueville and Nietzsche to Spengler, Heidegger, and beyond, are "now in the process of being fulfilled. They are now even in the process of being theorized in 'postmodernism,' whose displays of self-contentment are as arrogant as they are stupid."[6] His critique of contemporary culture was based on a view of radical democratic politics as a struggle for autonomy, and of art and philosophy as a continued

---

5. See Castoriadis, "Retreat from Autonomy," 20. Castoriadis typically praises high modernism—"As concerns substantive culture, the era of great modern creativity reached its end around 1930" ("Crisis of Western Societies," 264)—while denigrating postmodernism—"What could there ever be *after* modernity?" ("Retreat from Autonomy," 15).

6. Castoriadis, "Culture in a Democratic Society," 347.

creation of new forms, an active negation and refashioning of the natural and social worlds. Ironically, "the service rendered by 'postmodern art' has been really immense: to show how great modern art had truly been."[7]

The modernist critique of the new era naturally applies to the mass media. In "Culture in a Democratic Society," Castoriadis argued that the new closure in the democratic process takes the form of a generalized conformism induced by "teleconsumption, which is made up of consumption, television, and consumption simulated via television" (346). The pleasure of the contemporary "teleconsumer" includes a minimum of sublimation coupled with a maximum of passivity, in contrast to the active engagement involved in the reading of a great novel, "a strange and multiple psychical and mental activity that stimulates me without tiring me" (347). Contemporary cultural creation suffers from "the loss of the *object* and the loss of *meaning*, which go hand in hand with an abandonment of the search for form (form always being infinitely more than form since, as Victor Hugo said, it is the bottom that rises to the surface)" (347).

Unlike Castoriadis, Henri Mendras provided the reader with a very precise date for the beginning of what he calls the "second French Revolution": 1965. Like the first, the second revolution had lasted about a quarter of a century, ending in 1984, and represented as "profound a disruption" of the country as the events of 1789–1814.[8] In *Social Change in Modern France*, Mendras argued that May 1968 was the symbolic expression of a "profound transformation that had been taking place for three years.... Only a fundamental transformation of society could explain why such a movement emerged in France.... Both ideology and symbolism contain their own dynamism that can slow down or accelerate movements within society; they became the central moving forces of the May 1968 social uprising" (9). A long list of events and statistical trends made the year 1965 a turning point in French postwar history, in Mendras's view. The simultaneity of seemingly unrelated phenomena was endowed with a sort of chronological necessity, a precipitate

---

7. Castoriadis, "Retreat from Autonomy," 21.

8. Mendras argued that all the major sociopolitical upheavals in French history took place within a quarter century, a kind of magical number: "A revolution always lasts about a quarter of a century. The upheavals lasting from the siege of La Rochelle (1627) to the Fronde (1653), by destroying the remnants of feudal society and parliamentary institutions, gave rise to the classical and monarchical absolutist France of the old regime. The revolution of 1789, followed by the empire, destroyed the old regime and put in place the principles and institutions of peasant, industrial, bourgeois, and republican France. The twenty years we have just gone through (1965–84) have swept away the foundations of that France to make room for a new society." *La seconde révolution française*, 9–10. This section of the book was not included in the English version. The page number refers to the French original and the translation is mine.

of historical mutations in the making. The birth rate, the productivity of fixed capital, and the length of the workweek all start to decrease concurrently, the president of the Republic is elected by universal suffrage for the first time in French history, the Second Vatican Council ends in Rome, the number of supermarkets and the number of immigrants register a significant rise, the University of Nanterre, the future hotbed of student unrest, opens its doors in the fall, and naked bodies appear for the first time in magazines and on movie screens.

In *The Making of Modern France*, Emmanuel Todd also selected 1965 as the beginning of a "mental revolution" driven by the development of secondary education, and responsible for the retreat of Catholicism as a viable political and cultural force. For Todd, the fall of the birth rate, the rise in the number of children born out of wedlock, and the rapid transformation of sexual mores due to scientific innovations (e.g., *la pilule*, the contraceptive pill, was legalized in 1967) did more in the space of a few years (1965–82) to weaken the moral teachings of the Church than a century of republican secularization and anticlerical politics. Catholicism, however, is not the sole casualty of the definitive "structural mutations" that ushered France into the "postindustrial age."

Painting a quasi-apocalyptic picture of the new France, Todd argued that during the two decades following 1965, the traditional French political system, marked by strikingly resilient patterns of regional voting blocks (conservative in the West and East, liberal-republican in the Parisian area, Socialist in the Southwest, and Communist in the North and South), had imploded and entered a phase of rapid decomposition. Voting behaviors that had been stable since the late 1970s were no longer predicated on spatial location, in large part because of the increased mobility of individuals across the country. The dislocation of traditional electoral blocks was only matched by the accelerated dissolution of the political ideologies they had supported for almost a hundred years. In terms of vanishing influence, communism had gone the way of the Catholic Church (and its Christian-democratic political relay), while the National Front benefited both from the concurrent disintegration of the revolutionary Left (communism) *and* of the republican Right (Gaullism). Disenfranchised voters, many of them from the working class, having lost faith in the ability of the labor movement to advance their economic interests and of the moderate Right to articulate their nationalism, were increasingly turning to the National Front, hoping it would protect their jobs and restore their identity.

Todd argued in the introduction of *The Making of Modern France* that in the course of five years (1981–86), century-old structures had been "liquidated" by the sweeping tide of historical change (2). To gauge the combined effects of an industrial counterrevolution and a cultural revolution occurring in such a short period of time, one had to imagine "the French Revolution and the Industrial Revolution taking place *simultaneously* within the space of twenty years" (3). A process of deindustrialization and unprecedented violence had brought about the end of the working class, eroding the electoral base of the Communist Party. Meanwhile, as previously mentioned, the democratization of secondary education (itself a consequence of strong demographic pressures in the late fifties and early sixties) had led to the collapse of Catholicism.

The two churches (the divine and the secular) that had shaped the social and political history of France for a good part of the twentieth century were gone. While the new media culture challenged the Church's former control over the minds of the people, birth-control technology ensured the "sexual security" of women and rendered the moral order championed by Catholic priests and politicians obsolete. Both the Church and the Party had been vectors of national cohesion, socializing the peasantry and the working class into the Republic after World War I, and creating ideological identifications that cut across class lines. The disappearance of the two major institutional providers of collective identities, Todd said, would leave France more polarized in the years to come, torn between the tolerant liberal cosmopolitanism of the educated elites and the new racist populism of the working class.

Todd contributed to the postmodern debate by arguing that the crisis under way did not represent a break from two centuries of modernization. The process could be termed postindustrial, but not postmodern. "Hypermodern" was a better word for it, since it represented the passage to "a superior order of modernity. . . . The present crisis is merely Phase II of a permanent and many-sided revolution, in which mass literacy, demographic changes, and the Industrial Revolution constitute the whole of Phase I" (136). Todd's diagnosis was devastating. Now that the dust of the second French Revolution had settled, most of the monuments erected in the aftermath of the first one were in ruins: the political system was in shambles; the two historical *frères ennemis*, Catholicism and the Jacobin-Communist tradition, were moribund; and Gaullist republicanism, the heir to the Bonapartist legacy, was faring no better. The National Front offered nothing to its electorate but a doctrinal void, and the elections of 1981, "a masterpiece of historical false consciousness" (183), had revealed the absence of ideological identification in the electorate.

The new national consensus in foreign policy (later confirmed at the onset of the second Iraq war in 2003) meant that the catchall Socialist Party had become the great conservative force of contemporary France. And yet, like many other analysts of the crisis, the author, perhaps wary of the overly depressing consequences of such a dire prospect, ended his book in a confident, almost upbeat note. Although the ideological values that had made France what it once was had been divorced from their regional moorings, their influence was as strong as ever. It was as if individuals had taken them along wherever they went in the course of the unprecedented geographical mobility of the postwar period. The passing of the great authoritarian doctrines of the Left and the Right was a good thing, and if the traditional opposition between Catholicism and communism was a thing of the past, there remained a fruitful tension between freedom and equality.

Egalitarian liberalism, the finest product of the French political tradition in Todd's eyes, was still dominant, successfully keeping at bay the demons of dirigisme and free-market ideology: "The disintegration of the party system . . . does not imply that national ideological traditions have been abolished. The Left-Right oscillations will continue, more and more rapidly, and more and more lacking in real significance. France, however, will never deviate towards excessive state interventionism, uncontrolled liberalism, or racism. She will continue to be herself" (207). With Gaullist overtones, the author felt confident enough to argue that France remained, through thick and thin, true to itself, that the country's national essence transcended the accidents of history: "France existed before the Industrial Revolution and the 1789 Revolution. She will survive the disappearance of the working class and the terminal crisis of Catholicism" (3).

Post or Hyper?

Both Mendras's and Todd's accounts underscored the complex interaction of factors involved in the transition to hypermodernity. Todd made the sound methodological point that there is a large degree of autonomy among the different components (cultural, sexual, and industrial) of the modernization process. Mendras remarked for his part in the conclusion of *La seconde révolution française* that the economic crisis that began in the mid-1970s had little effect on the social and cultural transformations discussed in his book: "There appears to be no direct link of causality between a major reorientation of the productive system and social structures" (432).⁹ In an essay devoted to contemporary developments in France, Marcel Gauchet also confirmed the relative autonomy of the various aspects of what he terms "a turning point in the history of liberal democracies, a wide-range inflection in their trajectory."¹⁰

Confronted with the complexity of the analytical task at hand, Gauchet identified the rise of human rights discourse as the thread that might best enable him to unravel the convoluted tapestry of the new times. And yet he was conscious that no matter how central the ideology of individual rights is to liberal-democratic culture, the substitution of ethics for politics was only "the visible focus of a transformation that affects the entirety of the parts and machinery" of Western democracies. Privileging ideology did not mean for Gauchet endowing it with any kind of Marxian, deep-structural priority or causal efficiency "in the last instance." The evolution of political culture needed to be set in the larger context of a "global transformation under way since the beginning of the 1970s" (yet another attempt at chronology!), which was wrongly perceived at first mainly as an economic crisis (333). Gauchet repeatedly warned his readers of the impossibility to do justice to "the multiplicity of the factors and levels of analysis" implied in "the complexity of the real process" in the short space of an article. The problem, he wrote, "requires a book, and a voluminous one at that" (334).

Like Todd, Gauchet saw the present situation from the perspective of an "analyzer" of the long history of political modernity. His rejection of the notion of postmodernity was predicated on his refusal to conceive of the contemporary in terms of break or discontinuity. According to Gauchet,

> The period starting with the economic rupture of 1973–74 shows a strong consistency. It accounts for the success of the notion of "postmodernity." The latter has the advantage of capturing both the depth of the discontinuity and the unity of the multitude of changes of all kinds, social, technical, political, intellectual, that develop in the wake of the "crisis." . . . The one thing . . . the reorientation of history that started in the 1970s leads us to elaborate is the model of a major discontinuity compatible with an essential continuity, i.e., what the association "postmodernity" clumsily attempts to grasp. There is no postmodernity in the sense that one can find nothing in the after than

---

9. The conclusion of *La seconde révolution française* was not included in the English version. The page number refers to the French edition.
10. Gauchet, *Démocratie contre elle-même*, 333.

was not already in the before.... One is confronted with a fulfillment of modernity [*un accomplissement de la modernité*] rather than a wrenching away from its values.¹¹

The multidimensionality of the transition to "hypermodernity" calls for an approach that could illuminate "the coherence of a large specter of disparate phenomena, whose dependence on a common focus point is nothing but obvious."¹² "One can perceive now," Gauchet adds, "that the relations between politics and the law, for example, change everywhere alongside the breaking down of the old 'industrial state.' Human rights are the ideological center of gravity of this generalized recasting. Their relations to these different facets are patent, but not always easy to identify. How is it possible not to notice their affinity with the inter-individual space opened up by the network economy? How can we ignore their complicity with the advent of the 'information society,' i.e. the rise of the media's power?" (332). What is at stake, he notes halfway through his book, is a "transformation of the regime of ideology in our societies" (350).

For all its references to things industrial and technological, Gauchet's analysis remains centered on ideological processes. In fact, the same can be said of his entire philosophical project. Acknowledging his debt to Claude Lefort, Gauchet remarked in 2003 that one can only have "a theory of society as society, a truly general theory, if one turns Marxism upside down on one key issue: the political commands the global existence of society. Democracy is an irreducible phenomenon that needs to be explained in itself; more, it is the general phenomenon that provides locus and meaning to all the others."¹³ In *La condition historique*, Gauchet reverses Marx's reversal of Hegel with the help of Tocqueville, and interprets the most significant events in human and European history in spiritual/intellectual terms. The political history of religion? "The emergence of the state allows us to illuminate the passage from a type of religion to the next, namely from one organization of thought to the next" (81); Karl Jaspers's "'axial turn' constitutes a major break in human history" (82). The birth of early modern Europe? "The material revolution occurring in the eleventh century is at the same time a spiritual revolution"

---

11. Ibid., xiii–xiv. Many French analysts of the contemporary remain faithful to the modernist heritage, as opposed to Anglo-American critics who often rely on a paradigm of rupture between pre- and postmodernity. As a consequence, the French tend to favor notions such as "late modernity" and "hypermodernity" rather than "postmodernity" as expressions of the continued presence of modernity within emergent forms of the new.

12. Ibid., 374.

13. Gauchet, *Condition historique*, 48.

(141). The deployment of the modern spirit in the sixteenth and seventeenth centuries? The major drawback of Max Weber's notion of "rationalization" is that it "overshadows the metaphysical source of Western dynamics": "If you put capitalism at the center, you are prevented from seeing the whole dynamics of which it is a late product as well as the religious logic that informs that dynamics" (149). Again, the whole point is to find "an alternative to Marxism" (77), and Weber is said to concede too much to historical materialism.

Gauchet views ideology as what replaced religion as a vector of social cohesion by substituting an immanent justification for the former transcendental grounding of collective organization. In fact, the whole process of modernization in western European societies is conceived as this moving away from the religious structuring of collective life. At the end of the medieval period, social orders based on the reproduction of the past through the cult of tradition shifted to an open-ended, future-oriented movement of self-invention and self-production. In Gauchet's view, it is precisely this belief in the capacity of human communities to refashion themselves through political mobilization, state intervention, and scientific innovation (Lyotard's "metanarratives of emancipation") that is being undermined by the globalization of markets, the weakening of national and local political institutions, the decline in the authority of transcendental entities of all kinds, and the rise of acquisitive individualism.

In the words of Krzysztof Pomian, Western democracies are facing an epoch-making "crisis of the future."[14] It is not that we have reached the end of history; rather, history has simply become unpredictable, thoroughly secularized, its meaning cast into doubt, its orientation no longer teleological. Gauchet's own version of the collapse of historical transcendence recalls the voluntarism of Sartre's existential humanism, which proposed that we are condemned to invent our own values: "The opacity of the historical element is nothing but the unfolding of its basic principle in all its consequences: there is nothing else in the history of men than what men do."[15] Gauchet's diagnosis is as sweeping and as devastating as that of Todd in *The Making of Modern*

---

14. Pomian, "La crise de l'avenir." Castoriadis shares a related view of the collapse of the dimension of historicity: "I shall limit myself here, as concerns the past, to underscoring the paradox in which contemporary society lives in relationship to 'tradition' and through which, in fact, it tends to abolish this tradition. Here we see the coexistence of a glut of information with a basic ignorance and sense of indifference, the collection of information and objects . . . goes hand in hand with the neutralization of the past: object of knowledge for some, a tourist's curio or a hobby for others, the past is a source and a root for no one. . . . Neither 'traditionalistic' nor creative and revolutionary (despite the tales being told on this score), the era lives its relationship to the past in a mode that itself certainly represents as such a historical novation: that of the most perfect exteriority." "Crisis of Western Societies," 263.

15. Gauchet, *Démocratie contre elle-même*, 346.

France. The disbelief in the main tenets of the modernist program, which stands at the heart of "the multiform crisis that broke out in the mid-1970s," affects the entirety of the political and social discourses previously elaborated to justify the movement of history: "Tradition, progress, revolution: there isn't a single one of the figures that allowed in a classical way to account for change, and answer the question: 'where are we going and why?' which is not called into question. . . . We will keep hearing all these discourses, of course, due to the inertia of custom, but they will increasingly sink into discredit and disbelief" (*Démocratie contre elle-même*, 346–47).

Again, the eclipse of the political does not mean that these constituents of the modern imaginary have simply disappeared, no more than the crisis of the future signals the end of history. They have simply lost "their magical aura, their ability to move forward, the power to mobilize and convince" that they possessed not so long ago, during the golden age of the postwar modernizing state (343). The singular fortune of the ethics of human rights in post-1968 France (and elsewhere) has filled the vacuum left by the retreat of the political. As a substitute for worn-out and disqualified political and social agendas, the rhetoric of rights fills the vacant place of ideology, whose role was to guide and clarify the work of the collectivity on itself in post-religious, historical societies.

Gauchet's explanation for the disappearance of class struggle in the contemporary context is reminiscent of Bauman's description of the advent of postmodernity. Bauman claimed that because of its increasing ability to fulfill the agenda of social management on its own, the state no longer needed the ideological function of the modernist intellectuals, who found themselves with no prince to counsel. In Gauchet's version, the collapse of the transcendental view of the social order as the symbolic communion of subjects guaranteed by religion has left modern societies deeply divided by class, race, and other antagonisms. The ideologies of modernity (traditionalism, liberalism, fascism, and socialism) were competing forms of "secular religion." They all addressed the anxiety of the breakup of the social by promising to restore and ensure collective reconciliation, while in fact perpetuating intolerance, civil discord, and mass violence. The ability of the postwar social-democratic welfare state to peacefully maintain the prosperity, educational achievements, social mobility, and cohesion of the collectivities under its tutelage, in addition to the creation of cultural homogeneity through consumption and the mass media, has rendered the anxiety of modernity obsolete, since "social unity has ceased to be a problem" (352). As a consequence, there is only one source of ideology left in contemporary social formations: the individual.

Individualism also figures prominently in Gilles Lipovetsky's narrative of the transition to postmodern times. In his view, both the high modernist culture of the late nineteenth and early twentieth centuries and the later consumption society are the consequences of the same historical development: the emergence of a new social form, a "process of personalization" that will gradually colonize ever-widening cultural spheres and social domains.[16] Lipovetsky resembles Gauchet (both men are philosophers by training) in his claim that the movement of modernity is ultimately ideological in nature. Underscoring the limits of sociological analysis, he argues that technique is not the main force behind the genesis of the modern, thereby opposing a Tocquevillian paradigm (based on the preeminence of the process of individualism) to the Nietzschean-Heideggerian genealogy of nihilism as the triumph of the scientific worldview. The deployment of *technè*, while contributing to the liberation of the process of personalization, did not produce that process. "Modernism," he writes, "could only appear because it was carried by a social and ideological logic so flexible as to allow the production of contrasts, divergences, and antinomies. . . . The revolution of individualism . . . is the leaven of modernism. Tocqueville had already shown that the individual . . . breaks the chain of generations, the past and tradition lose their prestige: . . . the cult of the new and of the present is strictly correlated with the individualistic disqualification of the past" (104–5).

Lipovetsky also subscribed to what we might call a paradigm of continuity regarding the genesis of late modern sensibility, while Bauman, Vattimo, Baudrillard, Lyotard, and Debray might provide various illustrations of a paradigm of rupture. Like Gauchet and Todd, Lipovetsky argues that postmodernism is both the prolongation and the crowning of modernism, not its deconstruction; and he refutes both Lyotard and Baudrillard because, "in the name of indetermination and simulation, or in the name of the metanarratives, [they] attempt to think of the present as an absolutely novel moment in history. By confining oneself to the short term and eclipsing the historical field, one overemphasizes the postmodern break, and loses sight of the fact that it continues the century-old work of democratic-individualistic modern societies, albeit with different means" (128).

The contemporary "culture of narcissism" is a result of the democratization of hedonism, an extension and radicalization of the basic principles of modern subjectivity first identified by Rousseau and Tocqueville.[17] Paradoxically, the revolutionary, transgressive dynamics of modern art were victims

---

16. Lipovetsky, *L'ère du vide*, 115.

17. On Rousseau's notion of "self-determining freedom" and its contribution to the "massive subjective turn of modern culture," see Taylor, *Ethics of Authenticity*, 26–27.

of their own success: the generalization of aesthetics as an extension of the domain of the mass media, as Gianni Vattimo has argued, undermines the subversive intent of art as social and cultural critique. As a consequence, Lipovetsky argued that "we need to revise the credo of the sixties: modern art is not the Other of the world of directed consumption. Revolutionary as it was, the profound logic of modernism remains nevertheless isomorphic to that of postmodern society as participative, fluid, and narcissistic" (116).

Lipovetsky's intervention in the postmodern debate was illustrative of the struggles within the intellectual field in the early 1980s occasioned by the coming of age of a new generation, which will be discussed in the next chapter. There was a political dimension to the above-noted analytical convergence between his approach and that of Gauchet. Lipovetsky published some of the pieces later collected as *L'ère du vide* in *Le Débat* between 1980 and 1982, and he thanked Gauchet in the book's introduction for his "friendship" and "the suggestions and bibliographical information he gave me" (18). Lipovetsky's critique of Baudrillard and Lyotard would earn him a place of honor, as a precursor and a reference, in Ferry and Renault's critique of the "philosophical sixties" in *French Philosophy of the Sixties*, published in 1985. The book, which heralded, and to some extent confirmed, a changing of the guard in dominant French intellectual circles, was an assault on four of the major figures of critical theory, described as epigones of German philosophy: Derrida as the French Heidegger, Foucault as the French Nietzsche, Lacan as the French Freud, and Bourdieu as the French Marx. Lipovetsky was praised by Ferry and Renault for having rejected the "hot," radical postmodernism of the early 1970s philosophies of desire in favor of a "cool," neoliberal version that restored the initiative of individual agency against the "processes without a subject" of the 1960s antihumanists. In Lipovetsky's words in *L'ère du vide*, "It is *homo clausus*, de-socialized, disengaged from the imperious principle to follow collective prescriptions, existing for herself and equal to others, who 'works on' or 'deconstructs' forms, not the primary process or the energy of desire" to be found in Lyotard's "'libidinal' interpretation of modernism" (108n10).

Lipovetsky's celebration of the emancipatory, exhilarating, and self-affirming aspects of contemporary individualism (which links him to the anti-authoritarian structure of feeling associated with at least some aspects of the sixties legacy) enabled him to discredit the avant-gardes, whether philosophical, literary, or artistic, by contrasting their belabored, jargon-filled, elitist academic essays with the fun, colorful, user-friendly commodities of consumer culture: "In fact, there is more experimentation, surprise, and audacity in the Walkman, video games, windsurfing, and commercialized, spectacular movies than in all the avant-garde films and the 'Telquelian' deconstructions of narrative and language" (136). The disparaging reference to *Tel Quel*—one of the main journals of the literary avant-garde in the sixties and early seventies, strategically situated at the intersection of Marxism, post-structuralism, and Lacanian psychoanalysis—left no doubt as to Lipovetsky's opinion of critical theory.

And yet, for all his appreciation of the hedonistic qualities of "life lived as a self-service," Lipovetsky was not a single-minded celebrant of the new times. He was wary of a disquieting, underlying tension between mass culture and the new individualism, between the consumer's uninhibited self-expression and the threat of a Foucaultian "total and microscopic regulation of the social." "The accelerated logic of objects and messages," he warned as early as 1983 in *L'ère du vide*, "brings to its peak the self-determination of men in their private lives while society loses simultaneously its previous autonomous depth [*épaisseur*], more and more subjected as it is to a generalized bureaucratic programming" (121). Once a critical intellectual, always a critical intellectual: it was as though Lipovetsky, despite his conversion to the virtues of the free market, was forced to bring back the Heideggerian paradigm he had previously rejected, as when he claimed that the consumer revolution implied "the final completion of the century-old design of modern societies, namely the total control of society" (119). Even the most enthusiastic supporters of the postmodern turn felt pangs of nostalgia for the threatened project of Bauman's enlightened legislators.

Lipovetsky's early misgivings about the contemporary would only be confirmed in the following decades, as evidenced by his 2004 book *Les temps hypermodernes* (Hypermodern times), in which he argued that the notion of postmodernity has become somewhat old-fashioned, a victim of the quick obsolescence of things and ideas that follows from our obsessive quest for the new. In an interview published in the popular TV magazine *Télérama* (a sign of the willingness of the intellectual to engage with media and popular culture), Lipovetsky offered his own definition of hypermodernity as modernity raised to a superlative power. In his view, the new concept (complete with a new chronological framework, of course) signals the emergence of a structure of feeling distinct from the euphoria of the postmodern moment—that is, a melancholy, anxious, disenchanted mood. "Since the middle of the 1980s," Lipovetsky argued, "constraints have reappeared on the front of the stage. Fear is dominant in the face of proliferating commodification, economic deregulations, global warming, the precariousness of labor, unemployment, and the unleashing [*déchaînement*] of techno-scientific forces whose effects bring as many dangers as promises. Self-obsession manifests itself in the fear of disease and aging. How can we explain, for example, the attitude of the twenty-five-year-olds who took to the streets last year to defend their retirement programs?"

The philosopher's latest view of what lies in store for hypermodern democracies, unsurprisingly, is a variation on the familiar themes of the crisis of the future and the impossible closure of the social, complete with the obligatory reference to the death of modernity. "Democracy is a society based on pluralism and consequently on contradictions," Lipovetsky tells his interviewer. "We are going toward the light and the shadows, for we know today that progress in happiness does not exist. Hypermodernity has made people globally more free, they will have more and more satisfactions, more and more solicitations, but at the same time more and more anxiety. It is neither contradictory, nor exalting. . . . The great idea of modernity was reconciliation. Hypermodernity leads us to mourn the passing of such a utopia."[18]

In many ways, Lipovetsky's account of postmodernism in the 1980s (as distinct from his later writings on hypermodernity) mirrored the disenchantment of the post-1968 intellectual generation, who saw in the narcissistic demobilization pervading the society of spectacle an echo of their own disillusionment with revolutionary politics. Marcel Gauchet, born in 1946, briefly joined the ranks of student radicalism, in his case the movement known as *ultra-gauche*. In *La condition historique*, he recalled the successive disappointments—political, pedagogical, and theoretical—felt by those who had previously harbored "lyrical illusions" about "the end of history, meaning the beginning of true history, the one that would make humanity pass on to the consciousness of itself" (40). Gauchet's point was that in the 1980s a new kind of history was beginning, but "not the one we were expecting" (41). The interpretive blindness regarding what was happening was only matched by the "terrible feeling of failure" that followed the conceptual frenzy of the early seventies. "The theoretical hangover of the '68 generation" was a consequence of its earlier unrealistic ideological investments (45).

Gauchet ascribed the subsequent crisis of the human sciences in French academic circles to the same unfinished work of mourning on the part of the orphaned children of the theoretical sixties as was discussed in the previous chapter. The inability to squarely face the loss, grief, and frustration associated with "the movement" meant that the attempt, by Gauchet himself and

---

18. Lipovetsky, "Tout est hyper."

his colleagues at *Le Débat*, to go beyond the intellectual models of the sixties would ultimately be unsuccessful. "The structuralist-critical paradigm," Gauchet regretted, "was never really questioned or criticized for what it was. It collapsed, became old-fashioned, but it remain in place for a long time, because of the inertia of the academic system. The most skillful minds were able to adapt it, like Bourdieu for example. Traditional ways of doing things took over, little by little. But no one drew the consequences of its failure in an open, public, and thoughtful manner. Hence the current atmosphere of decline. The prolonged stagnation of the human and social sciences seem to me to come from this refusal to look" at all these issues (46). Gauchet concluded somewhat wistfully that "the book on 1968 remains to be written," suggesting that something was lost in the middle of all this unfinished business, a meaning that no historian has yet been able to recover in order to put the past to rest, once and for all: "The soul of the event has vanished without leaving any visible traces" (32). The sixties are still undead, like the zombies of horror films, roaming the world of ideas in quest of redemption. There is, it seems, no end to the spectral nature of the event, the haunting of French consciousness by the ghosts of an enigmatic era.

Chapter Three

LE DÉBAT, YEAR ONE
The Generation of 1980

In his sociological study of French intellectuals during the Fifth Republic, Rémy Rieffel notes that the first issue of *Le Débat* went off the presses the day Jean-Paul Sartre died, April 15, 1980.[1] The coincidence was highly symbolic, since the new journal would be instrumental in redefining the parameters of ideological debate in France and ushering in a new generation of intellectual figures highly critical of the Sartrean legacy of commitment to revolutionary politics. A year later, on May 21, 1981, François Mitterrand took office as president of the Republic. On June 21, the Left won the legislative elections. The new government, headed by Socialist Pierre Mauroy, included four Communist ministers, despite the intense ideological campaign of the "antitotalitarian front" of the late 1970s (a coalition of journalists, political activists, labor leaders, and public intellectuals who had done all they could to prevent the French Communist Party from coming to power). Many of the collaborators of the new journal, whether from the liberal Right or the noncommunist Left and far Left, had been active participants in the antitotalitarian movement of 1974–78.

The extent to which *Le Débat* succeeded in setting a new intellectual agenda in post-1968 France is related to the two events, Sartre's death and Mitterrand's election, that frame the first year of the journal's publication. On

---

1. Rieffel, *Tribu des clercs*, 391.

the one hand, the new review discredited the model of the critical intellectual embodied by Sartre and Foucault, and provided a testing ground for many of the ideas championed by a new generation of talented young men and women born in the late forties and early fifties. Many of them went on to successful careers in academia, the media, and politics, from Alain Finkielkraut and Pierre Rosanvallon to Blandine Barret-Kriegel and Luc Ferry.[2] In the words of Michael Scott Christofferson, "*Le Débat* was the primary beneficiary of [the] reconfiguration of allegiances and divisions within intellectual politics," and became "the principal forum for centrist reformist intellectuals in the 1980s."[3]

The electoral success of the Union de la gauche coalition in the spring of 1981, however, clearly shows the limits of the intellectual realignments that had taken place after the publication of Solzhenitsyn's *Gulag Archipelago* in 1973. Not only was the intense anticommunist rhetoric deployed by the antitotalitarians in the late seventies unable to break up the Socialist-Communist coalition, but the unexpected (and short-lived) alliance of former *gauchistes* turned "new philosophers" (Glucksman, Lévy, et al.) and reformist Socialists failed to persuade the traditional electorate of the Left that the PS-PCF alliance posed a threat to democracy. A majority of voters took the chance and sent Communists to the government.

The discrepancy between the intellectual class and the electorate was only matched by what appears in retrospect to have been a gross misjudgment, on the part of the former, of the real power and influence of the PCF in late modern French society. Not only did the country not become a Western gulag or a Soviet republic, but by mid-1984 the Communist ministers had been ousted, Mitterrand had declared his support for NATO in his famous Bundestag speech, and the Socialists had reversed their aggressive nationalization policies, repudiating their original intent to break away from capitalism. By the time Laurent Fabius replaced Pierre Mauroy as prime minister in July 1984, it seemed as though the Socialists had, for all practical purposes, converted to the market economy.[4]

2. Finkielkraut became one of the most outspoken critics of postmodernism in the late eighties; Rosanvallon, director of research at l'Ecole des hautes études en sciences sociales, and professor at the Collège de France, was secretary-general of the influential Saint-Simon Foundation; both Barret-Kriegel and Ferry were later appointed to important positions in the Chirac administration, one as special counsel for media issues, the other as minister of education. Their trajectories exemplify in various ways *Le Débat*'s original goal of translating ideas into political reforms, or, as Pierre Nora put it, "to help those who do to understand what they do." "Dix ans de *Débat*," 11.

3. Christofferson, *French Intellectuals*, 269.

4. Years later, Lionel Jospin famously contrasted *l'économie de marché* (market economy), which the Socialists had learned to live with, and *la société de marché* (market society), which remained unacceptable for the Left.

The strikes of December 1995 in the public sector further dashed the reformists' hope to turn France into a consensual, socially pacified, "Anglo-Saxon" kind of neoliberal democracy. The radical model of intellectual commitment they had hoped to eradicate in the early eighties came back with a vengeance when Pierre Bourdieu took up the cause of the striking workers, lent his rhetorical talents to the critique of neoliberalism, published a series of old-style, critical theory best sellers (*Distinction* and *The Weight of the World*), and championed an anticapitalist, antiglobalization agenda. *Le Débat*'s undeniable contribution to the reconfiguration of French intellectual life needs to be weighed against the inability of the antitotalitarian movement to prevent the Socialist-Communist coalition's victory. The reformist camp was more successful in influencing decision makers, both in the political and economic spheres, than it was in helping to overcome the chronic divisions of French society. The rejection of the European Constitution by almost 60 percent of the electorate in May 2005, for example, showed that the nationalist Right and the anticapitalist Left were still powerful forces at odds with the consensual, liberal-democratic views traditionally associated with *Le Débat*'s orientation in the 1980s.

Setting the Post-Sixties Agenda

The journal's project to set a new intellectual agenda for the post–cold war era rested on three distinct and related strategies: (1) to discredit their predecessors' philosophical views and modes of political intervention, (2) to promote a new generation of intellectual leaders, and (3) to provide the latter with a site where they could circulate new ideas and invent a different style of intellectual engagement. Cultural dynamics often involve a generational struggle between the old guard, whose views have dominated the field for some time, and the newcomers, who often ground their dissent on a set of cognitive principles or aesthetic convictions that reverse those of their opponents. The Romantics' delegitimization of their neoclassical elders, for example, rested on the contrast, stated ad nauseam in the literature of the time, between reason and imagination, or religious sensibility and positivistic scientism, or monarchic convictions and liberal-republican views.

This set of binary oppositions rarely worked in practice, but was a very efficient tool in the struggle for the dominant definition of the right way to be a poet, a painter, or a philosopher.[5] Once the Romantics as former rebels

---

5. Zola's aesthetics, for example, combined detailed, at times sordid, descriptions of ordinary social life with an imaginative, often lyrical, style of exposition, effectively fusing "classical" and "Romantic" principles, and this in spite of the scientistic, anti-Romantic outlook of the Naturalists' agenda. Similarly, Baudelaire combined the neoclassical, symbolist lack of affect with pervasive Romantic ennui.

had become the cultural establishment, they found themselves under attack from a younger generation (that of 1848), who advocated "realistic" principles of representation, a radical change in the objects of that representation (ordinary life as opposed to the sublime), a return to the creed of the neoclassicists, and in the case of many in the new "Naturalist School," militant republican beliefs. Thirty years later, the Fauvists "rediscovered" Romantic aesthetics, lamenting the naturalistic excesses of their realist predecessors, and so on and so forth. In this context, the function of the literary, artistic, or philosophical manifesto is to serve both as a rallying platform and as an expository tract for the newcomers, as they attempt to assess their popular support while providing one another with arguments to further discredit the ruling orthodoxy. In many ways, the first issue of Le Débat was such a manifesto, calling for a new kind of intellectual culture, based on democratic exchange rather than agonistic excommunication, ridiculing the erring ways of the sixties critical theorists, and proposing different conceptual and methodological tools and new objects of inquiry.

The first line of the opening page of the inaugural issue summed up the challenge faced by the new journal: *"Le Débat*, parce qu'en France il n'y en a pas" (The Debate, because in France there is no such thing). The raison d'être of yet another publication in the already crowded field of French intellectual journals was to open the possibility of a genuine dialogue within a social world famous for its propensity to condemn rather than argue.[6] Most of the themes that would be addressed in the months, and indeed years, to come were present in the initial manifesto: the opposition between the shopworn discourses of the past and the "free spirits" that refused them, the rejection of "intellectual terrorism" and *esprit de système* in favor of the open inquiry of communicative reason, the cultivation of impartiality rather than blind passion, the denunciation of the vacuity of previous intellectual exchange, the need to wed scholarly competence and public communication (as opposed to the sixties philosophers' combination of an elitist, obfuscating jargon and a view of knowledge as oppressive power), and an acute sense of the crisis of democratic societies, which called for a lucid and fearless examination. What we need to do, the anonymous first page proclaimed, is "to understand that the muddled free-for-all [*la mêlée confuse*] is the truth of our historical

---

6. The major intellectual journals in the postwar era included, from far Right to radical Left: *Nouvelle Ecole* (the organ of the new Right), *Preuves, Contrepoint*, and *Commentaire* (center-right), *Esprit* for the Catholic Left, Sartre's *Les Temps Modernes*, the PCF-affiliated *La Nouvelle Critique* and *Clarté*, and avant-garde reviews such as *Arguments* (until 1962), *Socialisme ou Barbarie* (until 1965), *Critique*, and *Tel Quel*.

moment. To understand ourselves, as we no longer know whose children we are, or what we will be fathers to, condemned as we are by a century blown to pieces to live only in the present."[7]

The first issues of the journal would start implementing the new program in three major areas: new social and cultural developments in contemporary society ("the present"), reflections on the rise and fall of communism ("the century blown to pieces"), and the contributions of foreign books to the understanding of the historical moment, beyond the sterility of the parochial, self-absorbed *débat franco-français*, to use a phrase that has enjoyed a lasting influence. One section in the first issue, titled "Library: A Foreign Book?" was introduced in the following way: "We asked several personalities to tell us briefly which foreign volumes recently published deserved to be brought to the attention of the French public." The list of contributors reads like a who's who of postwar academic excellence: Cornelius Castoriadis (on biology), Eric J. Hobsbawm (on Barrington Moore, Jr.), François Jacob (on Stephen Jay Gould), Leszek Kołakowski (on Isaiah Berlin), Emmanuel Le Roy Ladurie (on Enzo Bettiza's study of European communism), Claude Lévi-Strauss (on Japanese intellectual history), and Jean Starobinski (on Reinhart Koselleck). The choice of reviewers is illustrative of the journal's intention to cross national and disciplinary borders, since the old intellectual life was perceived as ridiculously insular. Two philosophers, two historians, a biologist, an anthropologist, and a literary critic, both native and foreign, reviewed books by German, Japanese, Italian, and American authors, commenting on topics that would figure prominently in the next issues, from the history of ideas, science, and the epistemology of historiography to the fate of communism and the comparative study of cultures.

Contributions to the understanding of contemporary societies in issues 1, 2, and 3 included a study by Robert Castel and Jean-François Le Cerf of the development of a new psychological culture (*le phénomène psy*), essays by Alain Minc and Pierre Rosanvallon on unemployment and the underground economy, and Marcel Gauchet's influential article on human rights as the new ideology of post-Marxist western Europe. As for the ongoing analysis of totalitarianism, André Glucksman wrote on Vietnam and Cambodia, Michel Bonnier on Communist China, and Mona Ozouf on the persistence of utopia in Western thought, while Edouard Kouznetsov argued for a new status for political prisoners in the Soviet Union. Reviews of seminal foreign publications included a piece by Lawrence Wylie, a *livre-montage* on Polanyi's *Great*

---

7. *Le Débat* 1 (May 1980): 1. This first page, unsigned, was obviously a statement of the entire editorial team.

Transformation, and articles by promising young scholars such as Roger Chartier on Vigarello and Patrick Fridenson on the French translation (almost twenty years after the book's publication in 1963!) of E. P. Thompson's *The Making of the English Working Class*. Rediscoveries and overdue translations suggested that French intellectuals were in dire need of catching up with the movement of ideas that had unfolded during the past quarter century, during which time they had been absorbed in their own internecine wars.

This long overdue aggiornamento of the national conversation was the topic of Pierre Nora's influential essay "Que peuvent les intellectuels?" (What can the intellectuals do?). The author combined a sweeping indictment of the corporation with a programmatic blueprint for a democratic life of ideas. His point of departure was the then much-debated notion of "intellectual power," recently introduced in the public conversation by Régis Debray's book *Le pouvoir intellectuel en France*, though Debray's name is never mentioned. While Nora did not deny the existence of intellectual influence, he distinguished the latter from the kind of power that "belongs to the register of politics and the vocabulary of the state" (3). The distinction enabled him to propose a new definition of intellectual engagement, away from radical political commitment, thereby disassociating *Le Débat*'s agenda from Debray's explicit connection between political power and intellectual authority.

Nora's argument combined a genealogy of the traditional intellectual in France since the Enlightenment with a review of the recent cultural changes that had severed the privileged relationship between the intellectual and the political fields. In other words, public intellectuals no longer influenced the political as they had in the past. Their use of the media, for example, far from extending traditional forms of intellectual power into the contemporary moment, was a radical break from former modes of intervention, revealing the impossibility of "the intellectual as oracle": "It is still possible that today, in view of a complex organization of the market of symbolic goods, and in restricted circles, intellectuals and politicians share some of the magic of this small number of individuals who seem all-powerful. But it takes the confusion of the moment or the envy of the frustrated to confuse the one and the other and to dare speak of an *intellectual* power as an element of *power* per se" (4).

Echoing François Furet's famous claim that "the French Revolution is over," Nora issued a series of death certificates, attesting to the profound transformation of traditional models and institutions of intellectual practice. The list included the end of the "civic role of the intellectual," the disappearance of the rhetorical ideal that was the backbone of the French learned tradition ("the world of the literati is crumbling"), the demise of the "leisure class," the secularization of the intellectual, and the loss of sacerdotal prestige. The passage from literary to (social) scientific principles of legitimacy, the decline of the republican-bourgeois cultural and educational matrix that had "led directly from the schoolmaster to the great writer," the professionalization and institutionalization of intellectual work (from the salon to the classroom), all of these related developments were said to have turned the prophets of old into functionaries of the state, and replaced the once-heroic civic role of the clerics into a more prosaic social function. No more posterity, no more tradition; the intellectual, understood as the one "in whose discourse the public hears directly or indirectly the echo of ultimate ends," was dead. One of the programmatic tasks of *Le Débat* would be to create a new type of intellectual project on the ruins of the old.

In Nora's view, the problem with the intelligentsia was that they didn't know, or didn't want to know, that they no longer existed. Like ghostly spirits outliving their own death, they persisted in playing a role that the new conditions of democratic life in late modernity had deprived of meaning and justification. The master thinkers were doomed to oblivion by the movement of history, and yet they refused to silently go away, finding in the instant celebrity manufactured by the mass media ways of salvaging, in a phantasmagorical manner, the worst traits of their despotic persona. The battles of the seventies were of a political nature; the complicity of the critical intellectual with the horrors of totalitarianism had been successfully revealed. But denouncing a behavior is not the same as renouncing the deep-seated ethos that had made it possible. Intellectuals had repented, but not yet converted. They had not yet "performed their democratic revolution" (12). The content of their discourse had changed (from the proletarian revolution to the democracy of human rights), but not its form. They still listened to their old demons, resorting more than ever to the rhetoric of intimidation, the terrorism of authority, and the duplicity of style, haranguing the people in a "language whose affectation or obscurity performs so many symbolic murders" (18). Building on the philosophical critique of totalitarianism in the seventies, the task of the eighties would be psychological: to eliminate all that the intellectual ethos still owed to the absolutist conflation of political power and spiritual domination. "There is a close link between the status of the intellectuals and the imagination of absolute power," wrote Nora. "It's that link that needs to be destroyed" (12).

Nora's iconoclastic conclusion was that in an intellectual democracy, history mattered and should be placed "at the core of our enterprise not because of a professional bias, but because *our history* calls for history: a resolutely contemporary history, political and conceptual, that frees the present from its false mysteries and artificial magic" (19). Outlined in these few sentences was the epistemological program of a group of historians, philosophers of history, and political philosophers who in the following decade would use a thorough investigation of the past (from ancient religions to the French Revolution) to make sense of the great transformation of their time, the advent of a world "that we do not understand because we believed it was impossible," as François Furet had put it in the same issue of *Le Débat*.[8] The centrality of a *historical* kind of hermeneutics, and the necessity of a *conceptual* kind of historical narrative, would lead the analysts of the present to uncover, beneath the various social and cultural developments on which Nora anchored his genealogy of the death of the intellectual, a broader, foundational, quasi-metaphysical *break* with previous ways of conceiving the movement of history. Nora referred to this new philosophical paradigm as "the second age of historical consciousness," a measure of the ambitious scope of the interpretive work that lay ahead. The magnitude of the object of study (the momentous recent changes in collective consciousness) lent great importance to the analytic project, crowning the practice of history as the dominant discipline of the new times, and validating the younger generation that felt called to undertake it.

In many ways, the epistemological project of the new generation was as ambitious as that of the post-structuralists they were eager to displace. Although "theory" was taken to task for its hubris, its claim to achieve a unified science of man and society based on the symbolic operations of language, Gauchet described the new intellectual agenda of the eighties in highly comprehensive, interdisciplinary terms: "The basic question was that of the nature of the human sciences, of their excessive compartmentalization. More and more of us wanted to reconstruct an interpretation of Western history since the sixteenth century, the beginning of the post-religious times."[9]

The End of History and the Rise of Historians

The new historical consciousness was presented as a radical departure from preceding forms of modernity in the sense that contemporary individuals

---

8. Furet, "Editorial," 125. Furet also recommended using the past to illuminate the present: "In the face of a world that we do not understand because we believed it was impossible, will we ever recover the understanding of the political? I suggest, as a start, to go back to the good old authors of the nineteenth century."

9. Quoted in de Montrémy, "Marcel Gauchet," 69.

were no longer able to imagine the future as a meaningful, thinkable, and knowable deployment of rational, or at least foreseeable, events. Both classical liberalism and orthodox Marxism implied a belief in the predictability of economic developments and assumed the capacity of society or the state to orient and control the future. Whether the movement of society was the result of the spontaneous harmonization of a multiplicity of individual decisions, the enlightened planning of the state, or the inexorable unfolding of the laws of history, the modernist assumption was that there lies in the heart of "post-religious" social formations a meaningfully oriented power of self-fashioning.

The world-historical paradigm outlined by Nora, and exemplified in the works of Furet, Gauchet, and their colleagues and students during the following two decades, was that this conception of history as the unfolding of society's self-production no longer structured the representations, practices, and value systems of either the cultural elites or the citizenry.[10] The passing of the three major post-Enlightenment concepts of the response to historical becoming—restoration, progress, and revolution—illustrates for Nora "the historical liquefaction of these traditional landmarks that had insured the fate of society since the French Revolution." One more "end" needed to be added to the list, that of a thinkable, predictable, meaningful *avenir* as opposed to the contingent *futur* of late modernity, which simply happens, without any kind of rational necessity. Instead, the world was faced with the advent of "a future [*futur*] forever nameless and faceless, uncontrollable, indefinite.... We are experiencing the end of finite history" (17).

The specific task of *Le Débat* would be to explore this "second age of historical consciousness that has already started." The themes and rubrics outlined in the first issue were central to this emerging interpretive program. The focus on communism past and present served to illustrate the waning influence of the modern philosophies of history as a rational, meaningfully oriented process, and to assess the chances of Marxism's survival in eastern Europe and East Asia. The critical sociology of the intellectuals uncovered

---

10. On the political and sociocultural consequences of the emergence of the second historical consciousness in France, see, for example, Furet, Julliard, and Rosanvallon, *République du centre*; Hartog, *Régimes d'historicité*; and Gauchet, *Démocratie contre elle-même*. Many early collaborators of *Le Débat*, such as Gilles Lipovetsky and Paul Yonnet, offered significant analyses of the "postmodern" turn, some of which were discussed in the previous chapter. See Lipovetsky, *L'ère du vide* and *L'empire de l'éphémère*; and Yonnet, *Jeux, modes, et masses*. Tocqueville's views on the unstoppable forward march of democratic individualism (in *Democracy in America*), and on the specific role of the public intellectual in France (in *The Old Regime and the French Revolution*), were central to the new interpretive paradigm.

their profound complicity with the first age of historical consciousness, from Rousseau to Sartre and from Robespierre to Mao. The reading of foreign authors underscored the extent to which the French national tradition, from the Enlightenment and Jacobinism to positivism and republicanism, had been uniquely informed by the interplay of restoration, progress, and revolution, by the belief in the readability of history and the plasticity of society.

Nora's own monumental historiographical enterprise, the multivolume *Lieux de mémoire* (*Realms of Memory*), would be a major contribution to the acknowledgment of the French nation form as the flowering of self-confident modernity, and to the analysis of its withering away as a source of meaning and social cohesion.[11] The end of finite history provided the backdrop for the demise of the prophetic intellectuals. As self-appointed interpreters of historical becoming, philosophers and social scientists ranked high as sites of national memory. They had been the oracles of the future, "both in and out of history," as Nora put it, "secreted by historical sensibility and charged to express it" ("Que peuvent les intellectuels?" 13). But the party was over. They could no longer survive the collapse of the collective consciousness they had made it their mission to proclaim.

In fact, the "master thinkers of the sixties" had done more than anyone else to deconstruct the belief in the inevitable stages of universal history. Foucault, Derrida, and Lacan had proposed different versions of a generalized attack on the Marxist-Hegelian philosophy of history, paving the way for the new philosophers' distrust of historical progress and resigned rejection of emancipatory politics. In the words of Julian Bourg, "Some of the New Philosophers had been students of Louis Althusser, and the shift from theoretical Marxism to anti-Marxism was not much of a stretch. In fact, of the five characteristics of French theory . . . emphasis on language, suspicions about the unified self, doubts about historical progress, valorization of desire, and anxieties about power—only the second did not seem germane to New Philosophy since the self as ethical agent, resister, and dissident was to reappear in what Alain Touraine later called the 'return of the actor.' "[12]

Those who insist in painting the critical sixties with the broad brush of "totalitarianism" forget that the complex ideological configuration that defined the decade was as much anti-Stalinist as it was Marxist. It carried within it, in uneasy tension, Lenin and Rimbaud; collective organization and

---

11. For a brief discussion of Nora's role in the ongoing "memory wars" in France, see chapter 6.

12. Bourg, *From Revolution to Ethics*, 238.

individual rights; the need for discipline and the antinomian call for the liberation of all desires; angelic, utopian yearnings and the angry denunciation of police brutality; poetry and the scientific analysis of the social; metaphysical abstractions and prosaic, concrete demands for raising wages and improving working conditions; anti-consumerism and the narcissistic drive to have *tout, tout de suite* (everything, right now). Ironically, the historical skepticism of the generation of 1980 owed a lot to the deconstructive work of its predecessors, in part because the young Turks who contributed to the first issues of *Le Débat* had all imbibed the spirit of the sixties, whether they had temporarily embraced it or had rejected it from the start.

Burying the Sixties

All cultural revolutions imply both a broad, inspiring picture of the new times that calls for bold innovations, and a systematic critique of the ruling establishment, of its passé ideological categories and obsolete epistemological principles. While Pierre Nora's genealogy of the present set the stage for the much-needed reformation, Marcel Gauchet's ironical musings on "inexistentialism" fired the first salvo at the ruling orthodoxy. The title of Gauchet's article, "De l'Inexistentilisme" (About inexistentialism), was an obvious reference to Sartre and the immediate postwar generation, but its real target was the intellectual politics of the previous two decades. Jacques Lacan, Bernard-Henri Lévy, Paul Veyne, and Gilles Deleuze had demonstrated the propensity of the "best masters of the last decade" to proclaim the death of a plurality of constructs, from nature and the woman to the state, power, and politics. "To be acknowledged as a philosopher, and a profound one, in France, in the current conjuncture," Gauchet quipped in the first issue of *Le Débat*, "you only need to declare *inexistent* one or several 'natural objects' in whose reality naive people without diplomas believe" (24).

The political implication of the intellectuals' philosophical stance called for a critique, not only of the content of their belief systems, but also of the style of their pronouncements. Echoing Nora's complaint about the despotic nature of the intelligentsia and their elitist use of knowledge as a means of power over the hoi polloi, Gauchet claimed that "the entire herd [of ordinary readers] now needs to be kept at bay and forced to bow before an afterworld made to elude its grasp. . . . The supreme knowledge is by definition poles apart from what we, poor idiots, are doomed to believe, simple-minded as we are. The main thing to understand is that we will never understand what constitutes the exclusive fate of the philosophical minds. In the person of the clerics, we have to bend before a nothing that is everything" (24).

Reflecting on the best-selling success of Bourdieu's *Distinction* (1979) in the second issue of *Le Débat*, Gauchet pondered the obscure alchemy of intellectual power by which an academic book mysteriously answers the expectations of an elusive audience. "Who buys Bourdieu's books?" he wondered. How could fifteen hundred pages of a complex, arid sociological description of the subtleties of class relations in French society, complete with graphs, regressive analysis, and statistical tables, attract such a wide readership, in the era of mass-marketed popular novels, celebrity biographies, and watered-down journalistic essays? The paradoxical answer to that question had to do with the conjunction of a pseudo-scientific style of exposition and the continued demand for radical criticism amid the so-called neoliberal consensus. In his polemical, acerbic prose, Gauchet blasted the sociologist's "unforgiving pathos" and "rubber-like" academic writing style ("le caoutchouc increvable de la prose normalienne" [the puncture-proof rubber of the *normalien*'s prose]), as well as the "modernist compactness and dogmatic-critic rigidity of [his] system," replete with "a jargon mixing in an inimitable way the bureaucratic grayness and the bright neological colors of the great semiotic-structuralist decades." Bourdieu's publishing success was another opportunity for the self-styled historians of the present to "decipher the movements at work in our society." It simply proved, Gauchet concluded in "De l'inexistentialisme," killing two ideological birds with one polemical stone, that Régis Debray was wrong, that demagoguery and the quest for profit were not the only forces at play in the French editorial world, and that a difficult book, provided it advanced radical views, could "soothe the pain and bring euphoria to discontented minds" (32).

The survival of the radical critical intellectual in the post-Marxist era turned out to be one of the reasons Gauchet and his collaborators would later become so frustrated with the democratic individualism they had so enthusiastically championed in the early 1980s. Far from disqualifying the "professional enemies of bourgeois society," the new ethics of human rights provided them with a new lease on life, as Gauchet would argue twenty years later in a sequel to his 1980 seminal essay "Les droits de l'homme ne sont pas une politique" (Human rights are not a political program), 2000's "Quand les droits de l'homme deviennent une politique" (When human rights become political).[13] In a democratic society there is no end to radical

---

13. Both essays were reprinted in Gauchet, *Démocratie contre elle-même*, 1–26 and 326–85.

criticism, since the collapse of the revolutionary creed coupled with the belief in the open-endedness of the future imply that democratic ideals will never be fulfilled, that the struggle for rights will always need to be extended to additional disenfranchised groups. There will always be a gap between the goals and values of egalitarian individualism and the realities of cultural privilege, social injustice, economic inequality, racial prejudice, and the abuse of political power. There is no end to social critique in late modernity because in the new temporal paradigm there is no end to history, no Hegelian-Marxist final reconciliation of contradictions in a rational state or a classless communist society. In the new phase of historical consciousness, social critique, as Gauchet put it, "undergoes a major reconfiguration: it becomes criticism without explanation nor proposition. Forget the stages of universal history, the contradiction between productive forces and relations of production or the transition program, all these old-fashioned ideas that no longer interest anyone."[14]

All that is asked of the new radicalism is that it underscores the evils of the present, without "useless theorization or grand promises of solution in the revolutionary future." The intellectuals as self-proclaimed "specialists of radicalism" have become irreplaceable in the new context of democratic militancy: "Let's not fool ourselves, in the land of consensual ideology there is a cult of the rebel, and one enjoys the oppositional stance. . . . Following this logic of denunciation, the militant meets up with the journalist." The new oppositional logic "implies calling public opinion to witness, rather than raising the consciousness of an avant-garde, as in the old critique of bourgeois decadence. . . . It implies, in other words, information" (360–61). Pierre Bourdieu would remain a thorn in the social-liberals' side for the next twenty years, not only because of the ongoing success of his books, but also because he came to embody the infinite reproduction of radical critique in a media-driven public sphere.

The Class of 1980

Setting a new cultural agenda implies the constitution of a cohesive cohort of newcomers eager to spread the new gospel to the cultivated readership. A special issue of *Le Débat*, published in late 1980, was designed to acquaint the readership with the up-and-coming young philosophers, historians, and social scientists who would set the tone for the national conversation at century's

---

14. Ibid., 360.

end. The founders of the journal (Nora, Gauchet, and Pomian) showed they had an acute perception of the still-open dynamics of the post-1968 intellectual field, and of the emergent forces that were profoundly reshaping it. The three men held a strategic position within the Parisian world of ideas, at the center of a network connecting l'Ecole des hautes etudes en sciences sociales (where they taught), the prestigious Gallimard publishing house (where Nora directed the influential social science collections La bibliothèque des histoires and La bibliothèque des sciences humaines), and *Le Nouvel Observateur* (where Gauchet and Pomian were regularly featured, writing reviews of the significant contributions to the new intellectual configuration they wished to promote). This unique positioning enabled them to perceive the signs of the times, gauge the new intellectual ethos born of the failure of revolutionary politics, and identify the promising younger scholars and doctoral students who embodied that ethos and would later become regular contributors to *Le Débat*.[15]

The fourth issue of the journal, conceived along the lines of earlier "surveys" of the literary youth (the most famous one being *l'enquête d'Agathon* of 1912), registered the first tremors of the coming intellectual earthquake. The publication of twenty-two responses to the question "De quoi l'avenir intellectuel sera-t-il fait?" (What will the intellectual future look like?) amounted to a kind of performative act that *created* the new generation as much as it was *discovering* it, providing the younger authors with the patronage of a prominent group of elders.[16] Their collective contributions to the issue served to render visible the existence of a unified group of thinkers, a new school as it were, who would soon illustrate the rise of the democratic intellectual. The list of their names reads like a hit parade of the French life of ideas in the following two decades, a tribute to the editors' intellectual acumen and familiarity with the dynamics of the academic field. Most of the respondents would

---

15. In 2003, Gauchet contrasted the early 1980s, when "a new generation was very easy to locate," and the situation twenty years later: "We published in one of the first issues of *Le Débat* a survey of the intellectual future. Roughly all the names that were later confirmed are there. One cannot discern anything similar today." *Condition historique*, 166.

16. A similar strategy of legitimation took place fifteen years later in the American context with the publication by Princeton University Press of the New French Thought series, edited by Mark Lilla and Thomas Pavel. The first volume in the series introduced the English-speaking academic world to representative essays by many of the early contributors to *Le Débat* (Gauchet, Ferry, Renault, Raynaud, Lipovetsky, Kriegel, Manin, etc.). Subsequent volumes included translations of monographs by several of the same authors. In his presentation of the "new French political philosophy," Mark Lilla underscored the generational break behind the "legitimacy of the liberal age" in France: "The Paris events of '68 were no less a cultural and intellectual watershed than the Second World War, separating a younger generation from an earlier one shaped by its relations with the Communist Party and 'master thinkers,' from Sartre to Althusser." "Legitimacy of the Liberal Age," 25.

indeed become major participants in the coming ideological battles, from the controversies about postmodernism, republicanism, and multiculturalism to the struggles over the legacies of the French Revolution surrounding the 1989 bicentennial celebration.

The editors explicitly linked the survey of the new generation to Sartre's death, described as a major watershed in the French life of ideas and an opportunity to reflect on the end of the "national cycle of moral consciousness" associated with Anatole France, André Gide, and Sartre himself. Although the set of responses was in no way monolithic, a number of themes advanced by the most promising members of the class of 1980 dovetailed with the reflections of Nora, Gauchet, Furet, or Mona Ozouf in previous issues of the journal, reinforcing the sense of an emerging, coherent ideological paradigm. All of the respondents shared a sense of pessimism regarding the crisis of the Left ushered in by the retreat of revolutionary ideals, and stressed the lack of discernible ideological substitutes. Alexandre Adler compared the Left's electoral loss in 1978 to the military defeat of 1940, and bemoaned the passing away of a republican "culture that is cracking and to which I owe everything" (6), while Blandine Barret-Kriegel feared "war and the rout of democracy" (12). Pascal Bruckner and Alain Finkielkraut suggested that "the social order is decomposing," Christian Delacampagne claimed that "what is new is not that we are in a crisis, but that the crisis cannot be named" (19), and Jean-Pierre Dupuy conjured up the specter of nihilism, arguing that "there is no longer any transcendence," no absolute or sacred realm (29). For François Ewald, then Foucault's assistant at the Collège de France, "everything has become undecided because we are uncertain about the value of our values. . . . We know what we no longer want, without knowing what we could want" (33).[17] The theme of the *orphaned* condition of Western intellectuals was a recurrent one: "We have killed all the discourses of which we were the children" (Delacampagne, 19); "We are the orphans of a worldview, of an ideology" (Ewald, 32).[18]

17. Each participant in the "survey" contributed a few pages expressing his or her views on the country's intellectual future after Sartre's death. The citations refer to the following contributions to *Le Débat* 4 (September 1980): Alexandre Adler, "Malaise dans l'avenir d'une illusion," 5–11; Blandine Barret-Kriegel, "La Guerre et la crise des démocraties," 11–13; Pascal Bruckner and Alain Finkielkraut, "Déscolariser l'intelligentsia," 16–18; Christian Delacampagne, "Ce qu'Occident veut dire," 19–21; Jean Pierre Dupuy, "Les intellectuels, la patrie, les sciences et la gloire," 28–31; and François Ewald, "Il y a tant d'aurores qui n'ont pas encore lui," 31–33.

18. Three years before, as mentioned in a previous chapter, Jean-Claude Guillebaud had titled his influential memoir about the lost illusions of the class of '68 *Les années orphelines* (The orphaned years). The repeated use of the orphan metaphor was a telling sign of the elegiac, mournful mood of the times.

Nora's second historical consciousness was at the forefront of the new generation's concerns, and several respondents argued that a collective "we" shared this intellectual predicament. "The future no longer exists, except as the dead dream of the past" (Lion Murard and Patrick Zylberman, 68), and since "we share to such an extent today a feeling of no longer understanding anything, we are to this extent deprived of any law that can render intelligible the very 'course' of history" (Guy Lardreau, 41). Jean-Pierre Dupuy shared Nora and Gauchet's views on the connection between the decline of the intellectual function and the collapse of the sense of a meaningful future. "The role of the intellectual," he wrote, "everyone has noted, is born of the de-sacralization of the modern West. Since men have given up looking for the meaning of their history in a place outside of social space, a particular class had to be charged with telling [that meaning]" (29). Jean-Luc Marion proposed a philosophical account of modernity as "the closure of the future," the advent of a culture mired in repetition, unable to innovate, to give rise to any meaningful event: "The future unfolds, the present survives itself without anything—any thinkable event—happening within it" (55).[19]

Attacks on la pensée '68, in which many of the thirty-something pretenders had been raised as intellectuals in training, abounded among the responses to the survey. Emmanuel Todd called the fifties and sixties the "descent into hell of French thought," blaming Roland Barthes for his attempt to destroy the French language as the "necessary incarnation of the intellectual and national continuity" of the country, and predicting that the "christiano-sartro-bartho-marxisme" would quickly sink into oblivion, leaving only "the memory of a national hangover" (88). Pascal Bruckner and Alain Finkielkraut deplored the competitive nastiness of the Parisian intellectual milieu, claimed that modernity was nothing but "the Enlightenment gone crazy," and concluded that any intellectual wanting to be credible could "only wish for the defeat of what he is today" (18). Philippe Raynaud offered an early version of what would become the new vulgate of the eighties, the systematic refutation of the previous decades' style of philosophizing. "What the master thinkers of the sixties might have had in common," he argued, "was to destroy the conditions of communication and debate, and beyond, to prevent any issue of intersubjectivity, any meaningful investment in interhuman relations" (72).[20]

19. Citations refer to the following contributions: Guy Lardreau, "Ne pas céder sur la pensée," 40–45; Jean-Luc Marion, "Une modernité sans avenir," 54–60; and Lion Murard and Patrick Zylberman, "La révolution du pessimisme," 67–71.

20. Citations refer to the following contributions: Emmanuel Todd, "La vie intellectuelle française, du Néant à l'Etre," 84–88; Pascal Bruckner and Alain Finkielkraut, "Déscolariser l'intelligentsia," 16–18; and Philippe Raynaud, "Renaissance de la subjectivité et libération de la communication," 75–79.

Firing the New Canon

Within the dynamics of any intellectual changing of the guard, new high priests and new doctrinal beliefs require a new set of sacred scriptures. The young Turks called for the constitution of an alternative textual corpus to replace the obsolete trilogy of Marx, Nietzsche, and Freud. Emmanuel Todd advocated a return to "the strong individualities of nineteenth-century French thought" (i.e., Constant, Tocqueville, Le Play, Tarde, Durkheim, and Cochin), while Raynaud stressed the need to go beyond "hexagonal provincialism" and to read foreign authors, from logical positivists (Popper, Wittgenstein) to Frankfurt School theorists (Habermas, Adorno).[21] Most of this revisionist project would be completed in the following years, with the translations of works by German and Anglo-American authors, and the publications of numerous studies on Constant, Guizot, Tocqueville, Wittgenstein, and the philosophy of mind, not to mention Furet's rehabilitation of Augustin Cochin's views on the French Revolution.

Several of *Le Débat*'s early associates carried out this return to the classics of the French liberal tradition as members of the Centre de recherche politiques Raymond Aron, created in 1992 and housed in the Ecole des hautes études en sciences sociales (François Furet was president of the school from 1977 to 1985, a decade that proved crucial for the institutionalization of the new paradigm). The Center was a result of the fusion of the Institut Raymond Aron (founded by Furet in 1984) and of a research group headed by Claude Lefort. The new research program confirmed the intellectual convergence that had developed between the two historians in the 1970s regarding the interpretation of communism. The Center's scholarly publishing activities included a new edition of Constant's political writings in 1997 (edited by Gauchet), the publication in 1992 of a collected volume on the early nineteenth-century Idéologues (edited by François Azouvi), and the correspondence, memoirs, and complete works of Tocqueville in 2002–3 (edited by Françoise Mélonio).

Despite the pessimism of what might have appeared as yet another "lost generation," several respondents to the 1980 survey showed some confidence in their ability to rebuild a viable intellectual agenda on the ruins of what they described as philosophical terrorism. Olivier Mongin, who would become *Esprit*'s chief editor in 1988, called for another Aufklärung, "a new 'regime of reason' that would energize history [*dynamiser l'histoire*] rather

---

21. Todd, "La vie intellectuelle française," 84–88.

than master it or close it" (64). Bernard Manin, who would become one of the leading specialists of the history and theory of social democracy, drew the lessons of totalitarianism, arguing that the "Good Society" did not exist, that no individual, government, or party could presume to *make* the masses happy.[22] The idea of the fundamental pluralism of modern democratic societies, of the impossibility of the social order to reach a stable, tension-free, reconciled state of self-sufficient totality, quickly became a major component of the new developments in political philosophy, in France and abroad, including within Marxist and post-Marxist thought.[23] To acknowledge the phantasmic, and politically deleterious, nature of absolutist utopianism did not imply a fatalistic renunciation of all transformative action. "The Good Society does not exist," Manin argued, "but one should not be content with any order that sanctions the misery of some human beings" (51).

Philippe Raynaud welcomed for his part the emergence of a "new style" of intellectual practice, informed by a liberated attitude toward knowledge, the rejection of scientific theories of history, a strong sense of contingency, a return to the virtues of empiricism, and an awareness of the limits of historical objectivity, away from the "historical nihilism" of historians such as de Certeau. Hopefully, Raynaud argued, the reinsertion of the epistemological subject in her own discourse would insure that "in accordance with the best aspirations of the Enlightenment or the early Romantics, the critique of political, religious, or metaphysical illusion will not work against living individuals, but for the establishment of liberated relations among them" (79).

A Place of Their Own

The infusion of new blood to the existing cast of established public intellectuals and leading academics enabled *Le Débat* to carve its own niche within the space of intellectual reviews, especially in the increasingly crowded center, somewhere between *Commentaire* on the right and *Esprit* on the left. The recentering of the ideological debate implied a rapprochement between the liberal followers of Raymond Aron and a reformist, social-democratic camp that was fast renouncing the Jacobin, statist culture of the old Left, whether in its communist or *radical-socialiste* incarnations. Contributors to *Le Débat*,

---

22. Citations refer to the following contributions: Bernard Manin, "Eloge de la banalité," 49–54; and Olivier Mongin, "De la possibilité d'un avenir," 62–67.

23. See, for example, Laclau and Mouffe, *Hegemony and Socialist Strategy*; Žižek, *Sublime Object of Ideology*; and *The Ticklish Subject*.

Commentaire, and *Esprit* had forged common bonds during the heyday of the antitotalitarian campaign of the previous decade, and many of them published articles and book reviews in all three journals. *Commentaire*'s Aronian liberals, such as Pierre Manent, were welcome in *Le Débat*, as were younger members of the *Esprit* group, such as Mongin and Raynaud. This increasing collaboration between social democrats and liberals in the early 1980s provides the most tangible evidence of the restructuring of the ideological field, leading to the unique combination of anticommunism, antistatism, and neoliberalism their opponents soon denounced as the consensual, hegemonic *pensée unique*. *Le Débat*'s founders were faced with the perilous task of asserting their difference while championing ideological détente and the rallying of responsible minds around the new issues raised by the advent of liberal-democratic individualism.

Looking back on the earlier days of the enterprise, Marcel Gauchet described in 2003 the risky, but eventually successful, wager that allowed *Le Débat* to invent its own raison d'être within the field of existing intellectual reviews. Gauchet described the move, in retrospect, both as a necessity and as a creative solution, given the need to reinvigorate public debate. Asked about *Le Débat*'s relationship with its competitors, he replied in *La condition historique* that "they were excellent journals with whom we have fraternal relations, because we are all in the same boat. If one of them disappeared, it would be a bad sign for the others. We move within the same space, between Left and Right, rather right for *Commentaire*, rather left for *Esprit*, but with the same significant indifference for political divisions. Pluralism has become part of intellectual mores." Gauchet derived satisfaction from the fact that what Nora had described in the first issue of *Le Débat* as the challenge of the 1980s (i.e., to bring about the "democratic revolution of spiritual power") had been, for the most part, met. He went on to explain that while *Esprit* remained tied to the Catholic social movement and *Commentaire* was "the organ of the educated establishment," promoting the views of "the enlightened liberal fraction of the higher civil service and of those who teach at Sciences Po, law schools, and economics departments, . . . *Le Débat* was less determined by the sociology of a referential milieu" (170).

This professed free-floating position is what enabled the journal, in Gauchet's view, to fulfill its original function of intellectual go-between, linking various factions of the reasonable, constructive intelligentsia, and encouraging conceptual cross-fertilization and interdisciplinarity, via the dialogue between the social sciences and the experimental ones. Gauchet's academic home, l'Ecole des hautes études en sciences sociales, pursued a similar strategy of self-definition by stressing its difference from the Sorbonne's heavily compartmentalized disciplinary structure. The school's marginal position within the French higher education system allowed innovation in terms of curriculum and research agendas and links with foreign institutions. *Le Débat* would similarly pride itself on its detachment from immediate social-ideological interests linked to a particular class, social movement, institution, or national tradition, thereby fulfilling the very condition of the autonomy of intellectual discourse. According to Gauchet,

> We are more extraterritorial and we wished to be so. *Le Débat*'s concern is first and foremost intellectual, and that's what marks our major difference. What interests us, in politics, is the analysis and observation of deep-seated trends [*les tendances de fond*]. Our specific function is that of a laboratory of ideas, with as a consequence a wider encyclopedic openness. Our ideal is to embrace all that seems relevant and new in scholarly production, in order to inscribe it in living culture, whether it is science, art, sociology, philosophy, or history. We are looking to de-compartmentalize disciplines and domains of knowledge, at the highest level, at the same time as we are trying to insert intellectual renewal within the public debate, if only by making it accessible. (170–71)

Helping Those Who Do to Understand What They Do

Pierre Rosanvallon's response to the 1980 survey of new talent had addressed this issue of inserting intellectual renewal within the public debate. Rosanvallon was uniquely positioned, because of his social capital and professional trajectory, to promote such an agenda. Born in 1948 and a graduate of Hautes Etudes Commerciales, one of the most prestigious French business schools, he had served until 1977 as director of *CFDT Aujourd'hui*, the Socialist trade union's main publication and the site of frequent interactions between labor leaders, *deuxième gauche* politicians, and antitotalitarian intellectuals. A close collaborator of Edmond Maire and Jacques Delors, Rosanvallon had contributed essays to *Commentaire*, *Esprit*, and *Le Nouvel Observateur*. One of the leading theoreticians of the *autogestionnaire* movement within the noncommunist Left, he had written the group's ambitious and programmatic 1977 manifesto, "Pour une nouvelle culture politique" (For a new political culture), coauthored with Patrick Viveret, then editor of the socialist review *Faire*.

Coming from social Catholicism and the labor movement, and trained in economics and business management instead of philosophy, Rosanvallon perceived the limitations of the new generation's ideological creed. It was long on the critique of totalitarianism and short on any constructive proposal regarding a much-needed political theory of democracy. "It is not enough to think against Marxism," he warned, claiming that the post-seventies ideological void had its source in "the impossibility of thinking of the future except as repetition or decomposition."[24] Rosanvallon's proposal to find a way out of the predicament of the new Left combined serious analytical inquiry with a return to the public role of the intellectual. "One cannot be content with writing the history of ideas," he told his cohort of aspiring opinion makers. "One has to think historically about the role of ideas in a specific intellectual and symbolic field" (83). This belief in the political relevance and efficacy of ideas led him to an activist conception of intellectual practice. Since the aim of conceptual work was to make action possible, clear-sighted, and efficient, the task at hand was to write books that "articulate the fundamental and the instrumental," and reconcile the erudite with the amateur.

Gauchet, who shared a similar ambition for *Le Débat*, later clarified the distinction between the expert counsel of the Prince and the new version of intellectual engagement Rosanvallon had outlined. "I am fairly confident in the future of an intellectual role both more modest and much more effective [than that of the prophetic intelligentsia]," Gauchet said in *La condition historique*. "Our societies more than ever need to understand themselves—or should need to. No one any longer needs writers or philosophers to uncover the evil of colonialism or the horrors of the working-class condition or enlighten the people on their political choices. On the other hand, we are all lacking in the intelligence of what surrounds us, and the dilemmas we come up against every day. Purveyors of ideas are asked to intervene in a properly intellectual way in public affairs. They should not complain about that" (350–51). This did not mean, however, adopting the stance of the expert: "Expertise is necessary in a technical society. But it does not and cannot, by definition, answer the problems that require the kind of elucidation I call 'intellectual.' Expertise is part of the problem. It follows a logic of specialization" (351).

The project of influencing social movements and public policies by providing decision makers with serious, documented, historically grounded analyses of the present was nothing new in the French context. Rosanvallon's association with the CFDT (Confédération française démocratique du travail, or

24. Rosanvallon, "Oublier les modes," 83.

French Democratic Confederation of Labor) made him part of a long tradition of enlightened reformism going back to l'Ecole des cadres d'Uriage in the early forties. After the war, intellectuals, trade-union leaders, and technocrats had collaborated closely in the planning commissions of the Fourth and Fifth Republics and in think tanks such as le Club Jean-Moulin.[25] The blueprint for a redefinition of the public intellectual Rosanvallon had sketched out in 1980 naturally led to his active role in the creation of the Saint-Simon Foundation, of which he was secretary general from 1982 to 1999. Following Rosanvallon's earlier proposal, the new structure enabled *les gens de réflexion* to gain access to business leaders, policy makers, and media personalities, providing them with a unique opportunity to help those who do to understand what they do, as Pierre Nora had put it in the first issue of *Le Débat*. Many of the respondents to the journal's 1980 survey would later join the Foundation (Luc Ferry, for example), or teach "seminars" for members and invited participants.

A Social-Liberal Hegemony?

Conspiracy theories abound in the ideological debate today, and they tend to overestimate the ability of a particular institution or group of individuals to shape the collective imagination of the time. This is certainly true of the way *Le Débat* and the Saint-Simon Foundation have been described by some of their critics. A 1998 article in *Le Monde Diplomatique* refers to the Foundation's leaders as "the architects of social liberalism." A website titled Organizations of the Masters of the World (from the Bilderberg Group to the World Economic Forum) claims the Saint-Simon Foundation has "infiltrated the French Left and gradually converted it to economic liberalism and 'globalization.'" According to another website, Réseau Voltaire, the Foundation "has imposed a form of monolithic thought [*pensée unique*] in France."[26] These statements overstate the case. Despite its prominence, the social-liberal agenda never enjoyed a hegemonic position in the French life of ideas (whether it did in the political field is another matter). The very fact that there are opponents to it contradicts the claim of a monolithic ideological scene.

---

25. On the interaction between intellectuals and the state during Vichy France, see Delestre, *Uriage*; and Comte, *Une utopie combattante*.

26. See Laurent, "Enquête sur la Fondation Saint-Simon," 1, 26, 27; Jacques Kergoat, "La fin de la Fondation Saint-Simon"; *L'Humanité*, June 30, 1999; Denis Boneau, "Cercles d'influence atlantistes en France: La face cachée de la Fondation Saint-Simon," http://www.reseauvoltaire.net/article12431.html.

French society, as demonstrated by Le Pen's strong electoral showing in 2002 and the vote against the European Constitution three years later, remains highly polarized, and the far Left is alive and well. The various candidates to the left of the Socialists in the presidential elections of 2007 garnered more than 10 percent of the vote, while those on the far Right (Le Pen and de Villiers) received almost 13 percent. The divisions within the Socialist Party on Europolitics belie assertions that the Left has been thoroughly converted to neoliberalism. The antiglobalization, anti-free-market *altermondialiste* movement has been active in recent years, Trotskyist and other far-Left organizations still have a following, and the critical theory of the sixties and seventies has survived in the works of post-Marxist philosophers, Lacanian psychoanalysts, and promoters of a new kind of "public sociology." The bestselling success of Viviane Forrester's *The Economic Horror* or Pierre Bourdieu's *The Weight of the World* shows that the critique of capitalism continued to find an echo in parts of the educated readership. The vitality of the national-republican agenda, both on the Right and the Left, after 1989 hardly supports the thesis of the complete domination of an unchallenged, consensual neoliberal ideology in contemporary France. Moreover, the reformists themselves have become disenchanted with late modernity's decline in civic participation and with the rise of a "selfish," acquisitive individualism, which they see as major threats to democratic ideals. Even for the partisans of "modernization," all is not well in the post-historical era, and the end of French exceptionalism did not fulfill many of its promises. The antitotalitarian coalition of the late seventies, whose momentum had been so critical to *Le Débat*'s early success in setting the agenda for a postcommunist era, did not withstand the test of time.

The first rift occurred with the publication of Bernard-Henri Lévy's *L'idéologie française* in 1981. In the course of his discussion of fascism and anti-Semitism in French thought since the days of Drumont and Gobineau, Lévy accused Emmanuel Mounier, who founded *Esprit* in 1932 and was the leading figure of postwar social Catholicism, of having been attracted to Pétain's message. Lévy further portrayed the Ecole d'Uriage, whose agenda had been influenced by Mounier's philosophical doctrine *(le personnalisme)*, as the laboratory of a specifically French brand of fascism *(un fascisme aux couleurs de la France)*. Lévy's assertions sparked a heated debate in *Le Monde* (the daily's director, Hubert Beuve-Méry, had been a member of Uriage during the Vichy years), the Catholic daily *La Croix*, and, of course, *Esprit* and *Le Débat*. The controversy put an end to the antitotalitarian rainbow coalition between the social Catholic constellation so central to the "second Left" and the former

Marxist-Leninists, including Lévy himself, who had burst onto the intellectual scene in 1976.[27]

A second, even more significant rift occurred twenty years later, following yet another publication taking to task some of the most prominent representatives of the antitotalitarian galaxy. Daniel Lindenberg, a frequent contributor to *Esprit*, denounced in 2002's *Le rappel à l'ordre* (Call to order) the reactionary turn of the French life of ideas in the preceding decade.[28] Lindenberg described the new trend as a mixture of xenophobic populism, cultural neo-conservatism, statism, and neo-republican authoritarianism strongly critical of "May '68, mass culture, human rights, antiracism, and more recently Islam" (11). In other words, the French reactionary legacy within the Left, denounced by Lévy in the early eighties, was once again rearing its head, this time putting democratic individualism, sexual politics, and multiculturalism on trial. Although most of Lindenberg's critique focused on the openly racist, sexist, and elitist prose of writers such as Michel Houellebecq and Maurice Dantec, the last chapter of the book faulted Marcel Gauchet, among others, for his loss of faith in late modern democracy.

Lindenberg equated Gauchet's imputed "nostalgia" for a stronger, more assertive political and social order to an antidemocratic tradition including Georges Sorel's anarcho-syndicalism, Georges Bataille's *Le Collège de sociologie*, and, once again, Emmanuel Mounier. As with Lévy's book, Lindenberg's sparked a fiery debate, including a stinging response by Gauchet in *L'Express*. The main sign of the tensions raging within the republic of letters was that Lindenberg's book had been published by Editions du Seuil as part of a collection directed by Pierre Rosanvallon! Clearly, the antitotalitarian movement

---

27. The term "deuxième gauche" (second Left) refers to a new political culture within the French Left. This novel approach emerged in the 1950s in reaction to Stalinism and the Soviet repression of the workers' uprising in Budapest (1956), on the one hand, and the governing French socialists' support of colonial rule in Algeria, on the other. The second Left was made up of politicians, union members, and activists opposed to both components of the traditional, "first Left," that is, the Socialist Party (Section française de l'internationale ouvrière or SFIO), then in power, and the Communists. Key organizations involved in the rise of the second Left include the Parti socialiste unifié (PSU, created in 1960), a coalition of Trotskyists, left-wing, radicalized socialists not affiliated with the SFIO, and members of the CFDT union (Confédération générale du travail, created in 1964). The notion of "autogestion," or workers' self-management, which gave the rank and file more control over the process of production in factories, was crucial to second Left ideology, as distinct from the more hierarchical, top-down conceptions of labor organization and mobilization of the first Left. Representative figures of the second Left include political and union leaders such as Michel Rocard and Edmond Maire, as well as intellectuals such as Pierre Rosanvallon and Alain Touraine. The social-liberal wing of *la deuxième gauche* figured prominently in the antitotalitarian movement of the 1980s.

28. Lindenberg, *Rappel à l'ordre*. See also Anderson, "Union sucrée"; and *Pensée tiède*.

was no longer of one mind regarding the merits of late modernity, as the pressure applied by sexual and racial minorities and human rights movements continue to destabilize what was once taken to be a strong, cohesive national culture.

If anything, the latter skirmish confirmed the limits of the supposed hold of consensual neoliberalism among the French elites. *Le Débat* did not single-handedly "impose" on the intelligentsia the distrust of Caesarian socialism and bring about the liberalization of political creeds and social mores that have deeply transformed French society in the past quarter century. As discussed in the preceding chapter, these developments relate to long-standing sociological, cultural, and economic trends going back to the immediate postwar years, and were already well under way in the seventies, although very few people then were aware of their magnitude. Many on the Left, intellectuals and militants alike, still thought and lived according to a belief in the inevitability of a Marxist revolution, the coming collapse of capitalism, or the invulnerability of the welfare state. Intellectual journals rarely create change in collective consciousness; they mainly reflect them. The most successful among them contribute to the clarification of the new worldview, and in so doing, play a significant part in its legitimation. *Le Débat*'s founders skillfully assessed the cultural sea change that had taken place in the aftermath of May '68, and proceeded to provide an intellectual framework to make sense of it, while setting up academic and political networks that would support those developments within a "great transformation" they viewed positively. But the winds of change blew in all directions, including those where the members of the generation of 1980 were not willing to go.

Chapter Four

THE RETURN OF THE PROPHET
Bourdieu, Zola, and the Dreyfusist Legacy

One of the sixties' legacies was a considerable revision of the self-representations of left-wing intellectuals in France. The major figures of the critical intelligentsia who had in some way or other been involved in the political developments of the decade went on to propose various redescriptions of their own political practice in light of the new times. Jean-Paul Sartre, who had been both the promoter of the notion of engagement at the end of the 1940s and the embodiment of the oppositional intellectual during the Algerian War, was among the first to engage in self-criticism. In an interview with radical militants in October 1970, Sartre declared that the era of the "classical intellectual" he had long been associated with had run its course, having been thoroughly "contested" by the student movement. The only valid position left, he said, was to "do away with oneself as an intellectual."[1]

Concurrently, Michel Foucault and Gilles Deleuze proposed to substitute a new model, the local or specific intellectual, for the now-disqualified universal intelligentsia whose main function had been to "discover new political relations where no one had seen any before." The point for the specific intellectual was no longer to place oneself "a little bit ahead or a little bit aside"

Parts of this chapter were published as "L'exigence prophétique: Zola, Bourdieu, et la mémoire du Dreyfusisme," *Contemporary French Civilization* 24, no. 2 (2000): 321–40; and "'Refonder l'universalisme': Bourdieu, Balibar, et 'l'exception' philosophique française," *Contemporary French and Francophone Studies* 12, no. 3 (2008): 357–64.

1. Sartre, "L'ami du peuple," 467.

of the masses, as had been the case previously, but to fight against forms of power wherever she lived and worked: in the lab, the lecture hall, or the classroom, or in professional environments linked to the orders of knowledge, truth, consciousness, and discourse.[2]

These various reformulations of the classical role of the public intelligentsia had one aspect in common: they all questioned the right "to speak as masters of truth and justice" that the clerisy had traditionally claimed for itself.[3] Sartre urged his colleagues no longer to talk (down) to the proletariat "by doing theory," as they had done in the past (44). Classical intellectuals, Foucault argued, claimed to answer the people's need for awareness and expression; they told "the truth to those who could not yet see it and in the name of those who could not tell it." One of the lessons of May 1968 was that intellectuals could no longer speak for others, since "the masses did not need them in order to know" (Deleuze and Foucault, 4).

Sartre or Zola?

As discussed in the previous chapter, many historians, sociologists, and cultural journalists read this self-criticism as evidence that the prophetic function of the intellectuals, with its source in the biblical tradition, was dead. The modern prophet had taken up the cause of the oppressed and challenged institutional authority in the name of universal principles that undermined the rationales of power, but the eclipse of the political made such a stance impossible. The prophetic intellectual was one more item on the long list of the lost objects of late modernity.[4]

At the same time, however, the widespread mobilization in support of the Polish workers' movement Solidarność in 1981, the student protests of 1986, and the workers' strikes of 1995 seemed to refute the view that oppositional

---

2. Deleuze and Foucault, "Les intellectuels et le pouvoir," 4.
3. Foucault, "Vérité et pouvoir," 22; and *Essential Foucault*, 111.
4. The term "prophetic" refers to Max Weber's *Sociology of Religion*. The Weberian ideal type of prophecy includes the following elements: personal calling, charismatic authority, sense of a mission inspired by higher demands than individual interests ("prophecy is unremunerated," 47), opposition to the sacerdotal institution (the priests), concern for reform and social justice (in the case of Hebraic prophets), and the emotional tone of the predication. All these components can be found in the texts of Zola and Bourdieu discussed in this chapter, despite the transfer from the religious sphere to the secular domain. The public nature of their interventions also connects the secular prophets to their religious predecessors. Weber remarked that "the enterprise of the prophet is closer to that of the popular orator (demagogue) or political publicist than to that of the teacher" (53).

politics had breathed its last breath with the turbulent sixties. In fact, throughout the 1980s, prominent intellectuals such as Bourdieu and Foucault (until his death in 1984) publicly expressed their solidarity with eastern European dissidents, student demonstrators, and public sector employees. Bourdieu's trajectory as a public figure after 1980 provides an excellent opportunity to test the presumed demobilization of the cultural elites in the new, "postrevolutionary" France. The sociologist's relentless attacks against the "neoliberal scourge," and his interventions in favor of striking workers, illegal immigrants, the unemployed, and the "social movement" more generally, have inevitably invited a comparison with Sartre. In a September 1988 article in *Le Monde* titled "Examining the 'Bourdieu Case,'" Michel Contat, a renowned Sartre specialist, argued that "Bourdieu wishes to occupy the space Sartre left empty, that of the great intellectual standing up to the powers that be."[5] In other words, the ghost of the prophetic intellectual was still haunting the new liberal-democratic order.

Contat's claim seemed hardly debatable, and has been made time and again ever since, whether to celebrate or to deplore the survival of the intellectual prophet. And yet Bourdieu never missed an opportunity to distance himself both from Sartre's philosophy *and* his style of intellectual politics, devoting an entire section of *The Logic of Practice* to a refutation of Sartre's subjectivism. Sartre's public persona did not fare any better than his philosophy in Bourdieu's eyes: "What I like least about Sartre, is everything that made him not only the 'total intellectual' but the very ideal of an intellectual, and in particular his unmatched contribution to the ideology of the free intellectual, which brought him the recognition of all the intellectuals. . . . I could say that I constructed myself, as soon as I emerged from the educational system, against everything that the Sartrean undertaking represented for me."[6]

In contrast with this summary dismissal of Sartre's style of intellectual engagement, reminiscent of the post-1968 critiques of the universal/classical intellectual, Bourdieu's writings in the last two decades of his life were filled with references to another major figure of modern French literary history, Emile Zola. Bourdieu, the son of a postal worker from the small town of Béarn, once described his own trajectory as leading from the people to the elite. In his inaugural address as a newly elected member of the Collège de France, he told his colleagues that "the sociologist coming from what we call

5. Michel Contat, "Le 'cas Bourdieu' en examen," *Le Monde*, September 28, 1988.
6. Bourdieu, *Political Interventions*, 27, 26.

the people and belonging to what we call the elite can only have access to the special kind of lucidity associated with any kind of social displacement if he denounces both the populist representation of the people, which only deceives its proponents, and the elitist representation of the elites, likely to deceive both those who belong to them and those who do not."[7] Compare with Zola, caught between his right-wing critics, who blamed him for his populism (especially his use of the language of the streets), and his left-wing detractors, who deplored his *misérabilisme*—that is, his mostly negative, and hence politically demobilizing, depiction of the working-class condition. "*L'assommoir* is without doubt the most moral of my books," he wrote in the preface. "I have often had to put my finger on far more revolting sores. Only its form has upset people. They have taken exception to words. . . . But I am not defending myself. My work will do that for me. It is a work of truth, the first novel about the common people which does not tell lies but has the authentic smell of the people."[8] Bourdieu's social and spatial mobility closely resembled that of Zola, the orphaned child of an Italian immigrant, a Provençal and a provincial who had "moved up" to Paris, as the French say, to embark on a successful journalistic and literary career. Sartre, on the other hand, was the Parisian writer par excellence, the scion of a wealthy, highly educated bourgeois family.

One may wonder to what extent what Bourdieu says of Zola's oeuvre applies in part to his own epistemological project, or to the way he saw it, once transposed from literature to social science. "There is still the question," he wrote in *The Rules of Art*, "of how the 'creative project' can arise from the convergence of the particular dispositions that a producer (or a group of producers) brings into the field (due to his previous trajectory and his position in the field) and the space of possibles inscribed in the field (what one puts under the vague term of artistic or literary tradition)" (126). In the case of Zola, "one would have to analyze what in the writer's experience (we know in particular that he had been condemned to long years of misery by the early death of his father) might have favored the development of the rebellious way of seeing economic and social necessity (or even inevitability) that his whole work expresses, and the extraordinary power of rupture and resistance (no doubt arising from the same dispositions) that was necessary for him to achieve this body of work and to defend it against the whole logic of the field" (128).

---

7. Bourdieu, *Leçon*, 9.
8. Zola, *L'assommoir*, 21.

Bourdieu was much too aware of the workings of an intellectual's social habitus not to have been drawn to this contrast between Sartre and Zola. Moreover, his scathing criticism of the "neoliberal invasion" from the early 1990s was closer to the republican discourse of Zola in "J'accuse" and "Letter to France" than to the blend of Marxism and phenomenology that provided the philosophical background of Sartre's politics in the fifties and sixties. The space accorded to Zola's intellectual engagement in Bourdieu's later works illustrates the dialectics of loss and recovery I have examined throughout this book. The loss of the Sartrean kind of public intellectual as a source of left melancholy was largely compensated, in Bourdieu's view, by the recovery of the alternative model of intellectual engagement provided by Zola. The intellectual à la Zola was not as a total, universal, "free" consciousness, but a scholar involved in a struggle for democratic values and providing others with the knowledge she has accumulated over the years. Through his rescuing of the Zola legacy, Bourdieu also recovered a critical moment in France's republican past. From then on, he would frequently use this kind of anamnestic solidarity with Dreyfusism as a tool to criticize a present dominated by neoliberal capitalism.

Recovering the Dreyfusist Legacy

In many ways, the divisions of the French intellectual field in the last two decades of the twentieth century were comparable to the ideological struggles during the Dreyfus Affair, even though the balance of power between the intellectuals, on the one hand, and the state, the media, and the economic sphere, on the other, had changed considerably since the days of Barrès and Péguy.[9] Bourdieu saw the new social and economic conditions as favorable

9. The Dreyfus Affair was one of the most critical events in French modern political and cultural history. In 1894, Captain Alfred Dreyfus was accused of having provided sensitive military information to the German government. Although Dreyfus claimed his innocence, he was found guilty of treason by a military court, stripped of his rank, and sent to a penal colony in French Guiana. Because Dreyfus was Jewish, the nationalistic Right saw his trial as further evidence of Jewish treachery and French Jews' lack of commitment to the country. Although evidence surfaced in 1896 that exonerated Dreyfus, high-ranking members of the military suppressed the new information and fabricated documents destined to bolster the initial verdict against the captain. In 1898 Emile Zola, in a famous open letter to the president of the Republic published in the daily *L'Aurore* (known by its bold headline, "J'accuse"), denounced the military's cover-up and accused the government of sacrificing truth and justice.

The controversy divided France into two camps, the Dreyfusards and the anti-Dreyfusards, along ideological and philosophical rather than strictly political lines. The supporters of the Jewish captain defended the liberal, post-Enlightenment ideals of justice and tolerance against the arbitrary power of the state and the reactionary, monarchist leanings of the Church leaders. Their opponents

to those who advocated what he called the "involution of the social state." He claimed time and again that the power of the media, subjected as they were to the requirements of the new "economic Darwinism," severely threatened the autonomy of the cultural field that had emerged at the time of the Dreyfus Affair. The connection between the context of the late 1890s (the emergence of an autonomous academic field and the invention of the modern intellectual) and that of the late 1990s sheds light on both the practice of the intellectuals and their theoretical agenda, since the growing heteronomy of the life of the mind in the late twentieth century is usually viewed as a sign that the historical cycle that had begun with the publication of "J'accuse" is coming to a close.

In an essay devoted to the "cycle of hysteresis" of the Dreyfusist legacy throughout the twentieth century, Michel Winock wrote that "one can observe, if not straightforward repetitions of the Dreyfus Affair, at least a series of connections with it, insofar as the Affair was a revelatory-catalytic event, whose dramatic intensity laid bare a new kind of confrontation in French society."[10] This kind of "resonance" echoing throughout the Dreyfusist epic as a privileged site of memory prompted the historian to look for a homology between the Affair and some later events, "[one] that is imperfect in the details, but might be tenable as a whole" (20). The loose set of homologies posited by Winock extends to the contemporary situation. Four main areas of correspondence carry over from one fin de siècle to the next: (1) the structural homology between the competing "lists" of intellectuals involved in the struggle; (2) the common reference to the basic principles of republicanism; (3) the critique of the media and of backroom politics (what the French call la politique politicienne); and (4) the explicit connection, drawn by various actors in both cases, between the prophetic ethos and the necessary autonomy of the intellectuals.

---

championed a nationalistic, militaristic agenda fueled by the rivalry with Germany and the need to take revenge for the Franco-Prussian War of 1871, which had resulted in the territorial loss of Alsace-Lorraine, two provinces on the country's eastern border. Following several years of a bitter struggle between the "two Frances," Dreyfus was exonerated and reinstated in the French Army with the rank of major in 1906; he later served in World War I, a testimony to his previously questioned patriotism. The affair left a long-lasting imprint on the French national memory. The outcome of the scandal reinforced the republican, anticlerical Left, leading to increased opposition to the Catholic Church, which culminated in the law on the separation of church and state in 1905. In many ways, the Vichy regime of 1940–44 was a continuation of the Dreyfus Affair, with the Catholic Right taking revenge on the "enemies of the fatherland," from Jews and Freemasons to liberal republicans and communists. Marshal Pétain's Révolution Nationale abolished the Republic, dismantled the law of 1905, and collaborated with the anti-Semitic agenda of the Nazis by organizing the deportation of tens of thousands of French and foreign Jews to concentration camps.

10. Winock, "Les affaires Dreyfus," 20.

The permanence of the intellectual paradigm born in the 1880s implies that the model can be applied to changes in the situation of cultural producers throughout the following century. The reformulation of principles, in the form of adaptation without concessions, guarantees their conservation. As Christophe Charle put it, the complexity of the process of the birth of the modern intellectual explains

> the historical and theoretical persistence of this key notion of the culture and history of the French twentieth century. The structural conditions as well as the political circumstances that give the notion its multiple dimensions have been able to evolve without really affecting it, contrary to what happened to older representations of the intellectual craft. Every section of the intellectual field at each given time can use it again by privileging unilaterally such or such meaning justified by its multiple originary significations. Even the theme, periodically reborn, of its disappearance or decline, is a way of acknowledging its persistency. . . . Each intellectual generation seems thus to be rewriting Péguy's *Our Youth*. History provides us with many other examples of these starlike events whose light continues to reach us while the transmitting star is long dead.[11]

The thrust of Winock's argument is that the lines of contention that make up the Dreyfus Affair did not overlap neatly with the previous historical struggles between supporters and opponents of the old regime (the revolution/restoration political divide) or between bourgeois and proletarians (the socialism/capitalism economic split). The Dreyfus Affair was much more philosophical/ideological in nature. A moral conflict between recently created value systems, it opened up a new era in which the rise of populist, anti-Semitic right-wing nationalism (up to the 1880s nationalism had been mostly an ideology of the Left) prompted as a response the reactivation of the Enlightenment legacy, based on human rights, justice, freedom, and equality. This basic conflict, anchored in the two complementary and contradictory sides of political modernity, the nation and democracy, repeated itself at subsequent key moments of the French twentieth century: in the thirties, under Vichy, during the Algerian War; and since 1985, via the debates over immigration, Islam, and the National Front.

11. Charle, *Naissance des "intellectuels,"* 15.

In the words of Krzysztof Pomian, "When the time is right, an era of the past may serve as a screen on which new generations can project their contradictions, controversies, and conflicts in objectified forms."[12] "Screen" here may be taken to mean both a veil interposed between individuals and the traumas of their collective history, and a surface on which these distorted, fragmentary memories are being projected (the space of public debates). In his study of the "Vichy syndrome," Henri Rousso described the Pétain regime as the archetype of "la guerre franco-française" (Franco-French war).[13] The same can be said of the Dreyfus Affair, since memories have a way of feeding one another, or bleeding into one another, the revolution into the Dreyfus Affair, Dreyfus into Vichy, Vichy into the Algerian War, and the Algerian War into current race relations in France, from the successive affairs of the veil to the *banlieue* uprisings of fall 2005.[14]

The December of the French Intellectuals

Before examining the extent to which the events of 1995 and their aftermath can be inserted in this repetitive cycle of the Dreyfus Affair, let me briefly recall the circumstances that led to the most important series of strikes and demonstrations France had witnessed since 1968. The trigger for the movement was the Chirac administration's intention to propose a reform of the retirement and health care systems. In anticipation of the official disclosure of the plan, civil servants and transportation workers went on strike on October 15. Employees of the SNCF (Société nationale des chemins de fer français, or French National Railway Corporation) followed suit on October 25, blocking long-distance and commuter trains throughout the country and starting a debate in the media on the rights of the users of public services (SNCF is a state-controlled company). Following an agreement between all the major French unions a few days later, demonstrations for the defense of social security took place on November 14. The next day, the center-right prime minister, Alain Juppé, presented Parliament with a law to reform social security by creating a new tax, revamping the health insurance agencies, generalizing medical coverage, and limiting public health spending. The "Juppé plan," as the media dubbed the new proposal, was part and parcel of yet another effort to bring public spending under control through the reorganization of

---

12. Pomian, "Les avatars de l'identité historique," 117.
13. Rousso, *Vichy Syndrome*, 6.
14. On the interaction between memories of the Holocaust and other histories of victimization, see Rothberg, *Multidirectional Memory*.

the postwar welfare state. The disclosure of the government's agenda set off a series of demonstrations and the railroad strike was prolonged. By the end of November, most industries and services in the French public sector, including the postal service, the telecommunications industry, public universities, and civil service administrations, were involved in a combination of strikes and demonstrations that culminated in a rally of two million people in Paris on December 12. The government eventually withdrew the retirement component of its proposal but maintained the reform of the social security system. According to the Ministry of Labor, the accumulated number of striking days for all the participants totaled six million, most of them in the civil service.

The most remarkable consequence of the disclosure of the government's agenda in October was the splitting of the labor movement and the political Left. While the Confédération générale du travail (General Confederation of Labor, or CGT), the Communist Party, and the far Left denounced the reform as another conservative attempt to sacrifice workers' rights on the altar of globalization, the secretary-general of the Socialist union CFDT publicly supported some aspects of the plan, including the extension of health insurance to all those who had been hitherto denied medical care. The growing hostility of a large part of the union rank and file, notably among public sector employees, toward the proposals, and the disagreement among leaders of the major unions as to their interpretation, led the supporters of the reform to denounce the resistance to change of "privileged" state employees as a selfish, corporatist refusal to take the common good into account and include the excluded in the system of social protection. The increasing isolation of the CFDT leadership, accused by some of its own members and by "the Left of the Left" of aligning itself with a right-wing agenda, prompted a group of self-styled "intellectuals, militant members of associations, leaders, or experts" to sign a petition in favor of a genuine, thorough transformation of the welfare state into "a system that would ensure both solidarity and social justice."[15]

Inspired by Joël Roman, coeditor of *Esprit*, the petition praised the courage and independence of the CFDT and underscored the positive aspects of the government's plan (extension of medical coverage, focus on prevention, and vote by Parliament for the social security budget), while voicing some reservations regarding its more "questionable aspects." The text ended by condemning the "prevarication of the political Left," which had

---

15. Duval and others, " 'Décembre' des intellectuels," 18.

created an ideological void that the intellectuals had to fill. Once again, the intelligentsia voiced their distrust of the political class and reaffirmed their duty to make up for the politicians' shortcomings when they shirk their responsibilities. Several prominent scholars and writers signed the petition, among them Claude Lefort, Michelle Perrot, Paul Ricoeur, and Alain Finkielkraut. Many of the signatories were regular or occasional contributors to *Esprit*, *Le Débat*, or *Le Nouvel Observateur*; some were historians and sociologists teaching at l'Ecole des hautes études en sciences sociales, some of them with close ties to the CFDT, and some were members of the Saint-Simon Foundation. As mentioned in the previous chapter, the Foundation brought together academics, high-ranking civil servants, journalists, and political, economic, and administrative leaders with a goal to acquire "a better understanding of contemporary societies" and to promote the "modernization" of French society (i.e., its adaptation to the new constraints induced by economic globalization).

A few days later, another petition, signed by militants from the radical Left and the Communist Party, appeared in *Le Monde* in support of the strikers' resistance to the dismantling of *le service public*. The petition argued that the striking workers did not defend narrow, corporatist interests, but were struggling for the "most universal conquests of the Republic."[16] The signatories of this second petition were generally less prominent than those of its rival, and this deficit in social and symbolic capital led them to seek the backing of well-known personalities. Although they ended up securing the support of prominent intellectuals such as Pierre Vidal-Naquet, Etienne Balibar, and Communist Party economist Paul Boccara, it was undoubtedly Pierre Bourdieu who provided them with the greatest source of visibility. His support of the strike was the outcome of a marked, and remarked, evolution that had started in the early 1980s.

After being elected in 1981 to the Collège de France, France's most prestigious academic institution, Bourdieu became increasingly involved in politics, both at the national and international levels: support of Solidarność, participation in various educational reform commissions, and repeated calls for the mobilization of European intellectuals. He was instrumental in the creation of the journal *Liber*, an international review of books whose goal was to disseminate avant-garde literary, artistic, and scientific works to the general public by "overcoming temporal gaps and misunderstandings bound up with linguistic barriers and the slowness of translation . . . as well as the inertia of

---

16. Ibid., 19.

scholarly traditions."[17] Concurrently, Bourdieu shifted the main focus of his sociological inquiry from culture and education to the state apparatus and the economic sphere. *The Nobility of the State* (1989) and *The Weight of the World* (1993), whose best-selling success reached beyond the usual audience of social scientific monographs, even for an author as well known as he was, provided the theoretical background for his public interventions from 1995 onward.

The sociologist read the government's attempts at reorganizing *le service public* as the confirmation of his own analyses of the role played by "the right hand of the state" (i.e., the technocratic elites in the service of neoliberal modernization) in the destruction of the welfare safety net, leading to increased social and economic inequalities. By contrast, the public sector employees (utilities, railroads, postal service, and education) and their allies in the university and the schools expressed the needs and interests of the "left hand of the state," namely all those who had everything to lose from the disintegration of social democracy.[18] As an apt description of the diverging political and social interests among civil servants, the metaphor of the two hands of the state also implied that government cannot be expected to enact rational and efficient public policies, since the right hand does not know what the left one is doing, and vice versa.

Although the two petitions occasioned by the government's reformist agenda had not been conceived originally in opposition to one another (some individuals had even signed both of them, since approving the proposed changes did not necessarily mean rejecting the strike), the specific logic of media coverage quickly turned the whole issue into yet another "war of the intellectuals," a more entertaining topic for journalists than in-depth analysis of complex, boring social legislation.[19] The media-driven construction of a war between the lists prompted the intellectuals in both camps to rally around the critique of mainstream journalism inherent in the traditional ethos of the intelligentsia. Olivier Mongin, editor of *Esprit* and one of the instigators of the pro-reform petition, attempted to undermine the media's spontaneous sociology of the intellectuals by assigning higher motives to his fellow intellectuals than petty rivalry or competing self-definitions. "We did not get involved as intellectuals," he argued, "but as citizens concerned with these issues. The question of whether we are Sartrean intellectuals or not is

---

17. *Liber* 1 (October 1989): 2. See Bourdieu, *Political Interventions*, 205.
18. Bourdieu and others, *Weight of the World*, 183. See also Bourdieu, *Acts of Resistance*, 1–10.
19. Duval and others, "'Décembre' des intellectuels," 76.

quite ancillary to us. . . . Unfortunately, that's how it was portrayed in the media, who indeed love wars when they involve eggheads. On top of that, there is no risk involved" in spreading such characterizations.[20]

Mongin was obviously concerned with improving the less than flattering image of the intellectuals, given the number of critical essays on the "tribe" published in the preceding two decades. The claim that members of the cultural elite are ordinary citizens, sharing the same concerns and frustrations as the rest of the population, was meant to reverse the perception of the public intellectual as a carryover from less democratic times, when the intelligentsia pretended to speak for the masses and ritually weighed in on the future of the national community. Intellectuals might be citizens, but they are not ordinary citizens, if only because the reformation of the health care system did not affect them in the way it did most of their compatriots. Arguing, as many of them did, that their position was not determined by social and economic interests but by a disinterested concern with equity, justice, and democracy, was enough to turn them into citizens of a very specific kind, since the claim to be motivated by higher principles rather than base self-interest has always been the hallmark of the intellectuals' worldview.

To erase the social specificity of the signatories, or to deny that they represent a relatively autonomous section of the citizenry, is to ignore what sets them apart from other social groups as a consequence of their position in the field of cultural production, and to underplay their conflicted relation with the state, the media, and political and economic powers. There is a grain of truth in ironical comments about the "wars of the intellectuals," even though the journalists' delegitimization of the artistic and academic intelligentsia is rooted in their own corporate interests. After all, they too are busy waging a war against the intellectuals as their main competitors in the interpretation of the social world.

In the immediate aftermath of the strikes of December 1995, a group of young scholars close to Bourdieu published a critical analysis of the events to address, and redress, the official version popularized by the media. The book, titled *Le "Décembre" des intellectuels français* (The "December" of the French intellectuals), argued that there existed, beyond the empirical diversity of individuals and groups involved, "two major systems of resources opposing at one end of the spectrum actors who are relatively better endowed with media, political, and bureaucratic capital (the Reform list), and at the other end, actors relatively stronger in intellectual and scientific

20. Ibid., 77.

capital (the Strike list). . . . On the Reform list, the pole of economic and political power is distinct from its intellectual and media counterpart. As far as the Strike list is concerned, the opposition is between the militant and scientific polarities" (93).

From 1894 to 1995

This distinction between critics and experts, or between social scientists teaching in universities (the "Strike list") and economists and historians teaching in the more prestigious *grandes écoles* (the "Reform list"), or between *normaliens* on the one hand, and graduates of Polytechnique and Ecole nationale d'administration on the other, is reminiscent of the rival factions during the Dreyfus Affair. The anti-Dreyfusards were recruited mainly from the ranks of literary academies and salons linked to royalist circles and from a group of publicists close to the nationalistic Right and business leaders, while Dreyfus's supporters came mostly from *la république des professeurs*. As Christophe Charle has remarked, while the Dreyfusards represented the professorial and avant-garde literary elites, their opponents came from old-fashioned groups whose power was lost in 1880.

A very strong correlation between academic curricula and political opinions also existed in the student population. Students in law, medicine, business, and science were predominant in the anti-Dreyfusist camp, while most of the Dreyfusist cohorts hailed from the Sorbonne and the Ecole normale supérieure. In addition, the contrast between public and private sectors of the economy, between tenured state functionaries and self-employed business owners subject to the risks of the marketplace, induced similar ideological effects in 1898 and 1995. The Juppé administration's claim that government employees were moved by a corporatist, narrow-minded defense of their state benefits echoes the anti-Dreyfusard Right's attacks on the functionaries of the republican university, "revolutionaries drawing their salaries from the government payroll," as Ferdinand Brunetière famously put it. The analogy is not entirely adequate, of course. While the Dreyfus opponents came from reactionary, declining sections of the French elites, the reformist camp in 1995 presented themselves as "modernizers," and advocated the necessary adaptations of French society to the new conditions of global economic competition. The monarchist Right of the 1890s had looked to the past, while the neoliberal reformers of the 1990s claimed to be forward-looking.

That intellectuals had joined the fight in 1995 as autonomous agents with their own set of expectations is not enough to equate the rejection of neoliberalism and globalization with the paradigm of historical Dreyfusisme as defined by Michel Winock. At first glance, the 1995 struggle seems to be more akin to the traditional capitalism-versus-socialism divide Winock distinguished from the central impetus of the Dreyfus Affair. As a matter of fact, the 1890s socialists had argued with Jaurès that the whole thing was nothing but a quarrel among the bourgeois that would only lure the labor movement away from the centrality of the struggle against capital. Many of the academics who supported the striking workers one hundred years later were members of leftist parties and unions, which could suggest that the struggle was purely political and did not have the moral and philosophical overtones of the Dreyfus Affair. From a strict Dreyfusist perspective, the late twentieth-century intellectual militants, far from repeating the highly principled engagement of the class of 1898, would appear to have betrayed the moral ideal of the cleric in the name of class or party interests (following Benda's argument in *The Treason of the Intellectuals*), and sacrificed *mystique* to *politique* (to use Péguy's famous distinction in *Notre jeunesse* [*Our Youth*]). Was the ethical and philosophical dimension so crucial to Dreyfusisme and its legacy throughout the twentieth century lacking in the 1995 debate?

The fact that the CFDT leadership and several contributors to *Esprit* supported some aspects of the Juppé government's reform shows that the Left was as divided in 1995 as it had been (for other reasons, obviously) a century earlier, and complicates the argument that the social security controversy was a "classical" struggle between an antibusiness Left and a pro-globalization, neoliberal Right. In addition, the text of the pro-strike petition made explicit references to the constitutions of the Fourth and Fifth Republics, and to the equal rights of all "men and women, young and old, unemployed and salaried, . . . immigrants and French people," calling for "a radical reflection on the future of our society."[21] This kind of rhetoric inevitably broadened the scope of the conflict from a specific issue of social policy to a larger, more ambitious cultural struggle meant to safeguard the historical gains of the Republic. The original resistance to a particular piece of social legislation received additional weight, and increased legitimacy, from being associated with the universal principles of equality, solidarity, and justice.

In this sense, the social conflict of December 1995, as limited in time and scope as it was, can be said to belong to the space of resonance of the Dreyfus Affair. It allowed a small group of oppositional intellectuals to establish themselves, once again, as the guardians of the Enlightenment tradition. Bourdieu played a crucial role in broadening the initial pro-strike rhetoric from claims

---

21. Ibid., 19.

associated with a particular governmental policy to the larger issue of protecting human and workers' rights, which he explicitly identified with the historical struggles of the Left. Addressing the strikers and their supporters at a rally in Paris, he expressed his support for "those who have been fighting for the last three weeks against the destruction of a *civilization*, associated with the existence of a public service, the civilization of republican equality of rights, rights to education, to health, culture, research, art, and, above all, work."[22] Apropos the civil war in Algeria, he lamented the fact that many of his compatriots were engaged in a collective repression of the memory of colonialism and of the violence associated with the Algerian War, forgetting also that "in other times, France was a model for a certain number of things (including human rights), but it is in the process of becoming a model for collective regression into barbarism."[23] Looking back at what he had learned from the events of 1995, Bourdieu described the neoliberal turn as a "total war against trade unions, the social gains of past centuries, in short, against the whole civilization associated with the welfare state," the latter being gradually replaced by the "philistine platitude of a civilization of ratings, the best-seller, and the TV series."[24]

Bourdieu's formulations replicate, sometimes to the word, Zola's impassioned defense of the republican ideal of truth and justice against the double threat posed by the attacks of the reactionary camp and the complicity of the parliamentary Left for electoral reasons. In response to a journalist who asked him which reforms he would fight for if he entered the political arena, Zola declared in 1893 (five years before the publication of "J'accuse"): "Social reforms, of course. . . . but without indulging in the vile political scheming [*l'ignoble cuisine politique*] of the professionals—whom I continue to despise profoundly." Five years later, the novelist denounced again in his "Letter to France" the "base dealings of parliamentarism" and deplored the compromising stance of those ruling republicans who, instead of upholding civic virtue, tolerance, and human rights in the face of the anti-Semitic Right, contributed to "killing the ideal."[25] Similarly, Bourdieu blamed the Socialists and their allies for not taking a stand against the xenophobic discourse "which, for some years now, has been working to generate hatred out of the misfortunes of society—unemployment, delinquency, drug abuse, etc., perhaps for lack of convictions, perhaps for fear of losing votes."[26]

22. Bourdieu, *Acts of Resistance*, 24.
23. Bourdieu, *Political Interventions*, 266.
24. Ibid., 290, 291.
25. Zola, *L'affaire Dreyfus*, 138.
26. Bourdieu, *Acts of Resistance*, 16.

The Treason of the Intellectuals

A century apart, the novelist and the sociologist felt as though they were witnessing a turning point in their nation's history. Both of them denounced the powerful attempt at restoration that called for an immediate response from committed intellectuals: restoration of monarchy, clericalism, and militarism by social forces linked to the feudal past for Zola, restoration of liberalism and unfettered free-market ideology for Bourdieu. During the Affair, Zola repeatedly referred to "the return of the year one thousand" to denounce the reactionary agenda that threatened to take France back nine hundred years to the Dark Ages. "France, do you still know where you are going?" he asked in his "Letter to France." "You are going to the Church, you are going back to the past, this past of intolerance and theocracy, that the most illustrious of your children fought against, thought they had killed, by giving their intelligence and their blood.... True, the people still do not believe; but is it not the beginning of belief, is it not to begin again the intolerance of the Middle Ages, to burn the Jews on the public square?"[27] An acute sense of being at a crossroads, of *having to* raise one's voice at a critical juncture of the struggle for democracy, justified in the eyes of the writer and the sociologist the apocalyptic tone of their public statements.

Prophetic discourse also underwent some sort of restoration in the 1980s, returning after years of Marxist historicism and Nietzschean perspectivism to the rhetoric of Third Republic universalism in the form of a claim that France must show the world its historical attachment to the values of justice, equality, and "civilized" social relations. Facing the jury who was to sentence him to one year in prison and a three-thousand-franc fine for slander, Zola raised the Affair to the level of a moral struggle that went far beyond the personal fate of Alfred Dreyfus. No less than the salvation of the country's influence worldwide was at stake: "There is no longer a Dreyfus Affair, the point now is to decide whether France is still the France of human rights, the one that gave freedom to the world and should give her justice."[28] Zola was already defending the notion of the "French exception" a hundred years before it became a cliché.

French exceptionalism has become the target of all those who, in France as abroad, see it as the reassertion of Gallic arrogance, and a misguided source of a resistance to globalization that is futile and self-defeating. Although Bourdieu equated the French difference with the "republican equality of rights,"

---

27. Zola, *L'affaire Dreyfus*, 106.
28. Ibid., 132.

he parted company with the neo-republicans on the issue of nationalism, arguing for more internationalism, more universalism, and a supranational state, instead of advocating a defensive withdrawal within a besieged national identity. "I think that the dominated groups in society have an interest in defending the state, particularly in its social aspect," he told members of the Greek confederation of trade unions in Athens in the fall of 1996. "This defense of the state is not inspired by nationalism. While one can fight against the national state, one has to defend the 'universal' functions it fulfils, which can be fulfilled as well, or better, by a supranational state."[29]

Bourdieu's exhortations to counter the structural amnesia induced by electronic media were reminiscent of Zola's attacks on *la presse immonde*, the abject press intent on manipulating public opinion and substituting demagoguery for the rational examination of facts. Bourdieu's rogue gallery of "doxosophers," "television philosophers," and other "fast thinkers" he blamed for having switched from *la pensée Mao* to *la pensée Sciences Po* are very much like the "sectarians of the mind" Zola contrasted, in his "Letter to France," with "the free spirits, the big hearts who founded the Republic and should tremble to see her imperiled!"[30] In both cases, access to public opinion was seen as a key issue in the public intellectuals' competitive relationship with the media. The will to influence requires that the critical intellectual becomes a public figure. It is the cornerstone of the duty to get involved, and is the only reason why the writer, the philosopher, or the scientist should ever give up the seclusion of the study. Just as Zola tirelessly repeated that he only aspired to silence, only wished to go back to his novel writing and the privacy of an ordinary citizen's life, Bourdieu claimed that he had "little inclination for prophetic interventions," and that he had only consented to step onto the political stage because he was "forced into it by a kind of legitimate rage, sometimes close to something like a sense of duty."[31]

The competition with politicians and journalists in the struggle to influence public opinion requires claims of moral and ideological self-reliance on the part of the intellectual. From Zola's self-presentation as a free writer ("I did not work for any party, my own party was that of humanity") to Sartre's uneasy and contentious fellow traveling with the Communists, intellectuals like to define themselves as nonaligned, thus transferring to the political domain their notion of creative individualism in philosophical or aesthetic

---

29. Bourdieu, *Acts of Resistance*, 41.
30. Zola, *L'affaire Dreyfus*, 109.
31. Bourdieu, *Acts of Resistance*, vii.

matters. During his trial, Zola told the jury that he was motivated neither by political ambition nor by sectarian passion: "I am a free writer, who devoted his life to his work, who tomorrow will fall back into line and resume his interrupted labor."[32]

At the core of what Benda called the ideal of the cleric is a refusal to compromise on principles, which explains why leftist artists and writers save their harshest criticism for the politicians, essayists, and journalists in their own camp: having more to uphold, they have also more to betray. Zola himself proposed in 1896 that the reason why intellectuals are so critical of politics is that they are particularly unsuited for it: "It might be the case that our scorn for politics, all of us who make a living from art, literature, or science, simply comes from the fact that we lack what is needed to succeed in it."[33] In a letter to French President Emile Loubet, Zola, referring to the republicans, bemoaned the fact that "the friends of truth and justice, as soon as they are in power, find no other way but to save the country as well through lies and iniquity."[34]

The lack of enthusiasm with which Mitterrand's election to the presidency was received in the intelligentsia prompted the anger of the Socialists and the irony of the media reporting on the "silence of the intellectuals." The silence was soon broken, though, in protest against the repression of the Solidarność movement by the Polish Communist Party in the early 1980s. Both the silence and the subsequent clamor had their source in the clerisy's traditional hostility toward the Left when in power, whether the *républicains opportunistes* of 1898, cold war Atlanticists, SFIO (Section Française de l'Internationale Ouvrière) "colonialists" during the Algerian War, "social traitors" of May '68, or pseudo socialists of 1983 engaged in a realpolitik of appeasement with communism. Bourdieu's public stance in 1995 had its roots in his earlier collaboration with Foucault and some CFDT leaders and militants in the days of Solidarność. But the evolution of the CFDT's position during the following decade meant that the sociologist and the union leaders would part company and find themselves on opposite sides of the ideological divide, which could only confirm Bourdieu's views about the fateful drift toward social-liberalism of the anticommunist, reformist "second Left."

The logic of Bourdieu's positioning, his gradual conversion to the need for direct political action (as distinct from theoretical critique and scientific analysis), was a response to the re-centering of French political life between 1981

32. Zola, *L'affaire Dreyfus*, 131.
33. Ibid., 40.
34. Ibid., 201.

and 1995. The new rhetoric of consensus, in the media, the business world, state technocracy, and some quarters of academia, had reached such proportions by the middle of the 1990s that its opponents called it *la pensée unique* (one-track thought). As in the heyday of the Dreyfus Affair, the divisions of the intellectual field in 1995 were closely related to those of the political world, providing an environment conducive to the reactivation of the "mission of prophetic subversion" Zola had invented, promoted, and embodied in the highest degree in the eyes of Bourdieu.[35]

In other words, the homology between the two moments of crisis of the republican "civilization" accounts for the concurrent emergence of the oppositional position *and* of an individual ready, willing, and qualified to occupy it. As a consequence, both Bourdieu and Zola were inclined to justify their involvement as the product, not of historical necessity, but of historical contingency, and to describe it as a moral call for duty they could not evade. This correspondence in the social conditions of the production of the oppositional voice should not, however, conceal an important difference between the two moments: the difference lies in the relationship between the forces in the field and the process of modernity, and in the degree of autonomy of those whom Umberto Eco in *Apocalypse Postponed* called "apocalyptic intellectuals."

A hundred years ago, the Dreyfusard camp confronted old-regime France, with its royalist, clerical, and militaristic agenda. As a new century was dawning, the supporters of the Jewish captain were filled with positivistic optimism and looked to a bright future of racial tolerance, social justice, and scientific progress. The supporters of the social-republican state today are accused of defending conservatism, archaism, and corporatism, of refusing the unavoidable modernization of the country's outdated institutional and legal structures. The task of the 1990s republicans was more complex, and more perilous, than that of their forebears, as they were fighting on two fronts, against the populist, xenophobic, "ethnic" nationalism of the National Front (the contemporary version of the anti-Dreyfusards) on the one hand, and the new internationalism of the celebrants of global capital.

Whatever judgment one might pass retroactively on the events of December 1995 (short-term victory or long-term defeat, reversal of trends or precarious stabilization of inevitable transformations), one is struck by the difference in the mood of intellectual opposition from one fin de siècle to the next. Compare the lyricism of Péguy's *Notebooks* and Zola's conviction that "truth is on its way" with the disenchanted resignation, the *Kathederpessimismus*,

---

35. Bourdieu, *Rules of Art*, 129.

of many contemporary intellectual dissidents. Titles from the 1990s, such as Bourdieu's *Contre-feux: Propos pour servir à la résistance contre l'invasion néolibérale* (Fireback: Contributions to the resistance against the neoliberal invasion) or Debray's *Contretemps: Eloge des idéaux perdus* (Offbeat: In praise of lost ideals), suggest more than an oppositional stance; they call for resistance, for a counteroffensive against powerful, perhaps overwhelming forces.

The Zola Model

Bourdieu himself acknowledged this contrast between the republicans' confident progressivism of a hundred years ago and the bitterness of some of their descendants in his comparative study of the emergence of an autonomous intellectual field at the end of the nineteenth century. He argued in *The Rules of Art* that Zola had produced the new figure of the intellectual by "carrying to term the evolution of the literary field towards autonomy" and attempting to "extend into politics the very values of independence being asserted in the literary field." Paradoxically, Zola and the literary Dreyfusards relied on the freedom from politics the practitioners of art for art's sake had claimed for themselves after 1848 to justify the disinterested and emancipatory nature of "their prophetic rupture with the established order." In other words, "the intellectual is constituted as such by intervening in the political field *in the name of autonomy* and of the specific values of a field of cultural production which has attained a high degree of independence with respect to the various powers." The point was to intervene in the political field without becoming a politician (like Guizot or Lamartine), without acting "on the basis of a specifically political authority, acquired at the price of a renunciation of an intellectual career and values" (129).

Today, the public and the professionals of scholarly discourse are equally subjected to what Bourdieu called the media's symbolic oppression. The media's tight control over the production and dissemination of cultural works brings into the worlds of art and knowledge the constraints of the capitalist market and its commercial logic, symbolized by the competition for ratings. In that sense, we are witnessing the closure of the historical parenthesis that opened up with the Dreyfus Affair, the birth date of the modern intellectuals. The treason of those clerics who had put their talents in the service of the anti-Dreyfusards' nationalistic demagoguery take the form of "television thinkers" and "courtly intellectuals" who sacrificed the requirements of truth for the short-term profits of media-driven celebrity.

In his critique of the perverse effects of contemporary journalism, Bourdieu referred explicitly to Zola's way of dealing with the manufacture of public consensus against Dreyfus. To face the threat of the media, "two strategies are possible," he wrote in *Sur la télévision*: "to strongly demarcate the limits of the field and attempt to restore borders threatened by the intrusion of a journalistic mode of thought and action; or come out of the ivory tower (according to the model invented by Zola) to impose values born of the retreat in the ivory tower, and use every means available . . . to try to impose on the outside the gains and advances autonomy has made possible" (91). Zola and the Dreyfusard intellectuals had gone beyond the opposition between commitment and retreat, since they became involved in the name of values elaborated in and through the distancing implied by the quest for autonomy.

The parallel between Zola and Bourdieu is thus not only implicit, in view of their comparable social trajectory and their shared attachment to republican ideals, but explicit as well. The sociologist rejected the notion that there was no room left for intellectual engagement in late modernity and repeatedly referred to the lessons contemporary knowledge producers might draw from the example of the founding father of intellectual commitment. "There is a whole tradition of commitment in France initiated by Zola, which strikes me as perfectly respectable," he said in an interview in 1995. "The duty of communicating the truth is part of the business of the scholar; here again you can appeal to Max Weber."[36]

Zola's case is somewhat ambiguous in Bourdieu's genealogy of the intellectual, since the author of "J'accuse" stood at the intersection of the universal and the specific. On the one hand, Zola embodied the traditional or classical figure of the Enlightenment tradition (Voltaire), in that he championed universal values against the narrow interests of a class (the nobility, the bourgeoisie) or an institution (the Church, the army, the justice system, the government). On the other hand, he prefigured Foucault's specific intellectual in that he performed the autonomization of the scholar as having a personal interest in the universal, defined not only in ethical terms but in positivistic, scientific ones as well. Zola's commitment to truth was not only the application of abstract moral ideals, but also the result of a concrete professional practice.

Foucault himself considered Zola a complex transitional figure, since he represented "the type of 'universal' intellectual, bearer of law and militant of equity, but he ballasts his discourse with a whole invocation of nosology and evolutionism, which he believes to be scientific." It is worth noting that even

---

36. Bourdieu, *Political Interventions*, 268.

the nuclear scientist (the Oppenheimer figure), whom Foucault took to be the quintessential incarnation of the postwar specific intellectual, also represented a mix of the local and the universal (otherwise he would only be a scientist, not an intellectual). Since "the nuclear threat affected the whole human race and the fate of the world," the scientist's discourse "could at the same time be the discourse of the universal."[37]

Bourdieu's substitution of Zola for Sartre (and, in another national context, of Weber for Marx) implied the recovery of a particular strand of commitment within the larger tradition of the French public intellectual, a view more concerned with the autonomy of knowledge production than with the erasure of the distance between the intellectual and the masses. Bourdieu's committed scholar did not renounce his specificity as knowledge producer, as Sartre had advocated in the wake of May 1968, but used it as an instrument of liberation—liberation understood not as direct political action (that was the role of parties, trade unions, and the social movement), but as a release of the repressed truth of the social, especially in its historical dimension. "To really be a committed scientist, legitimately committed," Bourdieu wrote, "you have to commit your knowledge. And this knowledge is only gained in scientific work [*un travail savant*], subject to the rules of the scientific community. . . . The scientist [*le chercheur*] is neither a prophet nor a *maître à penser*. He has to invent a new role, and a very hard one; to try and assist those bodies that take as their mission—even the trade unions, though ever more weakly, I am sorry to say—resistance to neoliberal policy; he has to take on the task of assisting them by providing them with instruments."[38]

The Task of the Intellectuals

The contribution of social movements to the recovery of the past parallels that of the committed scholars, as both "have raised political objectives that the trade unions and parties had abandoned or forgotten, if not repressed."[39] Consequently, as Bourdieu told his audience during a public lecture in Berlin in 1992, the task of the intellectuals was "to pursue and generalize the work of historical anamnesis. To avoid being puppets of the past, i.e., of the unconscious (it was Durkheim who said that 'the unconscious is history'), we have to reappropriate the past for ourselves." Committed scholars had to be the voice of the voiceless and resurrect the old-regime figure of the public writer

---

37. Foucault, *Essential Foucault*, 314, 313.
38. Bourdieu, *Political Interventions*, 380, 381.
39. Ibid., 382.

(*l'écrivain public*), bringing "into public space the private discourses of those deprived of public discourse."[40]

In one of his last public lectures, Bourdieu placed Foucault squarely within the legacy of the Kantian Aufklärung, referring to Foucault's famous essays on "What Is Enlightenment?" and "What Is Critique?" "Fidelity to the philosophy of the Enlightenment, Foucault said, did not mean fidelity to a doctrine but rather fidelity to an attitude" that Bourdieu called the "critical attitude."[41] He saw Foucault's project as closely related to his own, which came as a surprise, or even a scandal, to those who persisted in opposing a positivist, Durkheimian Bourdieu and a nominalist, Nietzschean Foucault. Bourdieu was no more a naïve rationalist than Foucault was an unreconstructed irrationalist, as careless readings of their work would have us believe. They both favored a view of reason as a historical construct, as the product of specific social and intellectual conditions of possibility. Bourdieu wrote in *Pascalian Meditations* that "we have to acknowledge that reason did not fall from heaven as a mysterious and forever inexplicable gift, and that it is therefore historical through and through; but we are not forced to conclude, as is often supposed, that it is reducible to history" (109). Compare that with Foucault (apropos his book *Madness and Civilization*): "This book is neither Freudian nor Marxist nor structuralist. Now, as it happened, I had read Nietzsche . . . from a perspective of inquiry into the history of knowledge—the history of reason: how does one elaborate a history of rationality?"[42]

For Bourdieu, the historical nature of both cognitive and normative principles (reason and virtue) had to do with the emergence, in specific social and cultural situations, of a world in which disinterestedness is rewarded. Those who have interest in the promotion of universal procedures of understanding, evaluation, and actions, whether scientists, teachers, or citizens of a democratic republic, have made the progress of reason in history possible. Singular social microcosms such as the scientific community are historically improbable, "miraculous" sites in which "agents struggle, in the name of the universal, for the legitimate monopoly of the universal."[43]

As suggested by the title of the book in which he explored this conception of the universal to its ultimate consequences, *Practical Reason*, Bourdieu's argument was pragmatic in the sense that the rational worldview produces the empirical conditions of its own deployment via a kind of cost-benefit

---

40. Ibid., 224, 226.
41. Ibid., 384.
42. Foucault, *Essential Foucault*, 84.
43. Bourdieu, *Practical Reason*, 139.

analysis on the part of social agents: "The fact that there can be benefits from virtue and reason is undoubtedly one of the major engines of virtue and reason in history" (165). The views expressed in *Practical Reason*, published in 1994, provided him with a theoretical framework for the militant engagement of the last decade of his life. He became an advocate for a "realpolitik of reason" enabling scholars and their allies in the social movements to defend the social conditions of the exercise of reason, the institutional basis for intellectual activity, and, beyond, for a related politics of morality.

The moralization of politics was the result of the application of the Kantian test of universality to the resistance against neoliberalism. Bourdieu's view of democratic politics was a radicalization of the republican (Kantian) project to disseminate free will and turn every subject into an enlightened citizen. Knowledge was a source of power to counter those who had built their power on the monopoly of the universally valid protocols of knowledge formation. The agents who brought the state into existence (the king's jurists), he wrote in *Practical Reason*, "had an interest in giving a universal form to the expression of their vested interests, in elaborating a theory of public service and of public order, and thus in working to autonomize *the reason of state* from dynastic reason, from the 'house of the king,' and to invent thereby the 'res publica' and later the republic as an instance transcendent to the agents (the king included) who are its temporary incarnations" (58).

The democratization of reason, its extension to ordinary citizens and social militants, was meant to universalize the power of knowledge that had been confiscated by the servants of the state through their illegitimate monopoly on the res publica, and turn that newfound power against the state itself. The "politics of purity" inspired by Zola were the exact opposite of the reason of state. Bourdieu's realpolitik of reason, for all its democratic intentions, implied an extreme idealization of intellectual activity and of the committed intellectual, which, for many, smacked of elitism. Nothing could have been further from the egalitarian, anti-intellectual zeitgeist of the postmodernists. Bourdieu's reflections on Foucault's death, published in *Le Monde* in June 27, 1984, showed to what an extent the philosopher had been a kind of ego ideal, a model of intellectual commitment, for the sociologist: "For him, the critical vision was applicable first of all to his own practice, and in this respect he was the purest representative of a new kind of intellectual who has no need to mystify himself as to the motives and themes of intellectual acts, nor to foster illusions about their effect, in order to practice them in full knowledge of their cause."[44]

---

44. Bourdieu, *Political Interventions*, 139.

Bourdieu founded the journal *Liber* in the 1980s to provide a forum for the constitution of "an international of the intellectuals" and facilitate the insertion of academic researchers in the public debate, "so that it is not always those who know least who speak most."[45] The new mission of the committed scholarly community went beyond the opposition between "total" and "specific" kinds of clerics: "Intellectuals cannot rest content with the prophetic denunciations of the total intellectual in the manner of Sartre, nor again with the critical analyses of the 'specific intellectual' as defined by Foucault. They have to mobilize and organize themselves on an international scale (perhaps using the new technologies of communication), in such a way as to constitute a genuine collective intellectual." Bourdieu later described the *Liber* project as an attempt to reactivate on a world scale the communicative model of the eighteenth-century European philosophers, and to "gradually constitute a kind of great international popular encyclopedia in which activists from all countries will be able to find the intellectual weapons needed for their struggles."[46] This reappropriation of the Enlightenment's encyclopedic project, not as doctrine but as attitude, paralleled the promotion of Zola as the preeminent figure of intellectual autonomy, and entailed a reevaluation of three closely related elements of the project of modernity: the state, reason, and universalism.

Reassessing the State

Although Bourdieu's conception of the state retained an inner tension throughout his work, the opposition between its progressive and repressive aspects (symbolized by the contrast between the right hand and the left hand of the state) took a more acute turn in the final period of his life. The early works on education and public institutions, from *Reproduction* (1970) to *The State Nobility* (1989), were all written in the wake of May 1968. Informed by the anti-institutional mood of the times, they painted a mostly negative picture of the state apparatus. In these early books, Bourdieu underscored the state's hegemonic role in the production and imposition of the categories of thought its "subjects" apply spontaneously to the whole domain of the social, including the state itself. The sociologists' ambiguous relationship to state institutions was explicitly related to their social position within the state apparatus itself.

Social scientists, Bourdieu argued in *Practical Reason*, are caught in a double bind with regard to their employer and protector. Although they have

---

45. Ibid., 187.
46. Ibid., 236, 279.

historically relied on the state (as functionaries) to gain independence from the pressures of social demand that "is a major precondition of their progress toward scientificity," they also run the risk of losing their autonomy by assenting to the demands of the state, "unless they are prepared to use against the state the (relative) freedom that it grants them" (40). Bourdieu further described the process of state formation over time as the gradual concentration of all the other kinds of capital (military, economic, cultural, symbolic) within a kind of "metacapital granting power over other species of capital and over their holders" (41).

Consequently, the modern secular state holds "the place of God." It creates the nation as territory and collective self-image ("the national character"), submits all those under its authority to the established order, and produces itself as "a sort of common historical transcendental entity immanent to all its 'subjects'" (54), endowed with universal characteristics. The educational system is the privileged site of this process of collective indoctrination of the rational values embodied in the state, as schooling produces in each student incorporated cognitive structures that match the objective structures of society: "By universally imposing and inculcating (within the limits of its authority) a dominant culture thus constituted as *legitimate national* culture, the school system, through the teaching of history (and especially the history of literature), inculcates the foundations of a true 'civic religion' and more precisely, the fundamental presuppositions of the national self-image" (46).

Bourdieu called "doxa" this universal effect of the transcendence of the state, defined as "a particular point of view, the point of view of the dominant, presented and imposed as a universal point of view—the point of view of those who dominate by dominating the state and who have constituted their points of view as universal by constituting the state" (57). As self-appointed guardians of the doxa, the higher echelon of the civil service profession, the "nobility of the state," has historically produced itself while producing, and reproducing, the capital of the state and its "monopoly of the universal." That is why state functionaries (including academics as organic intellectuals of the public authority) are often described in Bourdieu's sociology as those social agents who have a vested interest in the universal. Universalism as the ideology of the agents of the state was a major component of French exceptionalism, and led to perverse forms of imperialism and "internationalist rationalism." "In the case of France," Bourdieu argued, "the nationalist dimension of culture is masked under a universalistic façade" (46).

Both universalism and rationalism, as key components of the Jacobin ideology, were frequent targets of Bourdieu's early work. A March 1966 lecture in front of an audience of Marxist intellectuals, significantly titled "Jacobin Ideology," laid the foundation for the critical sociology of culture and education he developed during the next decade, and underlined the basic ambiguity of republican pedagogy. "Those whom the school has liberated," Bourdieu declared in *Political Interventions*, "are more inclined than anyone else to believe in the liberating school" (38). He argued that the left-wing critique of public education in a capitalistic context is not radical enough, in that it contests the system while agreeing with its basic premises. The supposed neutrality of the republican school is a myth that ignores real inequalities and is complicit with an "ideology of the gift" (*l'idéologie du don*), which reproduces these very inequalities by rewarding performances based on skills (cultural capital) acquired outside the school itself (i.e., at home and in immediate social surroundings). "What might be called the charisma ideology (because it valorizes 'grace' and 'the gift')," Bourdieu had explained two years earlier in *The Inheritors* (coauthored with Passeron), "supplies the privileged classes with a legitimation of their cultural privileges which are thereby transmuted from a social heritage into individual grace or personal merit" (70).

The republican fiction of meritocracy transforms *social* inequalities, and particularly educational ones, into *natural* inequalities resulting from "unequal giftedness." This kind of misrecognition, Bourdieu contended in *The Inheritors*, is "part of the logic of a system which is based on the postulate of the formal equality of all pupils, as a precondition of its operations, and cannot recognize any inequalities other than those arising from individual gifts" (67). Bourdieu addressed the paradoxical nature of the republican pedagogical ideology in his 1966 lecture on the Jacobin ideology: "In a paradox that is quite surprising, the school devalues as scholarly [*scolaires*] the aptitudes that have been acquired at school, thanks to a scholarly effort, by those who have not inherited them from their milieu."[47] The school system, under cover of its progressive, egalitarian, emancipatory rationale, ironically contributes to the perpetuation of privileges without the privileged ones having to rely explicitly on the school system.

The liberal turn, the disenchantment of politics, the ascendancy of the media, and the weakening of social democratic agendas between 1981 and 1995 would cause Bourdieu to revise his former, critical view of the state and its nationalist-universalist ideology. He soon declared the need to defend public authority against the antistatism that was taking center stage in France and abroad. By 1992, he felt that it was high time to ask the state to "exercise a regulatory action able to counteract the 'fatality' of economic and social

---

47. Ibid., 37.

mechanisms that are immanent to the social order." Neoliberalism's goal was to reduce the action of a "minimal state" to the protection of the natural rights of individuals. The celebration of "ethics" masked the substitution of the private interests of isolated individuals for the public virtues of participatory democracy. Bourdieu quoted both Machiavelli and Kant in his defense of the threatened "civilization associated with the social state." "The ideal republic, according to Machiavelli, is a regime in which citizens have an interest in virtue," while Kant proposed in his essay on "Perpetual Peace" to organize egoistic interests in such a way that "they mutually counterbalance each other in their devastating effects, so that a man, even if he is not good man by nature, is forced to be a good citizen."[48] The republic of citizens, where everyone is compelled to have an interest in virtue, became the ethical double of the epistemological republic of letters (or sciences), in which everyone is interested (in both senses of the word) in the universal.

In "late" Bourdieu, the state is no longer solely a source of domination, but also a vector of resistance. The duality (and duplicity) of the Leviathan, whose nature is both repressive and progressive, accounts for the previously mentioned tension between the right hand of the state, made up of the higher nobility of media-savvy counselors to the prince and the technocratic experts who have demoralized the Republic and compromised the civic ideals of solidarity, and the left hand of the state, the lower nobility of school teachers and public sector employees who remain "the guardians of the whole tradition of public service, devotion, and disinterestedness that have [sic] been handed down by two centuries of social struggles." This civic tradition is described as the historical laboratory "for the invention of such institutions as social security, the minimum wage, etc., as well as virtues and ideals."[49]

As a consequence of this revaluation of the state, the pedagogical project of the early republicans also acquired a more positive dimension in Bourdieu's thought, and his previous critique of the Jacobin ideology gave way to a rehabilitation of reason as the emancipating faculty of a self-determined citizenry. The goal of democratic politics in the neoliberal age was to disseminate on a large scale "the symbolic weapons able to ensure all citizens the means of defending themselves against symbolic violence—liberating themselves, if need be, of their 'liberators.'"[50] Bourdieu's position remained original in that his critique of neoliberalism did not end up in a nostalgic return

48. Ibid., 194, 203.
49. Ibid., 200.
50. Ibid., 196. For Bourdieu's views on *laïcité* as a distinct contribution of French thought to the republican ideology, see his *Pascalian Meditations*. "It was only among some of the founders of the Third Republic, in France," according to Bourdieu, "that the idea of personal opinion, inherited from the Enlightenment, was explicitly associated with that of compulsory secular schooling, which

to some form of Jacobin fundamentalism, complete with its insular and anti-communitarian (i.e., racist) overtones. His use of the republican legacy was always strategic and contextual, given his own preference for the libertarian, antistatist, *anarcho-syndicaliste* tradition in the French labor movement.[51] Similarly, his defense of republican civilization never took the form of an absolutist, dogmatic, or elitist critique of the mass media. Unlike those who attacked television from an aesthetic-cultural position (e.g., Finkielkraut or Fumaroli), his quarrel with the medium was essentially political. What "the people" were deprived of by the social and economic structures of television broadcasting was not high culture, but political agency.

The Historicity of Reason

It should not come as a surprise that Bourdieu also reinterpreted the universalism of the national-republican tradition to fit the needs of the resistance to neoliberalism. Just as there are good and bad uses of the state, his political interventions after 1995 distinguished between two different kinds of appeal to the universal. Abstract, "egoistic" universalism, he wrote in *Pascalian Meditations*, "whether in the relations between nations or within nations, generally serves to justify the established order, the prevailing distribution of powers and privileges—the domination of the bourgeois, white, Euro-American heterosexual male—in the name of the formal requirements of an abstract universal (democracy, human rights, etc.) dissociated from the economic and social conditions of its historical realization, or worse, in the name of an ostentatiously universalist condemnation of any claim for rights for a particular group, and, consequently, of all 'communities' based on a stigmatized particularity (women, gays, blacks, etc.)" (71).

He was particularly sensitive to the deleterious consequences, notably in terms of ethnic and race relations, of the anti-communitarianism present in the most dogmatic positions of the neo-republican camp, even though he shared with some members of that camp a number of philosophical ideas and political beliefs. "The obscurantism of the Enlightenment," he wrote in *Pascalian Meditations*, "can take the form of a fetishism of reason and a fanaticism of the universal that remain closed to all the traditional manifestations of belief, and that, as is shown for example by the reflex violence of some

---

was thought necessary in order to give a real basis for universal access to the judgment supposedly expressed in universal suffrage" (*Pascalian Meditations*, 68).

51. See Bourdieu, "Rediscovering the Left's Libertarian Tradition," in *Political Interventions*, 127–30.

denunciations of religious fundamentalism, are no less obscure and self-opaque than what they denounce" (78).

In the same way that the culturally and historically conditioned nature of reason meant that one did not have to choose between an eternal, Platonic conception of the rational and "the historicist circle of the social sciences," the dogmatic nature of abstract universalism did not invalidate other kinds of universal categories as means of political mobilization or philosophical legitimation. In his view, it was possible to fight at the same time *against* the mystifying hypocrisy of abstract universalism and for the universal access to the conditions of access to the universal—that is, the access to democratic structures enabling all citizens to participate in the public sphere and determine public policy.

Reflecting on his support of Solidarność in the early 1980s, Bourdieu set the question of the intellectuals within the broader context of the redefinition of universalism and the historicization of the emergence of reason. The intellectuals "are not representatives of universality, still less a 'universal class,' but it does happen that, for historical reasons, they are often *interested in universality*."[52] As previously noted, he conceived of the present task of the intellectuals (and of progressive social movements) as both a continuation and a reformulation of what had been invented in the *sociétés de pensée* and scientific academies at the time of the Enlightenment, and later revived by the Dreyfusard intelligentsia: the institutionalization of the social processes that give rise to rational thinking and rational activity.[53]

Bourdieu did not share the belief that contemporary developments are absolutely unheard-of and require original ways of thinking. He looked at the challenges faced by radical democratic forces in the wake of globalization

---

52. Bourdieu, *Political Interventions*, 132.

53. Bourdieu's salvaging of specific forms of universalism in the face of the relativism of postmodern thought intersects with attempts to "refound" (*refonder*) universalism by Etienne Balibar or Jacques Rancière (who was also an early critic of Bourdieu's sociology). In *L'Europe, l'Amérique, la guerre*, for example, Balibar contends that postcolonial revolts and liberation struggles have effected a reversal of roles between the metropolis and the colonies, "particularizing" the former and "universalizing" the latter. The consequences of these developments "are felt in Europe itself thanks to racial mixing and population movements. It is therefore as impossible to impugn universalism as it is to be content with its 'European definition' or its appropriation by Europe" (163). Balibar contrasts this new and revised conception of the universal with the "universal sovereignty" of the United States, based on what Bourdieu would have called abstract universalism. However different these various redescriptions might be, they all point to a selective assessment of the role played by universalism in the democratic and republican imagination, in France and elsewhere. This unwillingness to reject universalism as a whole is based both on "universalizing" processes linked to globalization and on the drawbacks of such a wholesale rejection when it comes to the integration of distinct communities within a given political formation.

with a sense of déjà vu, which meant that old ideas, provided they were reexamined and cleansed of their undesirable aspects, could provide solutions to new dilemmas. "We are in a game where all the moves played today, here and there, have already been played," he told an Italian audience in 1989, "from the refusal of politics and the return to the religious to the resistance against a political power hostile to intellectual activity, through the revolt against the ascendancy of . . . the media or the disillusioned desertion of the revolutionary utopia. But the fact that we find ourselves at 'endgame' does not necessarily lead to disenchantment" (*Political Interventions*, 260).

The new political deal of the 1980s was neither unprecedented nor final; rather, it was merely a repetition within a difference. Rather than the passage to a new world, the contemporary situation was the unfolding of a new configuration of the same. Later in his lecture, programmatically titled "For an International of the Intellectuals," Bourdieu compared the illusions of 1848 with those of 1968, just as he had repeatedly linked the political challenges of his own fin de siècle to those faced by Zola's contemporaries. He was acutely aware of the losses suffered by the progressive camp, commenting in *L'Express* in 1993 that "besides the problem of unemployment, which everyone understands escapes political action alone, what [this government of the Left] is reproached for is the demoralization of the state, in the double sense of loss of both morals and morale."[54]

Remembering Foucault in June 2000, he deplored the fact that "we mourn for the critical intellectual," and described the intellectual world as having, "strictly speaking, lost its bearings, by losing its autonomy in relation to economics, politics, and of course journalism."[55] And yet he claimed that those "who we find on all sides announcing the end of the intellectuals and their function or mission, to use a big word, are seriously deceived."[56] Eschewing the debilitating effects of a melancholy rhetoric of loss, Bourdieu viewed the passing of the "revolutionary utopia" as an opportunity, not for disenchantment, but for a realistic vision conducive to a "rational utopia based on the defense of autonomy." Loss was not a tragedy, but an opportunity. "Our era is one of lost illusions," he said in a 1992 public lecture in Berlin. "In this sense, these are good times."[57]

---

54. Bourdieu, *Political Interventions*, 201.
55. Ibid., 385.
56. Ibid., 235.
57. Ibid., 274.

Chapter Five

DESPERATELY SEEKING MARIANNE
The Uses of the Republic

The first round of the presidential election on April 21, 2002, sent a shock wave throughout the French political system. In an unexpected turn of events, the leader of the far-right National Front, Jean-Marie Le Pen, took second place behind incumbent Jacques Chirac, edging out the Socialist candidate, Prime Minister Lionel Jospin. Forty years earlier, the French Constitution had been amended to allow the president to be elected by universal suffrage, according to a two-round or runoff voting system (if no candidate receives an absolute majority of votes, then all candidates, except the two with the most votes, are eliminated and a second round of voting occurs). For the first time since 1965, no candidate of the Left was on the final ballot, leaving representatives of the moderate and radical Right to square off for the highest office in the land. The immediate reaction to the unforeseen news was a mixture of panic and shame: panic at the threat that Le Pen's victory would pose to the functioning of democratic institutions, and shame at the image France was showing to the rest of the world. The Left had no other choice than to rally behind Chirac, a center-right politician whose first term had been mired in scandals; in fact, several of his close political associates had been brought to justice for corruption, electoral fraud, and misuse of public

---

A shorter version of this chapter was published as "Recherche Marianne désespérément: La République en minorité," *Contemporary French Civilization* 27, no. 2 (2003): 193–210.

funds. "Better a crook than a fascist," banners proclaimed in the dozens of demonstrations that followed the announcement of the first-round results.

One of the most striking consequences of Le Pen's strong showing in the polls (he received almost 17 percent of the vote in the initial ballot) was an immediate change in political rhetoric. Suddenly the call for a *sursaut républicain* (a republican awakening) was heard everywhere, from political talk shows and op-ed pages to campaign speeches and readers' letters to the editor. Left-wing voters as well as those who had stayed home on April 21 were urged not to watch from the sidelines, since only a "republican" surge of mobilization against the enemies of democracy would ensure Chirac's reelection. The incumbent president eventually received 82 percent of the vote, the kind of landslide victory more familiar to one-party states than pluralistic democracies. No matter: exceptional events (Jospin's early elimination from the race) required exceptional measures, in this case the sacred union of all democrats, right and left, against Le Pen.

During the two weeks preceding the second round, Chirac skillfully used to his own advantage the theme of *le rassemblement républicain* (the coming together of all supporters of the threatened Republic) against the anti-parliamentarian Right, reviving the memory of significant moments in the nation's history, from de Gaulle's alliance with the Communist underground in opposition to the Vichy regime to the struggle of all republicans, right and left, against the monarchists of Action française between 1880 and 1939. The equation "Le Pen = Pétain = French Algeria = fascism" helped seal the new alliance between Chirac and the Left, even though the National Front's electoral success owed more to the tensions and contradictions of contemporary French society than to Le Pen's admiration for the Nazis or involvement in the colonialist camp during the Algerian War.

On the night of the second round voting, Chirac rejoiced in the fact that "France had vigorously reaffirmed its attachment to the values of the Republic."[1] Assuring his "dear compatriots" that he had heard their message that "the Republic [must] live on," he described his reelection as the result of "a foundational choice, a choice that renews the republican compact [*le pacte républicain*]." In fact, the content of the "pact" was reduced to the ritual invocation of "the values of liberty, equality, and fraternity" and the usual rhetorical flourish about finding "solutions for problems that had been neglected for much too long." Chirac's strategy was to fill up the empty

---

1. Cited in Claude Dargent and François Platone, "L'éphéméride (1/2): Chronologie de l'élection présidentielle," Elections 2002, http://elections2002.sciences-po.fr/Ephemer/ephemeride.html.

frame of the three principles of 1789 with vague pronouncements meant to address the concerns and frustrations of a disoriented people, one-fifth of whom had cast a ballot for Le Pen (more than five and a half million people). The performative magic of the presidential word was supposed to breathe new life into the eternal values of the Republic, which had suddenly become the centerpiece of the government's new program.

The New Republican Rhetoric

Chirac proceeded to translate the revolutionary triad into the present concerns of the electorate. Freedom was another name for "security, the fight against violence, the refusal of impunity." Equality meant "the refusal of all discrimination, the same rights and the same duties for all." Fraternity implied "safeguarding retirements and defending the family." By redefining the meaning and content of the basic tenets of the republican creed in the context of the crisis of public institutions, Chirac attempted to reconcile the demands of the Right ("freedom" meaning being tough on crime) with those of the Left ("equality and fraternity" as being fair when fighting against crime). *Anti-laxisme* and *anti-racisme* were thus harmoniously welded together, their explosive tension briefly defused in Chirac's formulation aimed at shepherding back to the republican fold the once-divided flock, who were expected to keep him in power for another five years.

The president was hardly the only one to indulge in the exegetic reappraisal of the republican legacy. The media also picked up on the topic of the republican compact, and numerous variations on the theme found their way into political speeches, pundits' commentaries, journalistic pieces, and demonstrators' slogans: *barrage républicain* (republican roadblock), *renouveau républicain* (republican renewal), *élan républicain* (republican momentum), *refondation républicaine* (republican refoundation), and so forth.[2] Even police trade unions called for a "republican reaction" to stop the far Right in its tracks. Joaquin Massenet, secretary general of UNSA Police, claimed that la République had been held up to ridicule by Le Pen's second-place finish. "We will do everything in our power to make sure that the only republican candidate still in the running [i.e., Chirac] will be elected in the second round,"

---

2. The term *refondation* also became a staple of public discourse to signify the need to update those ideas and institutions that have proved less than adequate: "refoundation" of the schools, of universities, of *citoyenneté*, of public service, of the Socialist Party, and of course, last but not least, of capitalism. See speech by Nicolas Sarkozy, September 25, 2008, Toulon, France (widely available online).

remarked a representative of Alliance, another police organization. The union leader declared himself "stunned, as everyone in republican unions and associations, by the rise of the extreme Right."[3]

The volume of references to the Republic was matched only by the inaccuracy and semantic vagueness in the uses of the word. In public discourse, popular culture, and scholarly prose, the adjective *républicain* took on a life of its own, assuming a multiplicity of implied meanings, whose mobile boundaries overlapped and intersected. The word sometimes meant national, sometimes democratic, sometimes simply French, referring in turn to constitutionally guaranteed individual rights, or the state of law, or even citizenship. Its various connotations included that of a national identity, an institutional regime, a historical formation, a philosophical creed, a style of sociability, or a structure of feeling, a common set of values, memories, and images. *Citoyen(ne)* used as an adjective, another increasingly popular, and equally polysemic, lexical item in the new consensual lingo, has a similar ideological function. Municipal brochures and local social committees' (*comité des fêtes*) newsletters are increasingly fond of describing picnics, concerts, festivals, and other community events as *rassemblements festifs et citoyens* (festive and civic gatherings). The implication of the cliché is that the aim of these various events is to bring together individuals from all classes, races, and walks of life to partake in the shared feelings and memories of a local or regional "community." Citizenship, as an ideal and a code word, is used to counter the tensions threatening collective identifications with Frenchness.

Even more revealing was the attempt of the far Right itself to jump on the semantic bandwagon, thereby subverting a rhetoric aimed at excluding its supporters from legitimate participation in the national consensus. A minority of National Front members, dissatisfied with policies and orientations under Le Pen, had split from the party in the late 1990s. They named their new organization the Mouvement national républicain as a way to assert both their right to belong to the national community and the respectability of their political views. Bruno Mégret, the MNR's candidate in the 2002 presidential election, appropriated the newly minted rhetoric of its opponents, and loudly rejoiced about Le Pen's showing at the polls as an illustration of what he called "the spectacular scores of the national and republican Right."[4] No one could be excluded from the Republic. Mégret's rhetorical

---

3. Claire Guélaud, "Des syndicats de police appellent à la 'réaction républicaine,'" *Le Monde*, April 23, 2002.

4. Cited in "Le Pen ou le hold-up électoral du siècle," *Libération*, April 22, 2002.

move performed the phantasmic closure of a self-referential, self-contained ideological space (the nation as Republic and the Republic as nation) that included all the people within an institutional form conceived as a tautology.

The unexpected, shocking results of the April 21 election provided the media and the political class with an opportunity to reconnect France with its national tradition. But was the rhetoric an accurate reflection of reality? An excerpt from Jacques Chirac's speech on the night of the first round of voting shows the extent of the legitimation crisis of republican institutions: "Today, our national cohesion is in question, as well as the values of the Republic all French people are attached to. . . . I call all Frenchmen and -women to come together, to defend human rights to guarantee the cohesion of the nation, to affirm the unity of the Republic and restore the authority of the state."[5] Was there suddenly so much talk about republican principles because of the fear they might be lost and in dire need of recovery? The 2002 presidential and legislative elections broke the record of abstentions for a presidential election (28 percent versus 22 percent in 1995) or a legislative election (40 percent). Although the wake-up call might have led to Chirac's overwhelming victory, it never weakened the resolve of Le Pen's followers, whose numbers grew by another fifty thousand between the two rounds. Thirteen million individuals had refused to "save the Republic," either by persisting in voting for the candidate of the National Front or by staying home (still more than 20 percent of voters did so on the second round of voting), either because they had no doubt about the issue of the vote, or because their views were represented by neither of the candidates.

The campaign itself was proof of the problematic nature of the republican rhetoric. Most of the participants only resorted to it after the first round, with a mixture of panic and disarray. The only exception was Jean-Pierre Chevènement, the candidate of the Pôle républicain (Republican Pole). During the months preceding the election, he had tirelessly denounced the many threats to France's political identity. Chevènement's agenda, politically charged in a campaign largely devoid of any substantive ideological issues, revolved around a set of beliefs its opponents kept deriding as hopelessly passé—that is, until they were forced to include them, in a hurried and confused manner, when the chips were down. Chevènement only received a fraction of the popular vote, a measly 5 percent, much less than had been expected in view of earlier opinion polls.

5. Available online at http://www.jacqueschirac-asso.fr/fr/les-grands-discours-de-jacques-chirac.

Two reasons, one ideological, the other political, may account for the poor showing of the only explicitly "republican" candidate. These reasons are related, since the electoral weakness of the movement reflects the vulnerability of a discourse that fits with neither of the two major responses to the challenge of globalization—that is, the antistatist and anticapitalist views of the *altermondialiste* movement, on the one hand, and the neoliberal, transnationalist ideology of the "new world order," confident in the self-regulating virtues of economic markets, on the other. In addition, Chevènement's political program, by stressing national unity and the "integration" of immigrants, could not compete with the simplicity of the National Front's seemingly uncompromising response to the challenge of immigration.

Chevènement's sovereignist agenda was statist, nationalist, and antiliberal (in the economic sense) and did not fit with the main forces fighting over globalization. The republicans did not consider the nation-state an anachronistic form of social and trade relations. As a consequence, they had a hard time convincing either the supporters of the global market or the antiauthoritarian, "cosmopolitan" critics of state-based, civic nationalism. Neoliberals and *altermondialistes* are equally fond of multiculturalism, even though they often disagree over its meaning and content. To them, the space of the struggle is already global; it has already moved beyond the borders of an increasingly irrelevant nation form. They do not quarrel over the existence or desirability of globalization, but on the principles (economic for the one, social for the other) that will frame the reorganization of market relations on a worldwide scale.

The fragile coalition that brought together representatives of the sovereignist Right and champions of the Jacobin Left within the Pôle républicain did not survive the first round of the presidential election. Chevènement, a shrewd pragmatist and a seasoned politician, moved closer to the Socialists as the legislative elections drew near, causing the right-wing nationalists and the "historical" Gaullists to jump ship. Meanwhile, the antiglobalization wing of the movement blamed their candidate for making deals with a party whose leader (Jospin) had been so concerned with not appearing too "socialistic" (for fear of alienating the middle class) that he had lost a large part of the working-class vote. The 2002 elections confirmed the marginality of a principled national-republican agenda in public opinion, while opening up a significant rift within the Left, confirmed three years later during the debate over the ratification of the European Union's new constitution in the spring of 2005 (55 percent of the French voters, many of them on the Left, ended up rejecting the proposal).[6]

The Republic has rarely commanded unanimous respect in French history. Moreover, the republican form has long been an uncommon feature in Europe. In 1871, there were only two republics on the old continent (France and Switzerland), and even now seven countries in the European Union are constitutional monarchies or principalities (Belgium, Denmark, Spain, Luxembourg, the Netherlands, the United Kingdom, and Sweden). Germany had an emperor until 1918, and Italy a king as late as 1944. Among European republics, the French one stands apart with its Jacobin, universalistic, secular, and centralized legacy. By contrast, Germany and Switzerland have a federal structure, Italy is highly regionalized, and the constitution of Ireland recognized the special position of the Catholic religion until 1973. This unique situation accounts for several of the themes currently associated with the preservation of historical specificity. The notion of French exceptionality and the questionable equation between a particular institutional arrangement and the whole of French national identity (*La République, c'est la France!*) fly in the face of nearly two hundred years of civil wars fought over the legitimacy of that very particular, contingent institutional arrangement.

The Republic and Its Intellectuals

Although the theme of besieged republicanism does not seem to have resonated with a large segment of the electorate in 2002, it had become increasingly popular with the intelligentsia in the last two decades of the twentieth century. There is a long list of personalities of the academic and literary fields who have, since the bicentennial of the French Revolution, rallied around the defense of the republican legacy, from *laïcité* to public service and national sovereignty. We have encountered many of them in the previous chapters. Elisabeth Badinter, Pierre Bourdieu, Régis Debray, Alain Finkielkraut, Max Gallo, Marcel Gauchet, Blandine Kriegel, Pierre-André Taguieff, and Emmanuel Todd, to name just a few, have all in one way or another deplored the deleterious effects of the neoliberal consensus as a combination of acquisitive

---

6. The first casualty of April 2002 in the intellectual world was the coalition of neoliberals and center-left reformists (known as "antitotalitarians") who had contributed so decisively to the ideological reorientations of the late seventies and early eighties. See Lindenberg, *Le rappel à l'ordre*; and above, chapter 3.

individualism, globalization, and identity politics, even though these individuals might disagree on the proper response to the weakening of the republican reference. Meanwhile, new social and political developments show a growing divorce between many "national-republican" intellectuals and public opinion, as witnessed by Chevènement's modest showing at the polls. Régis Debray was both prescient and realistic when he wrote in 1999 that "for the time being, 'national-republicanism' could be compared with a minority protest vote, the kind we associate with the first round of an election, aiming less at obstructing (there are too few of us) than at bearing witness."[7]

Standing up for threatened values with a minority status can only be attractive to the intelligentsia, a social group that has made the prophetic denunciation of what Emmanuel Mounier called in the 1930s "the established disorder" the required posture of the progressive educated classes since the days of Voltaire and Zola. Their collective motto, to borrow a phrase from Gilles Deleuze, is that "one can never resist the present enough." The intellectuals' resistance to globalization as cultural standardization prompted them to reassert their ideological autonomy and to renew the tradition of the "end of French exceptionalism." To defend the Republic as the public space of political contestation is for many of them the only way to preserve their raison d'être, the privileged mode of their social being, since nowhere more than in France has the public intellectual been a model of self-definition for the cultivated elites.

The Republic, as the best way of achieving what the French call *le vivre-ensemble*, the art of living together, filled the space left vacant by the retreat of the revolution. Those who, almost half a century ago, reviled the Gaullist bourgeois capitalist state with the passion of youthful conviction, in the name of Mao, Trotsky, and Ernesto "Che" Guevara, today often honor the memory of the General. He has become, with the passing of time, the incarnation of national independence and an inspiration to those who wish to resist the Americanization of the global village. But while the revolution looked to the future, the Republic, even if it is recast along new lines, *refondée* as the current phrase goes, cannot but appear as an endangered relic of the past. Hence the accusations of archaism and nostalgia regularly directed at the guardians of the republican faith by their opponents, who ridicule them as political Neanderthals (*paléolithiques*) and neo-reactionaries.

The national-republican agenda brought together a constellation of former student radicals who had learned the lessons of the eclipse of a socialist alternative to capitalism. Refusing to give in to the sirens of liberalism, they

---

7. Debray, *Le code et le glaive*, 88.

moved back to the Republic as a democratic substitute for the revolutionary ideals they had believed in at first, and later turned against with a vengeance. Blandine Kriegel, born and raised in a prominent communist family, and a member of the Maoist group called the Union of Marxist-Leninist Youth as a student in the late sixties, went on to become a prominent political philosopher and a political aide to Jacques Chirac. She summed up the logic that led an entire generation from avant-garde to establishment in an interview published in the daily *Libération* shortly after Chirac's reelection in 2002: "I dropped out of the Left because the Left dropped out of the Republic."[8] Kriegel's evolution from Maoism to (conservative) republicanism is not so surprising, since the radical Left had always considered the revolution as a daughter of the Republic, and 1917 a repetition of 1793. To the revolutionary Left in the interwar period, the struggle against fascism, Nazism, and Vichy preserved both the communist hope and the Jacobin heritage. Their children, born during the Great Depression or the Occupation, raised in the cult of the Résistance and later disappointed in the failures of "real socialism," did not trade one ideology for another. Since the entire historical heritage of the Left was no longer acceptable, they settled for the better half. Once the revolution had evaporated, there remained the precipitate of the Republic.

The republican reference in its contemporary reformulations quickly became one of the major keys to recent French cultural and intellectual history, and it can be found time and again at the center of most of the major ideological debates of the last thirty years. The constant reappraisal of May '68 described in previous chapters underscored the corrosive impact of consumerism on the political culture born in the Third Republic but already under attack during the Fourth. In the fifties, two of the main pillars of the Republic were shaken: Parliament, rendered powerless by endless partisan bickering and ephemeral government coalitions, and the colonial empire, swept away by third-world nationalisms. The sixties only confirmed the political shrewdness of de Gaulle and Mendès-France, who had foreseen that the new middle classes produced by postwar prosperity would gladly trade the colonies for the stock market, and the flowery oratorical culture of the old Republic for television. The following debate on postmodernism (from 1979 onward) staged the same cast of characters in a slightly different play. The republicans were soon ridiculed as old-school modernists, unreconstructed sectarians of Enlightenment universalism. They were blamed for sticking to

---

8. Blandine Kriegel, "J'ai décroché de la gauche parce que la gauche a décroché de la République," *Libération*, November 15, 2002.

authoritarian notions of culture and politics, obsolete metanarratives about the people, reason, and the nation, and for advocating an anachronistic mixture of Caesarian Jacobin-Marxism, radical-socialist morals, and Kantian educational philosophy.

The quarrel of the "silence of the intellectuals" in 1983, sparked by the Socialists' frustration at the lack of support for their policies among the intelligentsia, revealed the intellectuals' growing dissatisfaction with the political Left, seen as nothing more than contenders for the management of a liberal state, barely distinguishable from their center-right competitors. Jean Baudrillard's ironic portrait of the "divine Left" of the early eighties captured both the disenchantment of former radicals, who viewed Mitterrand's reformism as a betrayal, and the condescension of the new liberals, who had nothing to expect from a socialist government still steeped in statism and whose policies were doomed, in any case, by the new world order.[9] The future national-republicans of the nineties, from Max Gallo to Régis Debray, remained for the moment within the Socialist Party, content with wagging an accusatory finger at the new treason of the clerics, perhaps still harboring the hope that the Left could dam the flow of what would later be called *la pensée unique*, the conquering ideology of the new times. The final year of the decade, which coincided with the bicentennial of the French Revolution, would add to the republican agenda a new, explosive entry—*laïcité*—and give the old doctrine an unexpected surge of energy.

I discussed in chapter 2 how the "centrist Republic" and the rise of democratic individualism were the talk of the town (Paris, in this case) in the early 1980s. Everyone seemed busy discovering the liberal tradition kept for so long on the margins of French thought, and almost overnight Tocqueville became the required reference of any analysis of the new France. After three decades of highly theoretical battles between phenomenologists and structuralists, moral and political philosophy was making a comeback, as in the good old days of the republic of the Kantian professors, but in a radically new context. In the historical disciplines, the old Annales paradigm, grounded, like structuralism, on the idea of a social *science*, also had to make room for the return of the political. The relationship between the individual and society, the foundations of the polis, and the genesis of the modern state became the preferred topoi of a new generation of public intellectuals and cultural journalists. Once a dominated worldview, the liberal model, redescribed in terms of the personalization of lifestyles and consumer choice, seemed to occupy the whole

---

9. On the "silence of the intellectuals," see Philippe Boggio, "Le silence des intellectuels de gauche," *Le Monde*, July 27, 1993; and Hazareesingh, *Intellectuals and the French Communist Party*.

of the intellectual scene, at least the one that was under the glare of the media spotlight.

The affair of the veil in 1989 was the call to arms of the republican camp, starting off the controversy over multiculturalism and communitarianism that was to define most of the following decade (see chapter 7). By placing the public schools at the center of the debate on national identity, the issue provided a perfect illustration of the way the Republic-nation-state complex dovetailed with the "French exceptionalism" motif. Five prominent intellectuals and academics called for teachers to resist communitarian threats to the school system in *Le Nouvel Observateur* in November 1989. Their manifesto became a defining moment of the crystallization of the fledgling national-republican crusade. Among the signatories were Elisabeth Badinter, Régis Debray, and Alain Finkielkraut, whose books had been influential during the postmodernism debate discussed in chapter 2. Quickly joined by others, they would be instrumental in the updating of the philosophical tenets of republican universalism, leading the resistance to the politically correct storm blowing in from the United States.

The Semantics of Melancholia

In the ideological context of the last decade, *République* and *républicain* (and their correlates, *citoyen* and *citoyenne* used as adjectives) have become empty signifiers, vacuous forms that can be filled with plenty of contradictory contents. They refer to a variety of domains, from legal dispositions and institutional arrangements to inclusive, tolerant modes of sociability, as in phrases such as *dialogue républicain* and *intégration républicaine*. In its greatest semantic expansion, the term ends up encompassing the whole of French national identity (another floating signifier it closely emulates), thereby becoming synonymous with France itself, a tautology about a tautology.

The semantic vagueness of the republican signifier illustrates the symbolic dislocation that is often associated with depressive psychological states. The melancholic subject is deprived of meanings and values, her speech repetitive and monotonous, her voice flat and affectless. The inability to imagine the future by reconstituting a new symbolic system on the ruins of the old one leads to what Julia Kristeva has called in *Black Sun* "the denial of the signifier." In Kristeva's words, "Signs are arbitrary because language starts with a *negation (Verneinung)* of Loss, along with the depression occasioned by mourning. . . . Depressed persons . . . *disavow the negation*: they cancel it out, suspend it, and nostalgically fall back on the real object (the Thing) of their loss, which is just what they do not manage to lose, to which they remain painfully riveted" (43–44).

The symbolic breakdown surrounding the word "République" points to a collective inability to find a stable, shared set of meanings to substitute for the lost imagined (national) community, now buried under layers of dead language. On the day of his inauguration as the first Socialist president of the Fifth Republic, François Mitterrand made a solemn visit to the tombs of Jean Jaurès, Jean Moulin, and Victor Schoelcher at the Panthéon, the church turned into a civic temple by the revolutionary government in 1791 to serve as the burying place of the Republic's most influential figures.[10] Mitterrand's televised pilgrimage inserted his presidency within the long history of the French Left, bringing together the memories of socialism, the Résistance, and the Republic (Schoelcher, a republican senator and an opponent to Louis-Napoléon Bonaparte, played a leading role in the abolition of slavery in the West Indies by the revolutionary government of 1848). Beyond the obvious political symbolism attached to the ceremony, Mitterand's visit to the crypt of the great ancestors manifested the mournful fascination for Kristeva's "Thing buried alive" concealed by the nostalgic, repetitive, dead language of the depressive patient (53). The spectral nature of the neo-republican nostalgia comes from its inability to re-symbolize collective meanings, to signify political and cultural community in a new way, as the obsessive-compulsive repetition of glorious past events and fascination for deceased legendary figures fails to give rise to a new national consensus.

The chain of equivalent identifications I referred to above (the Republic *is* France, the foes of the Republic are the enemies of France, etc.) derives some kind of empirical validation from the fact that, although republican institutions, dominant but contested between 1876 and 1940, were briefly dismantled during Vichy, their legitimacy was never seriously questioned after 1945. In order to correct the oversimplifications of the ideological debate, one needs

---

10. As a result of a vote by the Assemblée constituante in April 1791, the Sainte-Geneviève church became the Panthéon, destined to house the remains of major revolutionary figures. Mirabeau was the first to be buried, followed by Voltaire in 1791, Rousseau in 1794, Hugo in 1885, and Zola in 1908. The Left came to power in 1924 and transferred Jaurès's remains to the Panthéon that same year, ten years after his death. Jean Moulin's turn came in 1964 (during de Gaulle's presidency), and André Malraux, another figure of the Résistance, followed in 1996 (during Chirac's presidency). In 2002, Alexandre Dumas, born of a French father and a Creole mother of French African ancestry, joined fellow writers Hugo and Zola. A sign of the new challenges facing the nation, and a symbol of the inclusiveness of the republican ideal, a *métisse* woman riding a horse and impersonating Marianne accompanied the writer's coffin during the ceremony.

to foreground the polysemy of the word "republican," embedded as it is in a long series of struggles that have shaped the country's political unconscious since the end of the eighteenth century. Jean-Marie Colombani rightly claimed that those he called the "ultra-republicans," situated along the "Séguin-Chevènement-Pasqua-Debray ideological axis," do not have a monopoly on the legitimate definition of the Republic, which they identify with the "Jacobin Republic as it was recycled through the First Empire." Colombani favored a rival version patterned after the Girondists' conception, a modern, pluralistic, administratively decentralized regime based on the separation of powers and the independence of the judiciary. "The identification of the Republic with the nation-state that we believe has existed from all eternity," Colombani argued, "is nothing but a historical form among others. Sanctified by the Third Republic, this dated form cannot be taken as the basis of universalism and freedom."[11]

The current confusion does not only have its source in the multiple referents of the republican idea. It also results from transfers of meaning among distinct empirical social realities that Jacobinism has improperly mixed up, both in theory and practice, such as the state, the nation, and democracy. The republican compact of April 2002 was not a return to the roots of the *republican* project as conceived by Rousseau in the eighteenth century, Jules Simon in the nineteenth, or Alain in the twentieth. It was a rallying of all *democrats* against a candidate (Le Pen) tarnished, among other things, by his association with the anti-parliamentarian Right of the fifties. In the same way, to defend the schools against identity politics means confronting *laïcité* with contemporary conceptions of the complex relationship among faiths, cultures, and ideologies in a pluralistic, democratic setting. It is rarely a conscious attempt to recover the original meaning of the word, which implied the rational critique of religious beliefs and other "passions of the soul" as the source of "superstition" and oppression. The current notion of *laïcité* is reduced to being an argument against communitarianism, "diversity," and the threat of Islam. It is no longer about protecting the independence of public education and keeping the nascent reason of every pupil free from all pressure, whether from the Church, the state, business organizations, the press, or political parties.

The Republic is improperly equated with the nation, two realities closely connected within the Jacobin tradition, but not necessarily equivalent, since many nations are not republics and since France was not always a republic

11. Colombani, *Les infortunes de la République*, 39.

(and according to many neo-republicans, it is no longer one today). When fans of a Corsican soccer team or supporters during a game between France and Algeria boo the French national anthem, they are directing their anger at the symbol of the nation rather than at the republican regime per se. The Beurs' jeers and loud whistling signifies their attachment, e contrario, to the Algerian nation, a republic but hardly a democracy. An independent Corsica (presumably the cause championed by the jeering fans of Sporting Club de Bastia) would no longer be part of the French nation, but would most likely remain a republic. In the same way, the tricolor flags ritualistically displayed during demonstrations against the National Front are meant to symbolize democratic values (the refusal of racism and exclusion, the plurality of ethnic cultures, the respect for difference, etc.) rather than republican principles (after all, the July Monarchy accepted the tricolor in 1830).

Hieroglyphs in the Desert

In his essay on Freud and Rosenzweig, Eric L. Santner borrows from Jean Laplanche the notion of an "enigmatic signifier" to account for what he calls the "historicity of meaning": "We are . . . always haunted, surrounded by the remainders of lost forms of life, by concepts and signs that had meaning within a form of life that is now gone and so persist, to use Lacan's telling formulation, as hieroglyphs in the desert. We are thus always, in a certain sense, within the dimension of loss and abandonment. But what is more, we are in the midst of a loss we cannot even really name, for when you lose the concept you also lose the capacity to name what has been lost."[12]

Many versions of the current republican revival aim at countering this loss of meaning by reactivating the memory of "a form of life" (the all-encompassing, almost tautological meaning of the empty signifier "Republic") identified for almost a hundred and fifty years with the political and cultural specificity of the country. As with ritual and magic formulae, the value or affect of the enigmatic signifier exceeds its meaning, since the word lacks a referent, and since its content can always get lost in the sands of oblivion, as so many signs in the desert. Following Jospin's electoral rout in 2002, Jean-Luc Nancy deplored the "silence of the political voice" during the weeks leading up to the election. "The campaign was so pathetic," he wrote, "because it was not political. It was not because the Right and the Left both agreed with the erasure of the political. They agreed with it because they did

---

12. Santner, *Psychotheology of Everyday Life*, 44.

not perceive the urgency of thinking in a new way the politics that were discredited or supposed to be overcome by the economy. The missing voice was the voice of a thought."[13]

A politics inspired by thought (and, consequently, by thinkers who would then shoulder again the task of articulating the principles of the coming community): isn't that the definition of the Republic itself, the res publica of the ancient philosophers and the modern intellectuals alike, conceived as an enterprise based on a series of projects (Condorcet's *Lumières*, Comte's positivism, Jaurès's humanistic socialism, Durkheim and Mauss's progressive sociology, etc.)? A good deal of the conversation about "post-politics" in the past thirty years has revolved around the elusive figure of Marianne, not as the singular incarnation of a particular empirical regime (the Republic in its successive versions, the Marianne of 1848 as compared, say, to her 1945 version), but as the emblem of the public space, the allegory of the philosophical-political field per se.

Alain Badiou argued twenty-five years ago that politics had "become the appearance of its absence . . . , an automatic subject is tied up with it, disencumbered of any desire. . . . What the crisis of the political unveils is the fact that all sets of elements are inconsistent, that there are neither French people nor proletariat and that, as a consequence, the figure of representation [the nation] as well as its reverse, the figure of spontaneity, are themselves inconsistent, lacking the simple tense of presentation."[14] Disencumbered of its imaginary side (the French *ethnie* as organic community, the Barresian people as race and roots, the great nation of yesterday, "national preference" today),[15] the res publica lives on as a symbolic exigency, as an expression of the singular universal, a word, a concept or a right resistant to any form of totalization, whether by ethnicity or the economy.

Jean-Luc Nancy, drawing the lesson of April 2002 in his *Libération* piece, claimed that "politics is neither the parties' strategy to seize power or control the state, nor the epic vision of a nation. It stands at the point of a shared existence which is not a totalizing whole, which is in a sense an empty point (it's the specific nature of democracy: as Michelet said, its sole monument must be an empty square where people can assemble). But at that point,

---

13. Jean-Luc Nancy, "La voix qui a manqué," *Libération*, April 30, 2002.
14. Badiou, *Peut-on penser la politique?* 9, 13.
15. The notion of "national preference," first proposed by the National Front, and according to which jobs should be given in priority to French "natives" rather than to immigrants and their children, has its correlate at the subnational level in the demands by Corsican nationalists that civil servant positions held by "continentals" be reserved for ethnic Corsicans.

[politics] is the name for . . . the unity of this whole without totalization: it gives it a tone, a bearing, a voice." Nancy writes "democracy" in reference to Michelet, but one might substitute the word "republic," since Michelet's republic is the historical incarnation of the democratic project in postrevolutionary France. The space that must remain empty is that of the public thing, of Jacques Rancière's "part of those who have no part," the part that belongs to no one and cannot be returned to any majority or minority, to any professional category, interest group, or community: therein resides its universality.[16] The tension between the empty place of the democratic imperative and the various "identities" competing to fill its void reached a fever pitch around issues of memory, race, and difference during the first decade of the new millennium.

16. See Rancière, *Dis-agreement*, 11.

Chapter Six

MEMORY WARS

The official memory of the national past stands out as one of the most conspicuous of the lost objects of contemporary French culture. This may seem a paradoxical statement in view of the current memorial inflation marked by a proliferation of events, texts, and places of commemoration. In fact, the multiplication of claims to the past made by an array of social and political groups points to the disappearance of a *shared* representation of the nation, a sense of collective belonging in common to all those who felt included in it, which was accepted even by those who were excluded from it. Opposite camps now request equal representation in the struggle for memory, as shown by current controversies surrounding the transatlantic slave trade, colonization, and the Algerian War. While the 1990s were the decade of the "Jewish memory," the first years of the new millennium witnessed the return of other repressed pasts, as a growing number of pressure groups have contested the official version of national history, demanding that the state recognize the crimes perpetrated by public authorities against their specific communities.[1]

A shorter version of this chapter was published as "Transmission Problems: Memory, Community, and the Republican Idea in Contemporary France," *Journal of European Studies* 35, no. 2 (2005): 237–45.

    1. There is an extensive bibliography of books published in France on *la mémoire juive*. Among the most influential historiographical studies, essays, and testimonials, see Burrin, *Ressentiment et apocalypse*; Poliakov, *Histoire de l'antisémitisme*; Bensoussan, *Histoire de la Shoah*; Hilberg, *La destruc-*

The agenda of the minister for Veterans Affairs between August 2004 and February 2006, for example, testifies to the proliferation of the demands for memory in contemporary France. August 6, 2004: ceremony for the sixtieth anniversary of the Allied landing in Toulon; September 2: celebration of the ninetieth anniversary of the Battle of the Marne; September 7–9: commemorations of the 1944 liberation of Besançon, Dole, and Marseille; September 24: homage to soldiers from Africa and Overseas Departments and Territories; September 27: homage to Marshal Joseph Joffre; October 4: exhibition on the Résistance and the Deportation; November 5: homage to the Résistance in Grenoble; November 9: eighty-sixtieth anniversary of the end of World War I; November 24: inauguration of an exhibition in Aulnay-sous-Bois and lecture on the liberation of 1944; December 2: national day of remembrance for those "who died for the country" in North Africa; December 10: ceremony marking the discovery of French soldiers' bodies in Dien Bien Phu, Vietnam; December 15: presentation of a law on the *rapatriés* (citizens of the former French Algeria); January 11, 2005: official visit to Auschwitz, Poland; January 14: commemoration of the liberation of the Auschwitz concentration camp, in Paris; January 24: inauguration of the Shoah Memorial; January 31: homage to Jean Moulin, hero of the Résistance; February 7: launching of the national contest on the Résistance and the Deportation; March 9: sixty-second anniversary of the Japanese "coup de force"; April 1: Congress of the National Union of Deported and Interned Persons and War Victims; April 8: sixtieth anniversary of the liberation of children from the Buchenwald concentration camp; April 12: commemoration of the liberation from Nazi death camps; April 21: ninetieth anniversary of the beginning of the Armenian genocide; April 22: national day of remembrance for the memory of victims and heroes of the Deportation; April 27: award ceremony for the winners of the national contest "Biographies of WWI Soldiers"; May 6: sixtieth anniversary of Victory in Europe; May 31: memorial of the soldiers from Ivory Coast who died for France; June 6: sixty-first anniversary of the Allied landing in Normandy; June 8: sixty-first anniversary of the massacre of French civilians by the retreating German Army in Oradour-sur-Glane; June 16: sixty-fifth anniversary of General de Gaulle's famed radio address; September 14: visit to Auschwitz, public homage to Simon Wiesenthal; September 22: commemoration of the battles of 1915; October 11: advance screening of the movie *An Intimate Portrait of de Gaulle*; November 21: visit of an exhibition on the Mauthausen concentration

---

tion des juifs d'Europe; Friedländer, *L'Allemagne nazie et les juifs*; Lanzmann, *Shoah*; Pressac, *Les crématoires d'Auschwitz*; Vaisman, *Parmi les cris, un chant s'élève*; and Pechanski, *La France des camps*.

camp; January 10, 2006: inauguration of a monument for the Muslim soldiers who died for France; February 17: ninetieth anniversary of the beginning of the Battle of Verdun.[2]

Sites of Oblivion

The contest of memories and the controversies about recent political uses of the past gathered momentum during the years leading to the bicentennial of the French Revolution in 1989. The dominant reading of the revolution, based on Jules Michelet's republican version and later consolidated by the woks of pro-Jacobin historians such as Albert Soboul, was called into question from a variety of viewpoints that refused to take the revolution as "one block," as Clémenceau had argued in a famous speech to the Chambre des députés in 1891. Experts on the revolutionary period took a variety of conflicting political positions on the Jacobin Terror, replicating the ideological divisions of the time and reproducing the lines of fracture within the historiography of the First Republic, from de Maistre to Constant and Quinet, and from Tocqueville and Cochin to Agulhon and Furet. The historians' quarrel regarding the foundational moment of the republican tradition showed that although Furet had declared (in 1978) that the revolution was finally over, it did not seem to be the case when it came to professional historiography.

The first volume of the *Lieux de mémoire* (*Realms of Memory*), the influential, multivolume collection edited by Pierre Nora, was conceived as an illustration of the momentous shift in historical consciousness that had taken place since the sixties and was informed, in Nora's words, "by a sense that everything is over and done with, that something long since begun is now complete. Memory is constantly on our lips because it no longer exists."[3] But the massive historiographical enterprise turned out to be much more than a dispassionate, scientific assessment of the profound transformations in the way the citizens of post-historical liberal democracies relate to their collective past. The successive volumes revealed that many contributors to the project perceived a disturbing and growing cultural trend.

As years went by, the original project of desacralizing, through their historicization, the memorial loci associated with the official republican hagiography of the nation (*histoire-mémoire* and *nation-mémoire*) increasingly made way for the denunciation by professional historians of what Nora would call

---

2. See http://web.archive.org/web/*/http://www.memoire-france.com/.
3. Nora, "General Introduction: Between Memory and History," in *Realms of Memory*, 1:1.

la frénésie de commémoration, the frenzied demand for commemoration coming from public authorities and private associations alike. If the rise of the genre known as the "history of history" among professional historians had laid bare, "in a country like France, the subversion from within of memory-history by critical history,"[4] this dissociation of history from memory was in turn being subverted, and in some ways hijacked, by the new commemorative obsession.

In Nora's view, the "bulimic" consumption of memories not only had done away with the critical distance required by professional historiography, but had reduced *les lieux de mémoire*, originally conceived as *symbolic* objects, metaphors, or causes (as in "to fight for a cause"), to mere topographical places of remembrance (museums, monuments, or cemeteries)—that is, simple spatial markers, tourist-oriented remnants of what was once a lived connection with the past. While the intent of *Realms of Memory* had been to show how memory had been "grasped by history," the excessive "patrimonialization" of the past at work in French culture was now viewed as having perverted the whole project of critical historiography.

In his study of the postwar representations of Vichy France, published at the same time as the last volumes of *Lieux de mémoire*, Henri Rousso also deplored the deleterious effects of the commemorative obsession on the practice of history as the critical assessment of the past. In the book he coauthored with Eric Conan, *Vichy: An Ever-Present Past*, Rousso claimed that the public debate on the complicity of the French state in the Holocaust that raged throughout the eighties and nineties was fraught with "uncontrolled uses of the discipline of history," and a phantasmic rewriting of history that ended up in sacralizing the memory of the war years. He argued that through the successive trials of Nazis and their collaborators (Barbie, 1987; Touvier, 1994; Papon, 1997), the judicial institution had replaced both official and critical historiography as the country's main "vector of memory" (74). In Conan and Rousso's view, the replacement of critical distance by moral indignation on the part of those who demanded that the past be redeemed here and now, that a culprit be singled out and tried (in this case the French state), resulted in the erasure of the very stuff of history—that is, time, the difference that separates us from what is no longer. The collapse of historical becoming meant the triumph of anachronism, a process by which "the moral stance of posterity" is confused with the complex reality of past events (199). As a consequence, "the dark years [of the Occupation] become the symbol of a

---

4. Ibid., 1:4.

(universal) Evil, not the product of a specific history. 'Vichy' seems suddenly to be coming from nowhere, outside of time and the Nazi occupation, entirely born of the depths of the French soul, of 'the French ideology'" (203).

Beyond this allusion to Bernard-Henri Lévy's book bearing the same title I mentioned in chapter 3, the authors poked fun at the "late-coming militants of memory" who seemed to have discovered the Holocaust overnight, just as they had suddenly become aware of the Gulag in 1976, twenty years after Khrushchev's report to the Supreme Soviet on the crimes of Stalinism. Orphaned of a revolutionary future by the end of the 1970s, the former radicals "have converted themselves over from a prophetic political activism into an inquisitory and retroactive political activism" (207). This police officer's view of memory as ritual denunciation of secret plots was seen as the hallmark of a generation endowed with what Maurice Agulhon had called a "good moral conscience without any purpose."[5] Remembrance looms as the future fades away. Since they could no longer change the present, the sons and daughters of the World War II generation directed their resentment, in the words of Paul Thibaud, at "purging the past of its progenitors" (207).

In *Memory, History, Forgetting*, Paul Ricoeur reminds us that sorrow is "the sadness that has not performed the work of mourning. Joy is the reward for renouncing the lost object and the guarantee that one is reconciled with the internalized object" (94). The compulsion to repeat prevents the traumatic event from becoming conscious. As Freud pointed out, the patient repeats instead of remembering; repetition amounts to forgetting.[6] For Conan and Rousso, the melancholy fascination with "Vichy" fed on the failure of the myth of the Resistance, a fantasy designed to cover up and redeem the collective sin of collaboration, a secular form of "indulgence" (235). The national case of bad faith and the moral outrage of the younger generations stemmed from this belated rejection of the Gaullist indulgence, replaced by the sense of a collective debt owed to the sacrifice of those who had died fighting the Nazis and their French supporters.

Pierre Nora's somewhat disenchanted account of the shift from memory history to the tyranny of local, fragmented memories is also set against the backdrop of a collective feeling of loss.[7] "Museums, archives, cemeteries,

---

5. Cited in Conan and Rousso, *Vichy*, 207.

6. Freud, "Remembering, Repeating, and Working Through," cited in Ricoeur, *Memory, History, Forgetting*, 445.

7. On the evolution of Nora's account of the theoretical implications and public reception of *Lieux de mémoire*, see Ricoeur, *Memory, History, Forgetting*, 401–11.

collections, festivals, anniversaries, treaties, depositions, monuments, sanctuaries, private associations—these are the relics of another era, illusions of eternity. That is what makes these pious undertakings seem like exercises in nostalgia, sad and lifeless," Nora wrote in *Realms of Memory* (6–7). He began his general introduction to the English translation of *Lieux de mémoire* with references to "the disappearance of [both] peasant culture" (1) and *sociétés-mémoires*, "institutions that once transmitted values from generation to generation—churches, schools, families, governments," and to the end of ideologies "that once smoothed the transition from past to future or indicated what the future should retain from the past, whether in the name of reaction, progress, or even revolution" (2). The era of commemoration marks France's exit from "great history": "There is no longer a shared superego, the canon has disappeared."[8]

The proclamation by the state of the Année du patrimoine (Year of the patrimony) in 1980 put an official stamp on the fragmentation of national memory, as manifestations of the local and regional pasts flooded the media and, as a consequence, public consciousness. The lost solidarity of the past and the future had given way to the solidarity of present and memory.[9] Bastille Day, to be sure, had already shifted from historical event to official site of memory when it became a national holiday in 1880, "but the republican spirit, then very much alive," Nora argued in *Realms of Memory*, "made it something more than that: a genuine return to the source. But what does it mean today? . . . The loss of our national memory as a living presence forces us to look at it with eyes that are neither naïve nor indifferent. . . . So we no longer celebrate the nation, but we study the nation's celebrations" (7).

Legislating the Past

Faced with the proliferation of fragmented memories, the French state undertook a series of measures to try to control the political uses of history more and more prevalent in civil society. The debate surrounding the negationists' denial of the Holocaust prompted Parliament to pass the first "memorial law," the loi Gayssot of July 13, 1990.[10] Aimed at "repressing any racist, anti-Semitic, and xenophobic act," it made it a criminal offense to attempt to revise history by minimizing, denying, or ignoring evidence concerning

---

8. Nora, *Realms of Memory*, 3:614.
9. See Ricoeur, *Memory, History, Forgetting*, 534.
10. For a recent and comprehensive account of the "memory wars" in France, see Blanchard and Veyrat-Masson, *Les guerres de mémoires*. See also Prochasson, *L'empire des émotions*.

crimes against humanity as defined by the London Agreement of August 1945. This first law was soon followed by a series of similar legislative acts aimed at curbing the increased propensity of political organizations to reinvent the past according to their own agenda. In addition to criminalizing the denial of established historical "facts," such as the Shoah or the Armenian genocide of 1915, the legislators' objective was to promote awareness of ignored or repressed realities, to provide the symbolic recognition of the "wounded memories" of victimized populations, and to protect them from being submitted to the public celebration of crimes perpetrated against their ancestors.

In January 2001, the National Assembly voted a single article "recognizing" the Armenian genocide. A few months later, the Taubira law, named after the representative from French Guiana who successfully sponsored it, declared that "the French Republic recognizes that the transatlantic slave trade as well as the slave trade in the Indian Ocean, on the one hand, and slavery on the other, perpetrated . . . against African, Amerindian, Malagasy, and Indian populations constitute a crime against humanity."[11] The law was passed unanimously, a sign that political consensus could be reached concerning structures of oppression sufficiently removed in time. A similar consensus would prove impossible to reach four years later when the legislators' attention turned to colonialism and the Algerian War.

The second article of the loi Taubira represented a significant departure from the preceding pieces of legislation in that it mandated that slavery be given "the space it deserved in school programs and research programs in history and social sciences." By its inclusion in the pedagogical project of the Republic, the slave trade would become, in the eyes of the nation's representatives, an essential part of the country's collective memory. The expressive mandate from the government that school curricula reflect changes in France's official memory enacted by the new legislation did raise some concern among professional historians, but the protest remained limited in scope and intensity, given the fact that a large consensus, shared by most of the political class, the media, and the public, seemed to condemn slavery and its legacy.

The officially sanctioned condemnation of the slave trade in eighteenth- and early nineteenth-century French overseas possessions could only feed the demand for public recognition on the part of groups who felt their own past had been ignored or distorted by the dominant narrative of the Republic.

---

11. For the complete text of the various memorial laws, see the website of La documentation française, http://www.ladocumentationfrancaise.fr/dossiers/loi-memoire/lois-memorielles.shtml.

Expanding the *roman national* to include unacknowledged chapters of the colonial past, far from resulting in a liberal-pluralistic logic of reconciliation and *vivre-ensemble*, only ended up underscoring the extent to which colonialism had been a divisive institution, a site of protracted political struggles, which meant that the contest of memories triggered by the new piece of legislation quickly revived another set of interpretive battles.[12] Associations of veterans from the Algerian War linked to the nationalist Right had been increasingly vocal throughout the 1990s, demanding that a variety of individuals and groups involved in the conflict be recognized, financially compensated, and, in some cases, rehabilitated and amnestied. Among them were *rapatriés* (European colonists repatriated to France after the war, familiarly known as *pieds-noirs*), *harkis*, relatives of war victims, and even militants of the outlawed, factious Secret Army Organization.

There is a long list of these militant groups who have been claiming their "right to memory" (*droit de mémoire*) alongside other associations representing victims of past violence and discrimination. Most of these organizations are headquartered in southeastern France, where a majority of *pieds-noirs*

12. Like the Dreyfus Affair, the Algerian War has left a durable mark on French collective memory. In many ways, the current debates about immigration and the place of Islam in French society have their origin in nineteenth- and twentieth-century colonialism and in the postwar period of anticolonial struggles and decolonization (1945–62). Because postwar immigrants were also colonial and later postcolonial subjects, the social conflicts surrounding the "integration" of their children and grandchildren in French society are closely bound up with the traumas occasioned by the loss of the empire, of which the Algerian War (1954–62) was the bloodiest and most divisive illustration.

The Algerian War was a complex conflict that added the bitterness of two civil wars to the brutality of a war of decolonization involving indigenous guerrilla groups fighting a western European power with the support of foreign countries, from the Soviet Union to various Arab nations. The civil war in Algeria pitted militant nationalists of rival organizations, the National Liberation Front and the Algerian National Movement, often called *fellaghas*, against the *harkis*, Muslim soldiers who kept serving in the French Army. After the end of the war, several hundreds of thousands of harkis found refuge in France with their families, bringing to immigrant communities in the metropole the divisions born of the conflict abroad, since sympathizers of Algerian independence were also living in France.

The war also divided the military, the political class, and the public. The socialist government attempted to restore law and order in the colony after the beginning of the armed conflict in 1954 through a military campaign of "pacification," while the French Communist Party sided with the Algerian revolutionaries. The government's inability to resolve the political crisis and win the war led to the 1958 return to power of Charles de Gaulle, who gradually came to the realization that Algerian independence was inevitable. The colonialist Right's support of "Algérie française" led to the open rebellion of several generals against the government in 1961, and to the formation of the Organisation de l'armée secrète (OAS, or Secret Army Organization), responsible for bombings and assassinations on both sides of the Mediterranean. A 1961 referendum on Algerian independence supported by a majority of voters in France and Algeria led to the signing of the Evian Accords by the National Liberation Front and the French government and the subsequent cease-fire in March 1962. Ninety-one percent of the French electorate approved the Evian Accords in June 1962.

relocated in the early sixties, and where a large number of North African immigrant workers settled at the same time, resulting in an uneasy cohabitation among groups who had been on opposite sides of the decolonization struggle. By the time the Taubira law was passed in May 2001, these organizations had been actively lobbying the government for both recognition and compensation for the victims of the Algerian War and had disseminated alternative narratives of colonial and postcolonial history, in opposition to both the official discourse of the state and scholarly accounts provided by the historical profession.

The Politics of Monumentality

The Mémorial national des Français d'Algérie et rapatriés d'outre-mer (National memorial for the French from Algeria and repatriated people from overseas) was founded in Aix-en-Provence in 1965, only three years after the end of the war, in order to "perpetuate the memory of the dead who were buried abroad." A similar organization, Souvenir des Français disparus en Algérie (Remembering the French killed in Algeria), aims at "keeping the memory of the French people of all origins who died in the Algerian territory under French jurisdiction from the cowardly attacks of November 1, 1954, to July 2, 1962" (i.e., the entire war). The Comité pour le rétablissement de la vérité historique sur l'Algérie française (Committee for the restoration of historical truth on French Algeria), whose motto is "Veritas," presents itself as a "group of volunteers who have all chosen honorable ways of defending the memory of French Algeria and many of whom have played a major role during the tragedy that was to end with desertion [abandon], and suffered ill-treatment or been imprisoned because of their patriotic resistance." The goal of the association is to help others to "accomplish the necessary work of truth-telling" and "rehabilitate the *pied-noir* and *harki* communities, working without respite against the distortion [*dénaturation*] of history."[13]

SOS Outre-mer (SOS overseas), founded in 1991 and named in obvious (ironic?) reference to the antiracist militant organization SOS Racisme, has among its objectives to "fight against the disinformation that too often and unjustly surrounds the past of France overseas. Through its publications and public declarations, [the association] regularly denounces the gross caricatures of colonization and the insulting words found even in schoolbooks and hurled at generations who have written in blood these beautiful pages of history

---

13. See http://babelouedstory.com/veritas/00_accueil/00_accueil.html.

France has really no need to be ashamed of."[14] We are presented here with an ideological complex that mixes the patriotic cult of the dead (a traditional topos of the Right) with more recent discursive strategies linked to the postwar consolidation of the welfare state (a rhetoric usually associated with the Left). The demand for monetary compensation, the appeal to the rhetoric of victimization, and the production of counter-histories in order to legitimate the requests for public aid and retributive legislation goes hand in hand with the rejection of descriptions of the colonial past tainted with self-incriminating and defeatist "political correctness" (a theme common to nationalists on the Right and the Left).

The politics of monumentality that inscribe the symbolic memory wars in material sites and social practices (memorials, museums, *monuments aux morts*, statues, steles, commemorative speeches, flag ceremonies, etc.) has kept ideological tensions high in southern France and fueled the national debate. It has also raised serious doubts about the ability of the state to ensure the harmonious cohabitation of conflicting representations of civil and foreign wars within the space of a pluralistic public sphere. A number of monuments honoring the partisans of French Algeria have been erected in Toulon, Béziers, Perpignan, and smaller southern towns (e.g., Théoul, Pérols) in the past decade. On July 5, 2005, the Association for the Defense of the Moral and Material Interests of Former Political Prisoners and Exiles from French Algeria (Association pour la défense des intérêts moraux et matériels des anciens détenus de l'Algérie française, or ADIMAD) erected in Marignane, a suburb of Marseille, a stele commemorating "those who were executed and died so that French Algeria might live." Among those tried and sentenced to death in 1962 and 1963 were two major figures of OAS: Jean Bastien-Thiry, who tried to assassinate de Gaulle in 1961, and Lieutenant Roger Degueldre, leader of the Delta commandos, a paramilitary group responsible for the deaths of thousands of supporters of Algerian independence on both sides of the Mediterranean. Several organizations—including the Movement Against Racism and for Friendship Among Peoples (Mouvement contre le racisme et pour l'amitié entre les peuples, or MRAP), the League for Human Rights (Ligue des droits de l'homme), and the Charles de Gaulle Foundation—had asked the public authorities to forbid the display of the monument.

Although the minister for Veterans Affairs had publicly condemned the inauguration of the stele, which was declared illegal by the local authorities, it was nevertheless discreetly put in place. A few months later, on November

---

14. See http://www.sosoutremer.org/.

1, 2005, the fifty-first anniversary of the start of the Algerian War, the mayor of Marignane—a former member of the National Front who had allowed ADIMAD to build the stele on public land (fittingly, the town's cemetery)—attended a "private" ceremony during which a spray of flowers was placed on the monument. In a series of communiqués to the French press, antidiscrimination and civil liberties organizations denounced the government's increasing tolerance for activities that "turned murderers into victims, glorified a subversive political movement," and furthered "the historical revisionism," "negationism" (a term used for those who deny the existence of the Nazi gas chambers), and "Lepenization of memory" aimed at "glorifying the French colonial past."[15]

Michel Vauzelle, the Socialist president of the Provence-Alpes-Côte d'Azur administrative region, had also asked the representative of the French government in the area (the *préfet de région*) to forbid the inauguration of the Marignane monument, calling it a "racist, xenophobic, and antirepublican" initiative aimed at sowing hatred and discord in a part of France "where the National Front remains a threat." Significantly, Vauzelle ended his press release with a direct allusion to another site of memory located in the same area, the Mémorial du camp des Milles, a detention camp where 2,500 Jews had been interned during World War II before being deported to Auschwitz, illustrating the ways in which distinct, and sometimes competing, memories can also be linked as part of a specific memorial strategy. The completion of the Jewish Mémorial had been prevented by a lack of funding support from the French state, while local and regional authorities had kept their end of the bargain. Vauzelle's remarks underscored both the intense politicization of the memorial conflicts and the intense competition for the public funding of commemorative projects.

The Post-national State and the Management of Memory

The tensions surrounding the memorialization of white colonists, OAS militants, and Arab soldiers who had fought on the French side during the Algerian War also point to the limits of the public authorities' attempts to meet every demand for commemoration, giving activists free and equal access to redress. The war of memories is encouraged by the fact that the state increasingly wishes to project an image of impartiality and neutrality in the management of the competing needs, rights, requests, and expectations of the various

---

15. See http://mrap.asso.fr/communiques/stele; and http://www.ldh-toulon.net/.

lobbies that make up a liberal-pluralist civil society. Just as the memory of Vichy policies toward French and foreign Jews somehow won't go away, the open wounds of the Algerian tragedy prevent the forgetting, or forgiving, that would make it possible to commemorate all the victims of a double civil war. Just as the Gaullist version of the Occupation conveniently ignored that millions of French people supported the Vichy regime and did not join the Underground, the political class kept such a veil of silence over what was officially known as the "Algerian events" that the term "Algerian War" was only introduced in official public discourse in 1999.

The new post-national state is no longer as invested in grounding collective identity in the repression of past social and political divisions as the Gaullist regime was. But the more the public authority, following the new definition of its role as manager of the social, attempts to right the wrongs historically visited on an ever-growing array of "communities of memory," the more it makes itself vulnerable to the charge from any given group that it is rewarding their opponents or former oppressors, "turning murderers into victims." Public policies are perceived as either inadequate in redressing a given group's grievances or recklessly prone to manipulation by opposite or rival groups.

While the republican state of the pre–World War I period had the initiative in the elaboration and maintenance of national cohesion, effectively disseminating its centralized political principles and homogenizing cultural forms outward throughout civil society, the post-sixties neo-republican state has been on the defensive, clumsily reacting to, rather than integrating, the multiplicity of competing demands stemming from the political, professional, ethnic, or religious groups that make up an increasingly pluralistic social sphere. In other words, the nation-state no longer holds the monopoly of the pedagogical production of collective identity. Religious, cultural, and political groups are busy manufacturing their own genealogies regardless of academic accounts sanctioned by social scientific protocols. Since professional historians, and the schoolteachers they train in college, are no longer the only purveyors of collective histories, academic historiography has been increasingly "instrumentalized," as the French put it, by the competing demands for the recognition of rival versions of the past.

The logical outcome of the conflicts surrounding the Algerian War was for the Republic to pass yet another law codifying the way colonialism should be included in the national narrative. The new legislative act was patterned after the Taubira law, but its opponents called it "the revenge of the *pieds-noirs*" since it was sponsored by the Right, and since it mandated that the colonial empire be remembered as a positive accomplishment. Like its predecessor, the new law contained an educational provision. The soon-to-be extremely controversial article 4 required that "university research programs give the history of the French presence overseas, notably in North Africa, the place it deserves," and that elementary and secondary "school programs recognize in particular the positive role of the French presence overseas, notably in North Africa, and give the history and sacrifices of the French soldiers from these territories the prominent place they deserve." The second half of the statement sets article 4 within the larger context of legislation designed to bring justice to the *harkis*, since many of them were left behind by the French authorities at war's end to be executed as "collaborators" by Algerian nationalists. Article 5 explicitly forbade "all insult or defamation directed at a person or group of persons because of their true or supposed identity as a *harki*."[16]

Once again, the members of the National Assembly were caught in a double bind: how could they acknowledge the *harkis*' contribution to the nation without suggesting that their cause was honorable—in other words, that there was no "wrong side" in the Algerian War? The danger here was to formally acknowledge that the Algerian War was not over, that the dominant view that decolonization was a good thing (one shared by the Gaullists and the Left) was once again open to debate. Following the logic of the politics of recognition, the Socialists abstained from voting, not because the law glorified colonialism, but because it did not go far enough in compensating the victims who had fought on the French side. The Socialist position exposed the fundamental contradiction between an official liberal-democratic discourse asking that the nation "put colonialism behind us" (the postimperial Gaullist narrative), on the one hand, and the duty of heeding the demand by pro-colonial forces to have their memory legitimized by public recognition, on the other. Despite its explosive content, the law was passed on February 23, 2005, with complete indifference, on a Friday afternoon, at a time when most representatives are away from Paris in their constituencies. Only a handful of deputies were present, most of them from the southeastern part of France, where most associations defending *pied-noirs*' interests are located.

Who Owns History?

Some historians became aware of the law a few months later and a campaign to repeal article 4 quickly gained momentum in the spring of 2005, with a

---

16. See http://www.ladocumentationfrancaise.fr/dossiers/loi-memoire/lois-memorielles.html.

petition collecting a thousand signatures in three weeks. The text of the petition mentioned that the law imposed an official version of history, violating pedagogical neutrality and the principle of freedom of thought, which "stand at the heart of [republican] *laïcité.*" Moreover, by selecting only the positive role of colonization, it also imposed "an official lie about crimes, massacres leading all the way to genocide, about slavery, about the racism inherited from that past." The petition also explicitly inserted the law within the larger ongoing debate pitting republican universalism versus postmodern multiculturalism by stating that Parliament had attempted to legalize a kind of national communitarianism that was sure to trigger in reaction "the communitarianism of groups that were thus forbidden to have any past." Lastly, the text made a strong case for the necessary autonomy of the historical profession and its "specific responsibility" for the elucidation of the complex processes that led to an increasingly unified, globalized world that is at the same time racked by ethnic, racial, and religious conflicts.[17]

Influential professional organizations such as the Association of Teachers of History and Geography (the two disciplines are taught together in French secondary schools) and administrative entities such as l'Inspection générale (the corps of state-appointed inspectors who supervise the curriculum and evaluate teachers' performance for the Ministry of Education) also condemned the law, arguing that the government had never before so blatantly threatened the independence of the historical profession (the only other example was under the Vichy regime). Hamlaoui Mekachera, the French minister for Veterans Affairs, addressed the conflict of legitimacy that underscored the historians' resistance when he wondered publicly why "the representatives of the nation could not express themselves on topics that should be reserved for more or less self-proclaimed specialists." This remark attracted a swift rebuke from two professional historians who argued in a short piece published in *Le Monde* that "the representatives of the citizens," although they had a right to speak on historical issues, could not define the contents of school curricula, which are the sole purview of the "statutory power" of the state. The two scholars then suggested that the minister take a look at articles 34 and 37 of the French Constitution, where the respective roles of the legislature and of administrative regulatory bodies are clearly defined.[18]

---

17. The text of the petition, signed by a thousand historians, can be found at http://www.aidh.org/hist-mem/querelles-fen1.htm#1.

18. Claude Liauzu and Thierry Le Bars, "Colonisation: Réconcilier les mémoires," *Le Monde*, May 12, 2005.

One of the two authors of the article, Claude Liauzu, an emeritus professor at Université Paris 7 and a specialist in colonial history, was one of the six academics who had signed the original petition asking for the repeal of the law on colonial memory. Writing in the magazine *L'Histoire* a few months later, he warned that the passage of more and more memorial laws was a process fraught with risks. In response to the outcry caused by the new legislation, the minister of foreign affairs, Philippe Douste-Blazy, proposed that the government create a commission comprising French and Algerian historians, which would be charged with evaluating the role of colonization. Liauzu claimed that the new initiative, although it was a step in the right direction, still threatened the autonomy of the historical profession. The members of the commission, he argued, needed to be chosen by their peers rather than appointed by the government, and in any case historians, being neither judges nor counselors to the prince, should not be asked to assess the role of colonization.

Revealing how widespread the opposition to multiculturalism and its attendant "ideology of victimization" (made in America) remains among French academics, Liauzu brought up once again the issue of *communautarisme*—identitarian claims by ethnic minorities—as a threat to national unity. He warned that in the absence of proper training, high school teachers were likely to "condemn colonization in moral terms and reduce the history of colonized people to that of victims," which would run the risk of "pandering to communitarianism." Instead of encouraging the centrifugal aspects of racial, cultural, and religious diversity, "the teaching of history should answer the needs for recognition of a transformed society, traversed by pluralism, and inserted in Europe and the world" (52).[19]

Liauzu ended on an ironic note, remarking that, while the French ambassador to Algeria had acknowledged the responsibility of the government in the Sétif massacres of 1945, during which an estimated ten thousand to forty-five thousand pro-independence demonstrators were killed, members of the presidential majority had passed a legislative text giving satisfaction to *pied-noir* lobbies. "Sometimes, it's kind of hard to figure out what is going on," he quipped, appealing to his fellow historians' civic duty, and urging them to resist the manipulation of the past by antagonistic pressure groups who "swear solely by the duty to remember" yet whose discourse often ignores "the reality of historical events" (53). That most of the critics of the law shared their colleague's view of the practice of history as both scientific

19. Liauzu, "Non à la loi scélérate!" 52–53.

and civic-minded is clearly borne out by the title of an international colloquium, "For a Critical and Civic History" (Pour une histoire critique et citoyenne), that took place in Lyon in June 2006. The historians' necessary independence from political pressure for an official, state-sponsored narrative of the nation is only matched by their need to counter the influence of the fractious, solipsistic communities of memory who threaten the unity of the Republic.

Liauzu's reference to racial and cultural pluralism in the new France is all the more significant because it was published a few days before hundreds of ethnic neighborhoods went up in flames every night for more than two weeks in November 2005, as Arab and black youth rose up against police harassment, substandard housing and schooling, social and economic marginality, and job discrimination on the basis or race or religion. The debate on the memory of the Algerian War acquired a more pressing and dramatic dimension against the background of the uprisings involving the grandchildren of both *harkis* and *fellaghas*. The fact that words such as communitarianism, *laïcité*, and diversity inevitably crop up in discussions concerning issues of memory, race, sexual politics, or educational policy show how closely interrelated the various issues currently debated in France really are. In the aftermath of the *banlieue* uprisings, which triggered another soul-searching debate on the French malaise, the crisis of the republican regime, and the failure of its "model of integration," Jacques Chirac, after almost two months of unsuccessful attempts to convince the elected representatives of his own party to write another text eliminating the controversial passage, finally decided to bring the issue to the Constitutional Council (the French equivalent of the Supreme Court). The Council promptly declared that the text did not conform to statutory principles written in the 1958 Constitution, and the passage concerning school programs was struck from the law by statutory order in February 2006, a year after its initial promulgation.

History or Memory?

As the opposition to the law of February 2005 gathered momentum during the summer, another memorial crisis erupted, this time involving the Taubira law of 2001. This threat to the autonomy of historical scholarship came from the multiculturalist Left rather than the nationalist Right, and from activists rather than from the government. On June 12, 2005, Olivier Pétré-Grenouilleau, author of a well-received comparative study on the slave trade in global perspective,[20] which had just been awarded a prize by the French Senate, gave an interview in Le Journal du Dimanche, a popular French weekly. During the course of the discussion, the historian questioned the Taubira law's definition of slavery as a crime against humanity. He argued that slave trades were not genocides, since their objective was to use the labor force of the enslaved populations, not to exterminate them: "The Jewish genocide and the slave trade are different processes. There is no Richter scale of suffering."[21]

Prompted by the leading questions of the interviewer about the implications of his book for ethnic and racial relations in contemporary France, Pétré-Grenouilleau passed a series of judgments on the black movement, both in France and in the United States. He alluded to anti-Semitism among African Americans, reminded his interlocutor that Muslims had started the slave trade in the Middle Ages and that Africans had been both victims and actors of the practice, and questioned the validity of the "choice" of French artists and intellectuals who identify themselves as descendants of slaves. "West Indians were freed in 1848," the historian told his interviewer. "But if one goes back to Africa, one can say that the ancestors of their ancestors were either freemen, slaves, or slave traders. To present oneself as a descendant of slaves is to choose among one's ancestors." Clearly, the historian was equally guilty of "creating an identity between the past and the present," as were the militants of memory he was criticizing. Crossing the line between scholarship and politics, history and memory, he had brought his research to bear on extremely volatile contemporary issues in a climate of growing racial tensions. Instead of reading the past from the present, as the militants of memory do, Pétré-Grenouilleau was reading the present from the perspective of the past.

The day after the publication of the interview, Claude Ribbe, author of several books on Guadeloupe and the French West Indies, wrote an open letter to the "descendants of French slaves and to their friends" (widely available online), in which he took the French Senate to task for giving an award to the work of a "revisionist" historian. Ribbe asked the Senate president to reverse the jury's decision, and called on the minister of education to suspend Pétré-Grenouilleau and his revisionist colleagues from their teaching positions. He further suggested that the historian be brought to justice for his "revolting" comments to the press and the "abject theses" presented in his

20. Pétré-Grenouilleau, Les traites négrières.
21. Christian Saurage, "Un prix pour Les traites négrières," Le Journal du Dimanche, June 12, 2005.

book, in accordance with the law "protecting the memory of the slaves and the honor of their descendants." Ribbe concluded his open letter by stating that, "in case the Minister of Education refused to take the necessary sanctions, it would be up to . . . all of those who are revolted by the negation of colonial genocides and by revisionism to draw the consequences." The accusation of revisionism and negationism, the equation of slavery with genocide, and the use of the semantically charged term *déportés* (deportees), usually reserved for prisoners in Nazi concentration camps, to refer to the Africans displaced by the slave trade, were meant to draw an explicit parallel between slavery and the Shoah, an amalgamation Pétré-Grenouilleau had explicitly rejected in his piece in *Le Journal du Dimanche*.

Claude Ribbe was no stranger himself to the controversial politics of remembrance. In a book titled *Le crime de Napoléon*, published in the fall of 2005, he had portrayed Bonaparte as a forerunner of Hitler. The book described the reestablishment of slavery in 1802 (after its abolition by the French Revolution) and the brutal repression of the Haitian Revolution as a genocide perpetrated by means of systematic deportation and death squads, the use of gas for large-scale massacres, concentration camps (on Elba and Corsica), and racial laws forbidding interracial unions. The full title of the English edition, *Napoleon's Crimes: A Blueprint for Hitler*, explicitly linked Bonaparte, Nazism, and, by implication, the Holocaust, with a cover showing a swastika in the shadow of the emperor. The debate over posttraumatic identities sometimes takes the extreme form of a competition between representatives of rival wounded memories as to which population has been the most victimized by systematic, large-scale atrocities. In a conference later broadcast by a Jewish community radio station, RCJ (Radio Communauté Juive), Alain Finkielkraut described *Le crime de Napoléon* as "inspired by a kind of victimized rage, a way of telling Jews that they unduly occupy the place of the victim, which belongs to the descendants of slaves, sometimes self-proclaimed descendants, by the way."[22]

Napoleon's Crimes came out shortly before the controversial bicentennial celebration of the Battle of Austerlitz, which opened yet another front on the wars of remembrance. Several associations representing French nationals from overseas territories referred to Ribbe's book to oppose the official portrayal of Bonaparte's contribution to national history as relayed by the media. Pierre Nora publicly held Ribbe responsible for having forced the French

---

22. See Noël Blandin, "L'écrivain guadeloupéen Claude Ribbe porte plainte contre Alain Finkielkraut," *La République des Lettres*, January 9, 2007. Ribbe later sued Finkielkraut for defamation.

government to keep a low profile during the bicentennial: President Chirac even declined an invitation to attend the official commemorations organized by the French military. Nora also faulted Ribbe's interpretation for "judging history only in moral terms and tacking on the past interpretative grids that only apply to the present."[23] Nora deplored the fact that the government had legitimized Ribbe's positions by appointing him to the National Consultative Commission on Human Rights, echoing Ribbe's earlier complaint that the Senate had legitimated Pétré-Grenouilleau's book by giving him an award, and showing the extent to which the contest of memories is a struggle over the legitimate definition, in this case sanctioned by political institutions, of what constitutes the truth of the past. In his response to Nora, published in *Le Monde* a few days later, Ribbe countered that slavery did not seem to have a place in Nora's sites of memory and that for the *académicien*, Napoleon and France were one and the same thing. Ribbe also wondered why the Republic should celebrate the dictator that destroyed its first incarnation, opposing a conflictual view of French *history* to the consensual position of those who argued that the celebration of the national *memory* must be inclusive. He also inverted Nora's formula about the anticolonialists' anachronistic interpretation of the past, suggesting that the custodians of France's official memory tacked on the present interpretive grids conceived from the viewpoint of those who wield institutional power.

On September 2005, an association called the Comité antillais-guyanais-réunionnais, of which Ribbe was a member, filed suit against Olivier Pétré-Grenouilleau on the basis of the Taubira law.[24] Two months later, a number of prominent historians rallied to the defense of their colleague, determined to put an end to the criminalization of historical research. The mobilization eventually led to the constitution of an association for the defense of historians, chaired by René Rémond, former president of University of Paris X-Nanterre and of the National Foundation for Political Sciences, and, like Pierre Nora, a member of the Académie française. Under intense pressure from prominent representatives of academia to take a position in what had become a cause célèbre, Jacques Chirac conceded that "the law should not write history. In the Republic, there is no official history. . . . The writing of history is the business of the historians."[25] In February 2006, the Comité antillais-guyanais-réunionnais withdrew its lawsuit against Pétré-Grenouilleau.

23. Pierre Nora, "Plaidoyer pour les 'indigènes' d'Austerlitz," *Le Monde*, December 13, 2005.
24. The members of the committee were from Guadeloupe, Martinique, and French Guiana, as well as from La Réunion, an island off the coast of Madagascar. Together, the four territories make up the French overseas *départements*.
25. Quoted in Pervillié, "La confrontation mémoire-histoire en France depuis un an."

The Historians' Quarrel

Despite the favorable conclusion of their campaign to defend one of their colleagues, the historians involved in the movement did not agree on the role the profession should play in the new memorial configuration, and different answers to the question of who owns history were proposed in the course of the debate. Who will decide when there is a moral conflict regarding the interpretation of past events? The representatives of the people or a particular corporation? The initial "petition of the 1,001," in reference to the number of signatures it received in the few weeks following its publication in *Le Monde* on March 25, 2005, was soon followed by several interventions by historians or jurists condemning the state's control of school curricula. While the first petition had stopped short of condemning the principle of the legislation of memory, a second document, signed by nineteen prominent members of the historical profession, published in *Libération* in December 2005 in direct response to the Pétré-Grenouilleau affair, went one step further, demanding the repeal of all the articles of law constraining research and teaching in their discipline.

Titled "Freedom for History," the petition denounced the series of legislative acts going back to the loi Gayssot as unworthy of a democratic regime. It claimed that the practice of academic history was neither a religion nor a moral system, and that it should not be confused with memory and become the "slave of the present." Lastly, historiography was not a "juridical object" either. In a free society, neither the legislative nor the judiciary branches of government should "define historical truth" since "state politics, even with the best intentions, is not the politics of history."[26] The wholesale condemnation of memorial laws by historians endowed with considerable symbolic capital, given their association with influential intellectual institutions such as the Collège de France and the Ecole des hautes études en sciences sociales, prompted an immediate response in the form of yet another petition, this time published in *Le Nouvel Observateur*.

---

26. See http://www.ldh-toulon.net/spip.php?article1086. "The nineteen" included some of the most prominent representatives of postwar French historical research, including Alain Decaux, Pierre Nora, Mona Ozouf, Antoine Prost, René Rémond, Paul Veyne, Pierre Vidal-Naquet, and Michel Winock. Many of them belonged to the generation of the Algerian War and had been active in the antiwar movement, a political engagement some of them used as a badge of progressivism in order to distinguish their legitimate critique of the anachronistic antiracism of the multiculturalist "communitarians" from that of the nostalgic, imperial, colonialist Right who had sponsored the memorial law on colonialism.

Signed, among others, by Serge Klarsfeld, the well-known "Nazi hunter" who had been instrumental in bringing Barbie, Papon, and Touvier to trial in the 1990s, the text called into question the amalgamation between the laws concerning the Shoah, the Armenian genocide, and slavery, on the one hand, and the article regulating the teaching of the colonial past, on the other. Klarsfeld and the other signatories argued that in the first three cases, "the legislator did not encroach upon the historian's territory" but had rightly sanctioned practices, such as racism or defamation, that "threatened public order." The petition also admonished the nineteen historians for their corporatist, and ultimately undemocratic, conception of their craft. "Is the historian," the petition asked, "the only citizen to be above the law? Does he benefit from a title allowing him to transgress in an offhanded way the common rules of our society?" If that were the case, such a position would be incompatible with the spirit of the Republic, in which "according to article 11 of the Declaration of the Rights of Man and of the Citizen, any citizen can speak, write, and print freely, except to answer the abuse of such freedom in cases determined by the law."[27]

The suspicions of arrogant, elitist esprit de corps directed at his colleagues caused René Rémond to reply that the title of their petition did not demand freedom for historians, but freedom for history, which, if it did not belong solely to historians, did not belong only to members of Parliament. The existence of a rift between those historians who argued that the "scientific" character of their practice implies absolute independence from political institutions (as opposed to "memory," the messy, partisan, passionate realm of the collective imaginary) and those who saw the danger of denying the public sphere (the state and the citizenry) the "right" to construct a national past, led to the formation of the Comité de vigilance face aux usages publics de l'histoire (CVUH, or Committee for Vigilance Against the Public Uses of History), a "watchdog" organization whose founding statement distanced itself from an ivory tower view of the historians' contribution to the national conversation.

The CVUH argued that although historical research and collective memory are both legitimate practices in their own right and should not be conceived as entirely separate domains, their functions must remain different. History's goal was to understand the past, while memory's aim was to pass judgment on it. In an open society, historians were not supposed to "dictate to memory" (*régenter la mémoire*), but rather "nourish the critical spirit of the

---

27. "Ne mélangeons pas tout!" *Le Nouvel Observateur*, December 20, 2005.

citizens" and "enrich their political judgment." Unlike their colleagues who insisted on maintaining an absolute independence from public authorities, members of the newly formed committee hoped to bridge the gap between the producers and the users of historical knowledge (i.e., scholars, educators, and ordinary citizens), and to give rise to a public debate followed by "collective action."[28] In an interview in *L'Express*, Gérard Noiriel, a founding member of CVUH, sharpened the lines dividing the profession: "autonomy" was a better word than "freedom" when it came to the relations between historical knowledge, the state, and civil society, and no one should presume "to prevent the legislator from intervening in what has to do with memory."[29] Significantly, CVUH's response to the "petition of the nineteen" was published in the communist daily *L'Humanité*, anchoring its authors squarely to the left of the political spectrum, in keeping with their civic-populist agenda. The profession's "establishment," on the other hand, sent their comments to *Le Monde* and *Le Nouvel Observateur*.

The historians' quarrel rehashed many of the arguments advanced in the preceding two decades regarding the threat posed to academic freedom by a "thought police" patterned after American political correctness. Many in the "isolationist" camp (holding that historical research must be free from politics) had been involved in the antitotalitarian movement of the eighties and had opposed the politicization of the university associated with May 1968. They viewed any meddling of the state in academic matters with extreme suspicion, as evidenced by their constant references to the Stalinist perversion of scientific knowledge illustrated by the Lysenko Affair in the 1950s. Their refusal to distinguish between an article of law mandating the teaching of the positive aspects of colonialism, and legislative acts condemning racism, Nazism, and slavery, showed the limits of their purely epistemological position. They seemed reluctant to condemn the "negative" aspects of the colonial enterprise (in order to avoid anachronistic value judgments), and, from their position of axiological neutrality, were equally dismissive of all "memorial pressure groups" from the Right and the Left.

The controversy was as much about the nature of historical research as about the uneasy relation between the "scientific" and the "political," to borrow a famous distinction drawn by Max Weber in *Science as a Vocation*.

---

28. See http://cvuh.free.fr/.

29. Jacqueline Rémy and Boris Thiolay, "Deux historiens face à face: Faut-il abroger les lois mémorielles?" *L'Express*, February 2, 2006. Gérard Noiriel and Jean-Pierre Azéma represented the two divergent positions regarding the politics of remembrance.

While the founders of CVUH refused to consider themselves "experts supposedly in possession of the Truth about the past," several of the texts condemning the legislation of historical research and teaching did so on the basis of a conception of history as a "scientific approach aimed at the establishment of facts" (*une démarche scientifique d'établissement des faits*), as one petition put it.[30] This positivistic view of the nature of historical knowledge is so prevalent among its practitioners in France today that it seems as though Pierre Bourdieu's critique of academic reason, or the whole debate about the amount of fictional literary tropes, narrative construction, and rhetorical devices constitutive of historical writing (Foucault, Ricoeur, Hayden White, etc.), had never taken place. Ironically, the affirmation by eminent historians that they alone produce the truth about the past is reminiscent of the Althusserian distinction between science and ideology. Gérard Noiriel perceived the epistemological vulnerability of the positivistic claim that historians produce the one legitimate truth about the past when he remarked, in a previously mentioned interview in *L'Express*, that "historical truth is an extremely complicated notion and historians are not all in agreement on the best way to demonstrate it."

The controversy that surrounded the bicentennial of the French Revolution provides a striking example of the inability of the historical profession to agree on the interpretation of the past. The historians' feud, as the debate came to be known, made the point that no amount of factual information can bring about an interpretive consensus about profoundly divisive events of the past. In the case of the French Revolution, for example, no matter how detailed and comprehensive an account of the Jacobin Terror you provide or receive, this "factual" information will not substitute for the "value judgment" implied in deciding whether it was a necessary evil to protect the threatened, besieged revolutionary regime or the demented prologue to the worst horrors of the twentieth century. If the science of history could provide an undeniable account of it, then why the lack of consensus? Are biologists divided about the structure of DNA? Momentous events of the past are meaningful, symbolic entities; they are themselves the products of ideological struggles, and so are their commemorations, regardless of how much epistemological vigilance goes into the recounting of these events.

As if to confirm the endless nature of the contested use of the past and the inability of the historical profession to stop the infinite regress of interpretive "judgment," one of the most recent episodes in the ongoing wars of memory

30. See http://www.clionautes.org/petitions/index.php?petition=3.

came from the highest reaches of state power, as the president of the Republic himself mandated that the letter written by Guy Môquet, a young communist *résistant*, to his father before his execution by the Nazis, be read every year, on the first day of class, in all high schools in the country. Sarkozy's decision touched off yet another firestorm, prompting now-familiar accusations of political gimmickry, exploitation of the past, and shameless poaching in the memorial treasure trove of the Left by a right-wing politician. Sarkozy was faulted for imposing an official memory aimed at creating the myth of a consensual national past through the erasure of historical contexts and political differences. As in the heyday of the Third Republic, but this time in a regressive rather than progressive context, public education had become a key strategic site of national integration, its "patrimonialization" leading to the transmission of a new state ideology some called "liberal neo-Bonapartism."[31] One of the president's replies to his critics (on March 18, 2007) underscored the conception of the national compact underlying his frequent references to leading figures of the Left in political speeches: "Those who dared to say that I did not have the right to quote Guy Môquet because I was not on the Left, I mean, I am stunned by such a display of sectarian thinking. Guy Môquet belongs to the history of France and the history of France belongs to all French people."[32]

The failure to impose the content of the history curriculum or to bring historians to court had confirmed the vulnerability of public authorities and activist groups alike in their attempts to legislate the use of the past. It also gave the historical profession a renewed sense of its importance in the context of a collective memory in crisis. Many historians had entered the fray, substituting practical, "civic" action for the theoretical misgivings about the duty to remember that some of their colleagues had expressed almost two decades earlier.

Custodians of the Past

The crisis of those institutions that once transmitted collective values from generation to generation, and the collapse of ideologies framing what the future should retain from the past, find an echo in the recent publication by Editions du Seuil of several small volumes bearing titles such as *La République expliquée à ma fille* (The Republic explained to my daughter), *L'amour de la*

---

31. Sylvie Aprile, "L'histoire par Nicolas Sarkozy: Le rêve passéiste d'un futur national-libéral," April 30, 2007, http://cvuh.free.fr/spip.php?article82.

32. See http://www.politique.net/2007102201-la-lettre-de-guy-moquet.htm.

France expliqué à mon fils (The love of France explained to my son), and *La Résistance expliquée à mes petits-enfants* (The Resistance explained to my grandchildren).[33] The model for this new didactic genre is quite simple, and easily reproducible, as shown by the formulaic nature of the titles in the collection. Take a polemical issue often debated in the media (e.g., racism, *laïcité*, or national identity); ask a renowned novelist, journalist, or public intellectual to direct his reflections on the matter at his son or daughter, and, beyond, at French youth in general in an accessible yet provocative manner aimed at informing, convincing, and entertaining all at once; and you have a highly marketable product that combines moral and intellectual edification with the pleasure of a good read.

The content of these books is less significant than their form, or rather their function in a general economy of cultural transmission. What is the point of this kind of writing and how can we explain the success of the editorial concept? By explaining the Republic or "France" or World War II to his son or daughter, the author (very often a man; i.e., a father) serves a pedagogical purpose, which is to clarify what has been obscured or even forgotten. This very need for the past to be "explained" points to a lack of collective memory, a fateful break in the temporal chain of cultural transmission. The assumption is that the younger generation *should* know what is meant by the Republic, the Résistance, or the love of country, but that they don't. Literary and academic celebrities are enrolled in a last-ditch effort to fill the gap, to repair the tear in the cultural fabric, in the hope that these books, because of their authors' notoriety, will succeed in communicating what should have been conveyed by other means.

There is a sense of urgency in the concept (and sometimes the tone) of these books, as if it might already be too late. At the beginning of the *L'amour de la France expliqué à mon fils* Gallo wonders whether his child will ever be able to share his own "relation to the nation" born of his experience of the German Occupation: "On the day of the Liberation, I ran from barricade to barricade, and my father wore a tricolor armband. Flower wreaths had been laid at the foot of streetlights, with a poster than read 'Morts pour la France' [Dead for France]. My childhood was patriotic, my Republic heroic, and my

---

33. Other volumes in the same collection include: The French Revolution explained to my granddaughter, Auschwitz explained to my daughter, The Great War explained to my grandson, The Left explained to my daughter, Immigration explained to my daughter, Islam explained to children, Racism explained to my daughter, God explained to my grandchildren, Death explained to my daughter, and Philosophy explained to my daughter. Authors include prominent historians (Michel Vovelle, Antoine Prost, Anne Wieworka), novelists (Tahar Ben Jelloul), philosophers (Sami Naïr, Roger-Pol Droit), and political figures (Henri Weber).

France fighting and victorious." Gallo notes that these childhood experiences constitute the way in which both the history and the love of France "entered into me." Echoing Pierre Nora's wistful meditations on the passing of the integrated memory of the republican tradition, Gallo is left with the ominous, melancholy foreboding that his generation "may be the last to live in such a manner its relation to the nation," as if the collective thread to the past has been severed forever by new means of communication and community building: "I look at my son, seated at his computer. He is surfing, as he says, from one 'site' to the next. He checks his e-mail. What is his 'territory'? The world? What are his 'roots'? The Internet?" (7).

More optimistic than Gallo, Lucie Aubrac contrasts the will to forget of the children of Holocaust victims and Résistance survivors alike with their grandchildren's desire to remember, as if the collective mind had gone blank for a generation because of the violence of the trauma. Aubrac presents her testimony, *La Résistance expliquée à mes petits-enfants*, both as a response to the demand for memory emanating from the younger generation and as a way of combating the loss of memory implied in the passage of time and the growing disappearance of witnesses. What goes for World War II is also true, in a more acute way, of World War I. Every commemoration of the Great War was an opportunity to interview the handful of survivors of the trenches. The last survivor died in March 2008, ninety years after the Armistice (he was 110 years old). The erasure of living memory accounts for the intense interest in monographs, historical novels, and films about World War I in France today. The celebrations marking the ninetieth anniversary of the Battle of Verdun lasted from February to December 2006, including theatrical representations, photographic exhibitions, and the inauguration by President Chirac of a monument dedicated to Muslim soldiers who died in the war. The box-office success of Jean-Pierre Jeunet's 2004 film *A Very Long Engagement* (it drew close to 4.4 million French viewers in the first two months) attests to the war's haunting presence in the contemporary French imagination. The main male character, fittingly, has lost his memory as a result of the war and never comes home. His fiancée, who refuses to accept, and consequently, to mourn, his death, spends several years searching for the lost soldier, whom she eventually finds, alive though amnesic.

The point of the series published by Editions du Seuil is that notorious writers and public intellectuals need to make up for a deficient institution (one of Nora's *sociétés-histoires*) that failed in its mission to pass on to French children a solid, documented, cogently argued illustration of core cultural values now threatened by oblivion. This faulty, inadequate institution is, of course, the public school. It is because the republican school no longer talks of la République, and because *l'education nationale* no longer teaches students about the nation, that Régis Debray, Max Gallo, and other prominent intellectuals must act as their substitutes.

In a 1984 report addressed to Education Minister Jean-Pierre Chevènement, Claude Nicolet—former aide to Pierre Mendès-France, renowned specialist of the Roman republic, and author of an influential intellectual history of the republican idea in France—lamented the disappearance from French school curricula of the civic education that once was the cornerstone of Jules Ferry's pedagogical project in the 1880s. In his report, which was reprinted in *La République en France: Etat des lieux*, Nicolet deplored the "deficiencies" of the public school system: "Fifteen or twenty years of 'liberal' and 'industrial' policies have paved the way for the triumph of consumerism: the thin content of official recommendations are aimed at the 'future consumer.' Nothing about 'public law,' institutions, civic duty, and politics; instead, a self-seeking promotion of conviviality and 'social' practices of 'consensus,' for the greater good of the market. No surprise there, after all, this was the ideology of 'the new society'" (72).

The Left was as much a target of Nicolet's criticism as the free-market, consumerist ideology championed by the Right: "More serious yet, to my mind, were the deviations that some unions, and even some left-wing parties, had made possible: learning 'democracy' at school and 'opening up' the latter (to whom?) were supposed to make up, thanks to a winning 'pedagogy,' for the lack of content with demagogic form. Last but not least, good intentions: civic duty, after 1981, was back in fashion; however, under the pretense of human rights, it only benefited antiracism (which is good) and the cultivation of difference (which is either questionable or insufficient)" (72).

The historian's diagnosis echoes traditional attacks by national-republicans against the "postmodern," "communitarian," and "humanitarian" (*droit-de-l'hommiste*) sectors of what Jean-Pierre Chevènement used to call the "American Left." The ascendancy of civil society over the state, and the replacement of the school system by the media as the major source of social values and behaviors, is viewed as a severe threat to the philosophical and political foundations of the republican regime, and especially the independence of public education from the political, religious, and economic forces at work in civil society. The much-debated notion of *laïcité*, so often misunderstood today, originally meant sheltering the public school system, conceived as a space for the free examination of knowledge, from the influence of churches, parties, associations, unions, business interests, ethnic groups, civic organizations, and "communities" of all kinds.

Memory Upgrade

The discipline of history, coupled with civic education, was charged with preserving the memory of the Republic by fitting the achievements of modern democracy within the legacy of the French Revolution, according to the official narrative provided by the mythical figures of Jules Michelet and Jean Jaurès. Today's republican intellectual, therefore, must become a historian, or rather, in Régis Debray's word, a "meta-historian," in order to combat the depreciation of history in a media-driven age. Alain Finkielkraut prefaced his critique of contemporary culture in *The Defeat of the Mind* with a long detour through the history of ideas leading from Kant and de Maistre to Fanon and Lévi-Strauss, by way of Ernest Renan.

It is hardly a surprise, therefore, that Max Gallo (a professional historian, and the prolific author of numerous historical novels) based his attempt to impart the values of patriotism to his son on a short overview of the triumphs, and shortcomings, of French history. In so doing, he acts as a substitute for society in general, and for public education in particular. Quoting Simone Weil's remark in *The Need for Roots* that "a certain part of the soul ... can only thrive in the national milieu," he fears that his son will be unable to keep this corner of his soul alive and will gradually become part of "another species," since "he is no longer told about France" (8). The national narrative stands as a last-ditch effort to prevent the transformation of the native species into the mutant, Internet-savvy creatures of the electronic global world. Lucie Aubrac (a leading figure of the French Underground during World War II) also takes on a pedagogical role ("I must be once again the history teacher," 47), performing her own duty to remember ("Let me remind you that on September 3, 1939 ... ," 9), mentioning important dates and places ("Koufra, Bir-Hakeim, El Alamein," 38), explaining acronyms, and remarking on the inscription of memory in the national topology: "Some of our streets, our squares and monuments, remind us of the names of men and women who died for freedom in France and abroad" (42).

The books by Debray, Gallo, and Aubrac present striking similarities, not only in terms of their form, which follows the dialogic structure common to all the volumes in the series, but also in their rhetorical strategy. All three authors rely heavily on historical memory, and both Gallo and Aubrac are particularly fond of quoting prominent figures of the French literary canon, especially those poets whose works were regularly taught, and memorized, in public schools: Eluard and Aragon (for Aubrac), Charles d'Orléans, d'Aubigné, Hugo, Péguy, Claudel, and Char (for Gallo). The recitation of poetry written during "tragic" moments of the country's past, whether civil or foreign conflicts (Hundred Years War, Wars of Religion, Franco-Prussian War of 1871, the two World Wars), was one of the preferred mechanisms by which the state ensured the passing of national memory from one generation to the next, and students' internalization of the basic building blocks of cultural identity.

Nietzsche spoke of the "metrical compulsion of rhyme and rhythm."[34] Poetry (like song) obviously lends itself very efficiently to the pedagogy of memorization, memorialization, and incorporation through repetition, because of its rhythm, lyrical and emotional tone, and the intense ideological and affective charge linked to love (of fatherland), death, and self-sacrifice. Poets always figure prominently in the pantheon of national and nationalist heroes. Three Résistance poems, one by Aragon ("Ballade de celui qui chanta dans les supplices" [Ballard for the one who sang under torture], dedicated to Gabriel Péri, poet and martyr), one by Eluard (the well-known "Liberté"), and one by Marianne Cohn ("Je trahirai demain" [I'll be a traitor tomorrow]) are appended to Lucie Aubrac's text. "In jail," she tells her youthful audience, "we tried to remember poems from the days of freedom" (21), adding that on D-Day, the BBC kept broadcasting verses of Verlaine's famous "Autumn Song" ("With long sobs the violin-throbs of autumn wound my heart with languorous and monotonous sound," 25). Aubrac also stresses the democratic, universal appeal of poetry: "You know, everyone is a bit of a poet. Verses, you can't forget them, you write them on the walls of your cell, you recite them in camps . . . Whether you were free, arrested, deported, these times of poetry were privileged moments, even if you were away from France" (22).

The children themselves volunteer bits of their own knowledge of the past, testifying to the successful, if incomplete, cultural work performed by the schools and the media. "We all know the famous 'Affiche rouge' [the Red Poster], Aragon's poem, and a song by Léo Ferré" (36); "we talked about [foreign volunteers] in class, when we discussed the Red Poster and Aragon's poem sung by Léo Ferré" (43); "we've heard of him [René Cassin]: he wrote the Universal Declaration of Human Rights and is buried in the Panthéon" (40); "we know [about D-Day], we saw the movie *The Longest Day* and visited

---

34. Nietzsche, *Basic Writings*, 209.

the Memorial for Peace in Caen" (51). Aubrac's narrative explicitly ties the cultural, artistic, and literary legacy of the nation to the struggle against Nazism because the occupying forces tried to destroy works of art, "the cultural patrimony of humankind," and because the Résistance fought for the universal values of the French republican tradition: "We knew that right and justice were on our side. They had stolen freedom and equality, but could not have prevented fraternity. . . . We were fighting for universal values, for all those we did not know, men or women, young or old, humiliated, exploited, to give them back, and also give ourselves back the right to think, to love, in short to live free in democracy once again" (39).

Even the decision to join the Underground is presented as resulting from the judicious use of deliberative reason, so central to republican pedagogy: "That's what the Résistance is about: to reflect, judge, choose, and commit" (40). The transmission performed by Aubrac's book, via a trans-generational connection, mirrors the very principles of republican teaching expressed in the political engagement of the World War II generation. "This little book," she writes, "is not a 'history of the Résistance,' it is a dialogue with my grandchildren, to inform them, to help them understand and then judge, and so to choose and to get involved in the defense of the universal values the Résistance salvaged and bequeathed to them" (8).

The dialogic structure of the three books raises issues of rhetoric and narrativity, since the figure of the addressee ("daughter," "son," or "grandchild") is a fiction produced by the author in the course of her demonstration, a discursive position whose voice is, in the case of Gallo's text, not strongly contrasted with that of the parent figure itself (both participants in the dialogue use the same lyrical tone and passionate intensity). The graphic inscription of the youthful addressee(s) and respondent(s) differs from one book to the next. In *La Résistance*, the grandchildren's interventions are short questions or comments printed in italics that accompany, rather than drive, the argumentation. Debray's text is a crisp, witty, playful conversation, each participant providing short, pointed, and often humorous contributions to the discussion on democratic institutions, republican law, the difference between nationality and citizenship, the principle of *laïcité*, and French exceptionalism (contrasted, unsurprisingly, with the American version of democratic republicanism). Gallo, on the other hand, alternates long oratory periods during which "father" and "son" rebuff each other by drawing on diverging citations from "classics" of the literary tradition, interpretations of historical facts, and recent developments in culture and society.

The Seamless Garment of the Motherland

The theme of memory as survival is everywhere in Gallo's *L'amour de la France*, from references to the ancestral rituals and burying sites of ancient cultures to the repeated claim that his son (and by extension, his younger compatriots) have a duty to remember: "When you walk upon this land, wherever it may be, remember that a man was there before you, that he hunted or ploughed a furrow, put up a fence, then another one came, who cut the stones to build a wall and raise a tower, and when they fall the stones are used again, to become a house or a basilica" (12). The recycling of the building material (nothing is ever lost) points to the continuity of national history, made up of those various human and cultural strata archaeologists keep on uncovering (a druidic ceremonial site under an early Christian chapel under a Romanesque church under a Gothic cathedral).[35] Gallo's France is a palimpsest, "an entanglement of histories, a superposition of men," genies of the place whose tombs dot the country (from the dolmens in the North to the painted caverns of the South), and whose ancestral remains have "seeded the earth," making up the "humus" of French history (10).

The status of memory, however, is somewhat ambiguous in Professor Gallo's history lesson. The past can only be resurrected through an act of forgetting that frees up the powers of imagination and summons the eternal, transhistorical presence of the natural world: "First, look at France. Forget the cities, the freeways, the railroads, the ports, the walls, the dikes, the airports, the pylons, and even the hedges. Imagine the forests and the rivers, the caves, the inlets, the clearings, the islands, the banks" (10). On the other hand, the son is repeatedly told not to forget. His duty to remember will stop the leakage of memory (induced by the Internet?) the father deplored in the opening pages of the book. Reacting to Paul Claudel's famous verse, "Take your place, honored Mother, at the great Easter meal of nations!" the youngster questions the old notion of *Dei gesta per Francos*, the belief that God distinguished France among all countries. "The French thought so for ten centuries," comes the parental answer, "and if you forget the certainty that dwelled in them, their faith, you cannot understand this nation, or the reason why she survived" (31).

---

35. France is a vast archeological space, its soil filled with innumerable artifacts. It is not rare for the government to delay the construction of a parking structure or a needed public facility because the digging of the foundation has uncovered precious remnants from the country's past that need to be preserved or at least examined before a decision to proceed with construction is made. To the celebrant of that past, the land, literally, becomes a museum, a treasure trove of history (and prehistory).

In response to his son's objection that the wars fought by France were not only patriotic defensive struggles but also military campaigns of conquest and domination, Gallo once again makes memory the necessary condition for an adequate understanding, and consequently an unquestionable love, of country. Quoting a famous line from Corneille's drama *Horace* ("Mourir pour la patrie est un si digne sort, qu'on briguerait en foule une si belle mort" [To die for one's country is such a worthy fate that all would compete for such a great death]), he argues that "if you forget this feeling, this heroism . . . if you forget this patriotism, the very history of France escapes you" (51). The summoning of memories is a rhetorical move aimed at sidestepping any attempt to bring up the dark side of national history, from the exactions of Bonaparte's armies throughout Europe to the brutality of colonialism overseas.

The negative aspects of France's past (that is, from the son's viewpoint) are not so much denied as they are woven into an all-encompassing symbolic fabric, a metaphor often associated, in the father's narrative, with the duty to remember:

> Which France is it, you asked? It's the country that you wish to see again when you are separated from it, the language you want to hear, speak, and read when, all around you, it is no longer in use. That's the moment when, willy-nilly, you do not wonder about the scrap of France that fits you more than others, or the part of your history you praise, you no longer root for either the white, the blue, the black, the red, the rose,[36] you see her as the garment cut from the same cloth you dream of, you say "France" and you understand the meaning of the words "one and indivisible." (20)

Interestingly enough, Gallo links patriotic identification to the loss of country through foreign travel or residence, as if the severance of the ties with the past experienced by his son's generation was the condition for a rebirth of the sentiment of belonging, albeit in the paradoxical form of melancholy: the object is never so cathected as when it is lost. The literary illustrations chosen by Gallo—Roland dying in Spain, his face turned toward the

---

36. "Les roses": an allusion to the Socialists, whose emblem is a hand holding a rose. "Les blancs" (the whites) were the monarchists and "les bleus" (the blues) the republicans, as in the title of Alexandre Dumas's novel. "Les bleus" are also the French national soccer team, in reference to their uniforms. The red and the black suggest the colors of the Communist and Anarchist flags, as well as the struggle between the Church and the eighteenth-century revolutionaries (priests wore black cassocks), not to mention the title of Stendhal's novel.

Frankish lands; Charles d'Orléans mourning his beloved country as a prisoner of the English in Dover in 1431; and, of course, du Bellay praising the charms of his little village in Anjou amid opulent Roman palaces—all testify to the virtues of exile in rekindling a nostalgic yearning for the fatherland.

The sin of contemporary multiculturalists—that is, their disregard for the profound and paradoxical unity of Frenchness (despite a succession of civil wars between Eduans and Arverns, Capetians and Albigenses, Burgundians and Armagnacs, Calvinist Huguenots and Catholic Leaguers, monarchists and revolutionaries, Jacobins and Girondists, Versaillais and Communards, *résistants* and collaborators)—stems from a lack of memory: "Everything is linked. And you must not, if you wish to untangle the tight weaving that is the history of our nation, forget a single thread. . . . Events ceaselessly follow one another, the embroidery changes, the woof itself evolves gradually, but the same threads are being woven first, even if their colors are different. And it takes decades, even centuries, tear after tear, killing after killing, stitch after stitch, constitution after constitution, before a new garment finally appears" (31, 35). Napoleon sewed back together the torn cloth of the postrevolutionary nation, after Robespierre had proved unable to do so with his cult of the Supreme Being—"an attempt to use the old weft in order to embroider a new political order" (36), a failed substitute for the God of the old regime, murdered along with what Kantorowitz called the two bodies of the king.

The Rhetoric of Cultural Transmission

The pedagogical function of the text itself supposes that the adult figure keeps control of the argumentation, and presumably has the last word. At the end of her history lesson, Lucie Aubrac asks her grandchildren what they have retained of her explanations: one child responds that she understood why ordinary people joined the Résistance despite the risks, another is "filled with wonder" by the fact that the freedom fighters were able to overcome the German Army and the collaborators, another mentions de Gaulle and Jean Moulin (thereby acknowledging the two sides of the Résistance, foreign and domestic), while the last voice to be heard assures her grandmother that "if need be, we would be ready to do the same as you" (54). In her case, the cultural work of transmission has been successfully performed.

Both Debray's daughter and Gallo's son are older than Lucie Aubrac's grandchildren (one of them is pictured alongside his grandmother on the book cover in an attempt to achieve some *effet de réel* by embodying the voice of the addressee), and much less amenable to their elders' point of view.

Their discursive position is patterned after the post-nationalist critique of the republican tradition Debray and Gallo have denounced in their writings throughout the 1980s and 1990s. Predictably, their children, as representatives of the complacent consumer youth—so prone to forgive and forget, fond of American pop culture and new technologies—contrast a relaxed, tolerant, liberal kind of cosmopolitanism to the centralized, homogenizing, monocultural nationalism of their forebears, and repeatedly oppose the lofty ideals of the republican tradition with their less than perfect application in history.

Debray's daughter blames her father for wanting "to line up young people four by four in front of the flag to listen to a sermon or make a pledge" (26), openly criticizes the forced repatriation by the French government of illegal immigrants back to their native countries, and defends the rights of nonwhites to "be different and stay together" (29). "When I buy CDs or go to the movies," she goes on, "I don't care whether it's French or not, as long as it's good" (31). In a passage eerily prescient of the *banlieue* uprisings in the fall of 2005, Gallo's son contests his father's celebration of a unitary, inclusive national legacy beyond the social and political divisions of the past ("*la* France"), and questions the difference between his elder's legitimate brand of nationalism and that of the National Front: "I see the fires in the suburbs where youth gangs—just like in Los Angeles, they say—are burning dozens of cars. This particular piece of France, what do I do with it? Am I supposed to shout, 'France belongs to the French!' march in the streets waving a blue, white, and red flag, join those who meet at the foot of Joan of Arc's statue?" (15).

The latest remark is an allusion to Jean-Marie Le Pen's fondness for the Maid of Orleans, a symbol of the undying virtues of the French popular classes, always at the mercy of their rulers' betrayal, and of their principled, unflinching resistance to foreign influence. Ironically, the cover of the book shows a picture of a crowd waving tricolor flags, an image that can suggest, in the absence of a caption, either the celebration of the French soccer team's victory in the 1998 World Cup or a demonstration of the National Front. This ambiguity points to the challenge Gallo faces in distinguishing his own brand of nationalism from that of Le Pen's supporters, since rival groups have appropriated the national flag for themselves throughout the history of the country (the tricolor of the Orleanists in 1830 is not that of the republicans in 1848). "Since we started talking about France," the son argues, "you only bring up the past, and you turn in on the nation. . . . In what way are you different from those who, in all the dark corners of the world, brandishing their racism and xenophobia, defend their identity, their roots, their 'race,' . . . their religion?" (21).

While Debray's dutiful textual daughter lets herself be gradually convinced by her father's argumentation, promising him, in her last words, to "keep an eye on the heritage" of the Republic, Gallo's rebellious son remains intractable until the end. The father has inscribed in his exhortation the possibility of its failure, as if he himself no longer believes in the power of the republican ideology to reverse the effects of post-nationalism. The son's last remark regarding the presence of black players on the French national soccer team (and black citizens in the country) suggests that the founding principles of modern France—the Republic and laïcité—might be mere "appearances": "You know as well as I do that there are French people whose face and name will always make them, in the eyes of some of those who pass them in the street, strangers, as soon as they leave the stadium where one consents in applauding them; they will incite fear, and so, scorn and hatred" (58).

Gallo's response, in typical national-populist fashion, is that the shortcomings of the French melting pot is not primarily due to what he calls "social difficulties," a telling euphemism for the economic and cultural dislocations of life in ethnic neighborhoods, but to the loss of national pride among the country's ruling classes. Enduring structures of social and economic inequality and job discrimination based on ethnic and racial origin are not to blame, but rather the ideological abdication of the new cosmopolitan, "one-world," transnational elites. "If France is nothing but an empty home, of which those who live in it say she no longer represents anything," the father rejoins, "then why want to become French, and why remain so? That is the fundamental question of this moment in our history." The implication here is that black and Arab youths refuse to become French, when many of those who rioted in 2005 did so to demand their rights as French citizens.[37] "France is hesitating, is plagued with self-doubt," the father continues. "Its elites, while celebrating patriotism during a few soccer games, declare that it can no longer be sovereign. Which means that it must disappear as a nation. That's why everyone, here, withdraws into oneself, forgetting the nation to think only of one's community" (58).

---

37. The demand for equal rights associated with the banlieue uprisings of 2005 was, in the eyes of Emmanuel Todd, who has written extensively on immigration in France from a national-republican standpoint, the paradoxical proof that processes of national identification were alive and well. Todd's optimism regarding the future "integration" of nonwhites in French society differs sharply from Gallo's pessimism and Debray's irony. See Todd, "Rien ne sépare les enfants d'immigrés du reste de la société," Le Monde, November 12, 2005.

Gallo is also plagued with self-doubt, acknowledging his failure to convince his own son, the representative of a "new species" of French people, of the validity of his argument, which is at times reminiscent of the pessimistic right-wing rhetoric of the 1930s about the decline of the West and the failure of the corrupted democratic elites to save European civilization from the twin threats of Americanization and Bolshevism. In an effort to stir patriotic fervor in the young man, Gallo appeals to the politics of mourning, quoting André Malraux's elegiac discourse during the ceremony honoring the transfer of the remains of Jean Moulin, the Résistance leader tortured and murdered by the Nazis, to the Panthéon in December 1964 (twenty years after Moulin's execution): "Listen today, French youth, what was for us the song of sorrow. It is the funereal procession of the ashes presented here. Beside those of Carnot with the soldiers of l'an II, those of Victor Hugo with the *misérables*, those of Jaurès with Justice watching over them. Let them rest together with the long retinue of disfigured shadows. Today, O youth, may you think of this man as if you had touched with your hands his poor deformed face on the last day, his lips that had never betrayed: on that day, his was the face of France" (61).

But this evocation of one of the most tragic moments of the German Occupation and Malraux's poignant plea to the younger generations never to forget fails to rally the son to the father's cause. In a final attempt, Gallo recalls the patriotic fervor with which young people celebrated the French World Cup victory, thereby conceding that sport might be all that's left of the national sentiment in the age of the World Wide Web. "You remain pensive," he tells his son. "Perhaps you refuse this image of suffering and war, already half-a-century old. I understand your feeling. Then, you and me, let's remember the shared joy in July 1998 when, suddenly, to the great surprise of those we call the elites, France draped herself in tricolor because her soccer team was the world champion" (62). The son remains silent, unmoved by the evocation of a rare moment of unity mixing athletic prowess and national pride, and the father, after warning that the people of France will refuse to exist only as a soccer team every four years, leaves the last word to Charles Péguy, yet another poet whose life was lost at war, and whose verses Gallo remembered upon seeing throngs of elated soccer fans pouring into the streets of Paris. Earlier in the book, pleading for the continuity of memory and ritual and underscoring the role of death and mourning in the rhetoric of national belonging, Gallo brings together, in a striking image, the Basilica of Saint-Denis (the "burial ground of kings") and the Grand Stade de France (the soccer stadium where the World Cup took place), also located in Saint-Denis, which therefore remains the site where "the new pilgrims go," reaching over the centuries to the pilgrims of old (34).

The dialogical structure of the texts I have discussed suggests that the debates surrounding the republican legacy in contemporary France is in large part structured along generational lines. Its most committed advocates cherish the images of a world gone by: the covered playground of the elementary schools, the grey smocks of the schoolmasters, the black-and-white movies, and the Citroen Traction avant. Hence the imperious need to salvage these memories and pass them on to their sons and daughters before it is too late, in the pages of the small volumes published by Editions du Seuil. It is no accident that Gallo's book ends with the *black-blanc-beur* image of France's multiracial soccer team, since ethnic pluralism has become one of the most salient issues of the politics of loss and recovery.

Chapter Seven

OLD WINE, NEW SKINS
Race, Laïcité, Frenchness

In March 2004, the French Parliament passed with an overwhelming majority (276 votes to 20 in the Senate) an article of law stating that "wearing signs or clothing ostensibly manifesting religious affiliation is forbidden in public elementary schools, middle schools, and high schools," while recommending that "the application of disciplinary action [should] be preceded by a dialogue with the student."[1] Although the new legislation officially targeted all "ostentatious" religious objects or dress (large Christian crosses, yarmulkes, and veils), its intention was to put an end to fifteen years of fierce debates regarding the right of Muslim students to wear a scarf in public schools. The controversy started in the fall of 1989, when several students at a middle school north of Paris refused to remove their headdress in class and were subsequently expelled. Parents and representatives of the local Muslim community protested the decision, the school principal maintained the sanction, and the event quickly became a cause célèbre, mobilizing the political class, the media, the intellectuals, and even the Conseil d'Etat, which provides the executive branch with legal advice and acts as the administrative court of last resort.

An earlier version of this chapter appeared as "The Dream of *Laïcité*," Occasional Papers Series, Department of European and Classical Languages and Cultures, Texas A&M University, vol. 1 (Summer 2005): 13–24.

1. *Journal Officiel de la République Française*, law no. 2004-228, March 15, 2004.

A few days later, five prominent intellectual figures published an open letter to the education minister, the Socialist Lionel Jospin, in *Le Nouvel Observateur*. The letter faulted Jospin for undermining the fundamental principles of *laïcité* by seeking a compromise with the expelled students and their parents. The word generally used to translate the French *laïcité* into English, "secularism," does not do justice to the configuration of meanings the term has acquired over time in French political culture. *Laïcité* not only refers to the idea of the separation of church and state as it is currently debated in several liberal democracies, from the United States to Germany. The notion often implies, at least in some of its historical incarnations, a philosophical critique of religious belief as superstition and alienation, based on Enlightenment rationalism. Secularism in France has historically meant much more than the protection of freedom of conscience and speech from churches or government, as in the dominant American liberal view. I will therefore retain the term *laïcité*, in lieu of secularism, in the following comments. Hopefully, the context will clarify some of the competing interpretations of the notion in contemporary France.

The open letter to the minister of education laid out the key arguments that would be used time and again in the following years. First, the veil is the oppressive tool of a patriarchal ideology that defies modern democratic conceptions of women's rights; second, it is a direct threat to the philosophy of public education and to the Republic itself. "The French version of democracy is called Republic," the authors of the article wrote. "It is not a mosaic of ghettoes where the rule of the strongest can be dressed up as freedom for all. Dedicated to free inquiry, committed to the growth of knowledge, and confident in the sole natural light of men, the Republic has its foundation in the schools. That is why the destruction of the school system would hasten that of the Republic."[2]

A mixture of outrage and irony, the letter had the makings of a powerful ideological bomb, sure to ignite political passions. A call to arms directed at fellow educators (its title translates to "Teachers, let's not give in!"), it also served as a reminder of the basic tenets of the republican educational ideology while alluding for the first time, through the use of the word "ghetto," to the threat of American-style communitarianism, a notion that would enjoy a long career in French public debates in the following years. The letter

---

2. Badinter, Debray, Finkielkraut, de Fontenay, Kinsler, "Profs, ne capitulons pas!" *Le Nouvel Observateur*, November 2–8, 1989, 30–31. I have briefly discussed the impact of the first "affair of the veil" in my *French Resistance: The French-American Culture Wars*. See also Gaspard and Khosrokhavar, *Le foulard et la République*; and Scott, *Politics of the Veil*.

also drew a sharp contrast between the weaknesses of contemporary liberal democracy, always inclined to compromise, and the strength of republican principles, based as they were on the authority of reason and experience. The dire prophecy that concludes the letter, warning of nothing less than the destruction of France's political institutions if the students were allowed to have their way, also set the apocalyptic tone of subsequent controversies. In many ways, the 1989 manifesto, which fired the first salvo in the war of *laïcité*, contained the seeds of the law of 2004.

The interminable debate on "national identity" points to yet another lost object of France's national narrative, that of the ethnic and cultural oneness made possible by the political institutions, legal system, and self-representation of the country as the "fatherland of human rights" (*la patrie des droits de l'homme*). Beyond the conception of an indivisible people, what is being mourned is a particular definition of Frenchness, whose boundaries are constantly displaced by the current debates on affirmative action that will be examined in the latter part of the chapter. Both *intégration* and *laïcité* refer to a cultural ideal now threatened by multiculturalism, claims for diversity, and France's own version of the "rise of the unmeltable ethnics."[3] If the depressive side of melancholy leads to desymbolization and acedia, its manic phase can be quite hyperactive, militant, and loquacious, leading to intolerance toward those who are made responsible for what has gone irreversibly wrong. Scapegoating is a central mechanism of cultural reproduction and a preferred, if often brutal, way to "heal" a community divided against itself. In the words of Julia Kristeva, "If the depressed subject does not commit suicide, he finds a release from his suffering in maniac reaction: instead of belittling himself, slowing down, or locking himself up in inaction, he mobilizes for wars, holy ones inevitably, hunting down an enemy, preferably an imaginary one."[4]

The fact that the intelligentsia played a central role in the debate on national identity, on all sides of the issue, is not surprising, given their self-appointed role as guardians of the national memory, framers of the national community, and heirs to the national rhetorical tradition. Denouncing the "stereotypes of stylistic and philosophical protectionism," Kristeva also pointed out that "the most subtly nationalistic and most slyly xenophobic

---

3. The first decade of the new millennium in France in many ways replicates the 1970s debate on the failure of the melting-pot theory and practice of American assimilation. For a plurality of approaches to the issue, see Glazer and Moynihan, *Beyond the Melting Pot*; Novak, *Rise of the Unmeltable Ethnics*; and Steinberg, *Ethnic Myth*.

4. Kristeva, *Dépression nationale*, 69.

milieus find a home and wield their power in the institutions that oversee the fate of belles lettres." "Whoever speaks 'the other language,'" she wrote in *Contre la dépression nationale*, "is invited to keep quiet . . . unless he or she joins one of the established clans, one of the current rhetorics" (72).

In "Mourning and Its Relation to Manic-Depressive States," Melanie Klein argued that the depressive position includes both "persecution (by 'bad' objects) and the characteristic defenses against it, on the one hand, and pining for the loved ('good') object on the other" (316). Acutely intolerant phases of nationalism and fundamentalism often exhibit both an intense idealization of the threatened mother(land) and a paranoid/schizoid search for interior and exterior agents (or objects) responsible for the threat, and the current debate on immigration and integration in France offers instances of both developments. Multiculturalism and its attendant set of claims for diversity is taken to represent the dismemberment of the once unified loved object, a process of violent disintegration that activates feelings of exalted omnipotence ("We will save the Republic!") and abject failure ("All is lost!"). The indivisible citizenry is, in Kleinian terms, "a 'perfect' object which is in pieces: thus the effort to undo the state of disintegration to which it has been reduced presupposes the necessity to make it beautiful and 'perfect'" again.[5] As we will see, the anti-communitarian argument rests on a highly mythical, because highly idealized, view of France's history. While the depressive subject is filled with anxiety for the fate of the loved object and guilt at her inability to render it whole again, the paranoiac sees the disintegrated object as what Klein called "a multitude of persecutors" in her essay "A Contribution to the Psychogenesis of Manic-Depressive States" (292). The fact that the struggles are about "identity" gives away the underlying mechanisms at work in the individual's intense investment in collective passions: in the depressive position, Klein writes, "the ego is identified with the suffering of the good objects" at the hands of the bad ones (293).

Laïcité as Dream Work

I will not rehearse here the successive affairs of the veil that followed the 1989 controversy, since the whole development has since been extensively recorded and commented on. Rather than approach the issue frontally, I propose to look at it sideways, as it were, by treating *laïcité* as a symptom of something else, a focal point for tensions and contradictions often ignored or

---

5. Klein, "Contribution to the Psychogenesis of Manic-Depressive States," 290.

silenced by the various participants in the dispute. The first notable aspect of the process leading to the passage of the law is the discrepancy between the cumbersome mobilization of political and legislative resources, including a book-length study by an expert commission and a two-month-long discussion in Parliament, and the rather limited scope of the issue itself. Some feared that the new legislation would trigger a significant increase in the number of students wearing the veil in school as a defiant response to the government's decision. In fact, there were a surprisingly small number of cases when school resumed in September 2004. Out of 639 students who came to class wearing a scarf, a bandana, or a Sikh turban, 538 decided to remove it after a few days. Only forty-three of the remaining hundred or so individuals who refused to comply were finally expelled from school as a result of the new law, a minuscule number given the hundreds of thousands of Muslim and Sikh students in the French public educational system.[6]

Why, then, did the French government choose to deal with such an issue by legislating rather than relying, as the Constitutional Council of the French Republic had recommended time and again, on school boards and local courts, which are better equipped to address cases involving specific individuals and particular situations? The French propensity to resort to the universality of law rather than to pragmatic, context-bound solutions appropriate to local situations is not enough, I think, to fully answer the question. The disproportion between the limited extent of the targeted behavior and the mobilization of the highest levels of the legislative branch points to the symbolic nature of the government's action. We are not dealing here with an adequate, proportionate response to limited student practice, but with a strong symbolic signal sent to the French public by its government, its political class, and a large segment of its intellectual elites, whether from the Right or the Left.[7]

The extent of the consensus surrounding the issue, in a country usually bitterly divided along ideological lines, should alert us to the real message

---

6. These figures, which can be found at http://citoyen.eu.org/doc/laïcité-exclusions.php, of course gave rise to opposite interpretations. Critics of the law argued that the small number of offenders shows that it was not really needed. Supporters saw it as a sign that the government's determination had paid off and solved the problem.

7. A similar disproportion between the number of offenders and the reaction of politicians and the media is true of the recent debate regarding the burqa, or "integral veil" covering the head and the whole body, worn by a small minority of Muslim women in France. Estimates of the number of masked and robed women vary from a few hundred to a thousand, out of millions of French Muslim women in France. Again, the government and Parliament are considering a law forbidding the burqa in public places, with the same set of arguments being advanced as in 1989.

conveyed by the legislative act. In an article titled "One Problem Can Be Hidden by Another," written in reaction to the first affair of the veil in 1989, Pierre Bourdieu argued that by "projecting onto this minor and soon forgotten event of the veil grand principles—freedom, secularism, women's liberation, etc.—those people who always stake a claim as *maîtres à penser* have revealed, as if it were a projective test, their unavowed positions on the problem of immigration." "The apparent question, whether or not to accept the wearing of the so-called Islamic veil in school," he continued, "hides the latent question, whether or not to accept in France immigrants of North African origin, and enables them to answer the latter in a way that should otherwise be unacceptable. In revealing their hidden thoughts in this incautious way, they contribute to raising the level of anxiety that a good many French people feel towards the phenomenon, and the irrationality such anxiety generates."[8]

Bourdieu's vocabulary (forgetting, projection, disavowal, hidden thoughts, etc.) is borrowed from psychoanalytic discourse, as is the distinction he draws between "latent" and "apparent" questions, echoing the classic Freudian opposition between "manifest content" and "latent thoughts" in his analysis of slips and dreams, and further, in his account of the general economy of the unconscious. Bourdieu's remarks implied that the debate over *laïcité* works as a dream or a symptom. It *condenses* a series of social dysfunctions into one issue while *displacing* onto the veil, a symbolic object par excellence, what cannot be revealed as such: the resistance to the integration of immigrants and their children (and grandchildren!) in a country fond of referring to itself as the land of human rights. Ideological work follows here a kind of euphemistic logic often brought to light in Bourdieu's analytical framework. In this case, a positively valued term, on which everyone, or almost everyone, agrees—such as pluralism, tolerance, or gender equality—is substituted for a negative word, subject to the censorship of liberal-democratic discourse—such as discrimination, segregation, or xenophobia—as if a "politically correct" strategy of euphemization were enough to remove the social, political, economic, and cultural tensions underlying the issue.

The new law received wide support in Parliament as well as in the public arena because it was conceived as a performative act aimed at reasserting the fundamental values of the national compact. Its goal was to reassure people that public authorities were determined to uphold the institutional integrity of the country and restore the vitality of the republican legacy. In the months

8. Bourdieu, *Political Interventions*, 253.

preceding the vote, an expert commission appointed by the president published a report that placed the notion of *laïcité* at the center of France's political culture, calling it "a unifying value" and the "cornerstone of the republican compact."9 The commission members reminded everyone that "the French Republic was built around the notion of *laïcité*," which they described as the "basis of national unity" (9). The argument rested on a chain of equivalencies including the Republic, the nation, democracy, and *laïcité* itself. In fact, the Constitution of the Fifth Republic (1958) names secularism as one of the fundamental principles of the national institutions, along with its "democratic" and "social" components.

The promotion of *laïcité* as the cornerstone of the republican consensus was meant to highlight the importance of educational and religious considerations in constitutional issues. At the same time, it underscored the specificity of secularist principles in French democratic life, a variation on the theme of French exceptionalism, coupled with considerations on the influence of French culture in Europe. In his presentation of the report, the commission's chair, Bernard Stasi, while acknowledging that "the experience of neighboring countries can be useful to us," noted that "our European friends have shown a lot of interest for the debate in France and, I say this without conceit, impatiently wait for the commission's proposals and the decisions that public authorities will take" (10). The construction of *laïcité* as one of the major building blocks of the French difference and influence abroad underplayed the extent to which all Western liberal democracies face similar challenges regarding the management of ethnic-religious pluralism.

The ritualized repetition of the founding myth of a unique national compact (*le pacte républicain*) masks the fact that both the state and civil society have been unable to bring a conclusion to the successive affairs of the veil. Public authorities can therefore maintain the illusion, in their own eyes and in the eyes of the citizenry, that they are safeguarding the country's cohesion at a minimal cost, since in fact local courts and school administrators will continue to deal with specific cases on an ad hoc basis, as they have always done in the past. The principle of *laïcité* becomes a kind of fetish that cannot be tinkered with for fear of triggering collective hysteria. It is the linchpin that keeps the nation together: remove it, and the whole thing falls apart. At the same time, the law banning religious dress in public spaces, by reasserting in a magical, phantasmic way that the government, as guardian of the Republic, remains in control, is supposed to provide a miracle solution to all the dysfunctions, malaises, and crises of late modern France.

9. Stasi, *Laïcité et République*, 12, 21.

Reading the Stasi Report

The Stasi commission's report drew up a list of all the issues that *laïcité* as dream work condenses under its name and displaces onto the signifier of the veil. In his address to Jacques Chirac, the head of the commission remarked that "the difficulties in integrating those who have entered our national space in the last decades, the living conditions in many suburbs of our cities, unemployment, the feeling shared by many of those who live in our country of being the objects of discrimination, even of being excluded from the national community, explain why they lend a complacent ear to those who incite them to fight against what we call the values of the Republic" (12–13). The report went so far as to acknowledge that communitarianism was often a reaction to exclusion and discrimination. If the "origin" of an individual was an obstacle to his or her social and economic inclusion, or even to the fair recognition of acquired skills, "it is not surprising that a kind of 'victimized' consciousness leads some to valorize this origin by contrast, going so far as to mythify it by exacerbating difference. The communitarian drift, at this point, is not far down the road" (107).

Though the diagnosis may have been accurate, the prescription for the cure has so far proved woefully inadequate. Most of the recommendations of the commission were largely symbolic, from banning religious dress and creating a school holiday for Yom Kippur and Aïd el-Kebir to allowing TV time to freethinkers and atheists. But even the recommendations directed at some of the serious social problems identified in the report were extremely sketchy. Violence in immigrant neighborhoods, which would flare up a year later, was summarily addressed by recommending "that urban ghettoes be destroyed by cities" and that "priority be given to shared sport facilities that favor social mixing" (147).

The law was in large part a response to the increasingly taxing, and sometimes downright dangerous, working conditions of teachers and other school personnel in "sensitive" neighborhoods. Banning the Islamic veil from the classroom, whatever symbolic meaning the measure might carry, did not address these problems, let alone begin to solve them. Assuming that students could be shielded, thanks to the new law, from the consequences of racism, unemployment, and the repercussions of the conflicts in the Middle East within the space of the public schools, they would still have to face these issues as they stepped into the street at the end of the school day. As regards the growth of anti-Semitic violence in France, the report rightly deplored that "children, because of their supposed religious adherence, are persecuted by classmates. Wearing a yarmulke after school, in the street or in public transportation, can be dangerous." During the hearing of 220 high school students by the commission, one of them declared, without being refuted by anyone, that no Jewish student could wear a yarmulke in his school without the threat of being "lynched" (106). The report suggested that emblems of religious affiliation be banned from the classroom, though it deplored that they cannot be worn in public without generating acts of racism. Should the state protect the free expression of belief in buses and subway trains while forbidding it in the schools? Would the banning of yarmulkes from the neighborhoods, as well as from the schools, effectively combat anti-Semitism?

The report extolled the traditional conception of *l'école laïque* as a social and philosophical haven, removed from the hustle and bustle of everyday life, shielding the child from the pressures of "clericalisms" of all kinds, as well as various forms of coercive power, whether religious, political, or commercial. The original notion of *laïcité* implied the coexistence of two kinds of public spaces, the one informed by the enlightened policies of the rational state and the other dominated by the corrupting influence of civil society. The members of the commission could not be unaware of the challenge involved in maintaining a watertight distinction between the two worlds in the age of the Internet and electronic media, amid an individualistic culture that constantly redraws the boundaries between the private and the public.

As a consequence, their report shied away from the most radical version of the neutrality of state education as it had been articulated by republican ideologues a hundred years before: "The State must prevent the minds [of the students] from being harassed [*harcelés*] by the violence and furor of society: without being a sterile room, the school should not become the echoing chamber of the world's passions for fear of failing its educational mission. . . . The school must not be sheltered from the world, but the students must be protected from 'the fury of the world': admittedly, it is not a sanctuary, but it must further a distancing from the real world to make learning about it possible" (33–34, 125). The inevitable compromise with the modern (real) world led to a rhetoric marked by hesitation, a kind of two-steps-forward-one-step-back approach. The report grudgingly made concessions to the arguments of the opposite camp (the pro-veil group) and to cultural change in general, while at the same time trying to salvage the fundamental tenets of the republican creed.

The authors of the report could not advocate a simple return to the old conception of republican socialization as assimilation, and of pedagogical work as the formation of rational subjects who commune in a secular, civil religion aimed at eradicating the last remnants of clerical superstition. As a result, they often gave the impression of conceding too much to their opponents, taking the ideological bite out of the republican revival they claimed to support, as in the pages devoted to "neutrality" with respect to the teaching of world religions in public schools. Trying to chart a middle course, the report noted that the teaching of "religions and spirituality in general . . . might help with the discovery of the revealed texts of the various religions without interfering in sacred interpretation [*s'immiscer dans l'interprétation sacrée*]" (34). The problem is that to posit a plurality of religious traditions and to study them from an external, social-scientific perspective is already to interfere with "sacred interpretations," insofar as they generally exclude (with the exception of liberal theologies) the external point of view itself. One cannot account for the subjective nature of religious belief and spiritual experience through an "objective," comparative description of all religious beliefs as if they were all equivalent. That is precisely the "secular humanistic" approach rejected by fundamentalisms of all kinds.

By presenting an overview of world religions and spiritualist philosophies, the curriculum would not be "neutral." It would be the site of a critique (which might be perfectly legitimate from a secular, pluralistic perspective) of sacred interpretations, since most theological views subject individual consciousness to the superior power of revealed truth and are based on the conviction that all faiths are *not* equivalent. The supporters of sacred interpretation (i.e., believers in divinely inspired religious truth and experience) are left with a choice between rejecting the history-of-religions curriculum within the public school (which is what some Islamist groups are doing) or opening private schools where the secular perspective on the plurality of beliefs has little or no place. The latter move raises a whole new set of issues, since private religious schools in France are under contract with the state and cannot teach a curriculum not approved by government authorities.

The problematic conception of *laïcité* holding the school as a privileged space of dispassionate inquiry into the human and natural worlds is nothing new. French high schools and universities in the sixties and seventies were the site of intense ideological, and at times physical, conflicts between communist, Trotskyist, Maoist, and far-right students who did not manifest any more respect for the neutrality of the educator state than their religious counterparts today. Political clericalisms of all kinds were flourishing within the presumed sanctuary of communicative reason (not to mention the heyday of the right-wing, antirepublican Action française during the interwar period). If the Republic of old has been so successful at instilling in the minds of its pupils the principles of moderation and tolerance that come with the cultivation of enlightened humanism, then how are we to explain the widespread hold on these youthful minds of such antidemocratic secular religions as fascism, Stalinism, or ethnic nationalism throughout the twentieth century? The irony, of course, is that many of the recent converts to the moderating, consensus-building, antitotalitarian nature of Third Republic rationalism are former sixties radicals who back then accused the republican state of advancing the interests of the bourgeoisie, described republican laws as upholding, at best, only "formal liberties," and blamed the republican school for reproducing social and economic inequalities.[10]

The *Sinthome* of the Veil

The report often displayed a fateful confusion between *laïcité* as a Kantian ideal of reason—a philosophical horizon that must guide the political process—and its always-already imperfect insertion in less than ideal historical institutional forms, fraught with social tensions and ideological contradictions.[11] In *The Ticklish Subject*, Slavoj Žižek argued that apparently universal ideological notions are always in fact "hegemonized" by "some particular content which colors its very universality and accounts for its efficiency" (175). Žižek cites as an example of this ideological process the "contamination" of the American New Right's general rejection of the welfare state by

---

10. Although the republican tradition in France has included a variety of philosophical and political doctrines, from liberalism to socialism, and from anticlericalism to progressive Catholicism, Enlightenment rationalism played a crucial role in the elaboration of republican principles throughout the nineteenth and early twentieth centuries. Rationalism is based on the philosophical premise that truth is derived from the innate faculty of reason rather than from information from the senses. The consequence drawn by many republicans was that since reason was a universal attribute, shared by all human beings regardless of their social status, it could be used to emancipate humankind from oppression and misery and form the basis of a just society. Education, viewed as the cultivation of reason in children and the formation of future self-determined citizens, free from prejudice and immune from political or religious manipulation, was the cornerstone of the republican attempt to replace the old regime with an enlightened democratic order after 1871. Today, the "return of republicanism" as a response to the current challenges facing French society has taken various forms. The use of a neo-republican rhetoric to address instances of institutional deadlock and social conflict—for instance, regarding issues of gender, race, or religion—goes hand in hand with the "rediscovery" of forgotten figures of nineteenth-century republican philosophy, especially in its neo-Kantian form. On the usefulness of the Enlightenment legacy to address current challenges in contemporary democracies, see, for example, Todorov, *L'esprit des Lumières*. On republican philosophy, see Fabiani, *Philosophes de la République*; and Kriegel, *Philosophie de la République*.

11. Those who wish to "adapt and modernize" the law of 1905 on the separation of church and state often advocate a decoupling of the ideal of *laïcité* (universally valid as a fundamental value of the democratic *vivre-ensemble*) from its outdated and inadequate embodiment in the current law of the land.

the "more concrete representation of the notorious single African-American mother, as if social welfare were, in the last resort, a program for single black mothers—the particular case of the 'single black mother' is silently conceived of as 'typical' of the universal notion of social welfare, and what is wrong with it" (125). Following Ernesto Laclau's concept of "readability," Žižek argues that the concrete content given to a general, abstract notion helps relate that notion to the agents' actual experience and add the force of affect to that of mental representation (idea, thought, point of doctrine, etc.). The specific content makes the everyday experience of those who subscribe to it more easily "readable," allowing them to more effectively "organize their life-experience into a consistent narrative."[12]

Žižek suggests other instances of this figuration of the abstract, this embodiment of a political cause in a single, "typical" representative. Antiabortion discourse in the United States often focuses on the paradigmatic figure of the single career woman (in many ways the polar opposite of the poor black mother of the welfare debate) who puts her own selfish professional ambition ahead of her maternal duties. The "typical case" proves to be largely illusory, since the majority of abortions in the United States concern lower-class married women with large families. Žižek relates the way the figures of the "single unemployed mother" and the "single career woman" work in antiwelfare and antiabortion discourse to Lacan's notion of *sinthome* or *point de capiton*. The typical case is

> a knot, a point at which all the lines of the predominant ideological argumentation (the return to family values, the rejection of the welfare state and its "uncontrolled" spending, etc.) meet. For that reason, if we "untie" this *sinthome*, the efficiency of its entire ideological edifice is suspended. We can see now in what sense the psychoanalytic *sinthome* is to be opposed to the medical symptom: the latter is a sign of some more fundamental process taking place on another level. . . . The *sinthome*, in contrast, is not a "mere symptom," but that which holds together the "thing itself."

The untying of the phantasmic "knot" is the aim of ideological critique as "theory" (from the Greek *theoria*, literally a different way of *looking* at things) in Žižek's perspective: "The moment we perceive as 'typical' the case of

---

12. On the notion of "readability" and the "constitutive impossibility of society," see Laclau, "The Time Is Out of Joint."

abortion in a large lower-class family unable to cope economically with another child, the perspective changes radically" (176).

The veiled Muslim teenager performs a similar function in French anti-communitarian discourse. She has become the *sinthome* of neo-Jacobin ideology, playing, mutatis mutandis, the same role as the "welfare queen" of U.S. conservative ideology. In the eyes of its opponents, the Islamic scarf stands in for what is wrong with French society today. It has become the quilting point on which are concentrated the entire set of values and customs and institutions currently under attack, because it is their exemplary negation. The veil/*laïcité* binary structure makes up the ideological "knot" in this case; the first term of the opposition is the negative counterpart to the second, positively valued term. The young Arab male also works as a *sinthome* in the Lacanian/Žižekian sense, but in a different context and with different ideological effects. As criminal and rapist, he is an iconic figure of national disruption who performs a similar ideological function for the nationalistic Right as his female counterpart does for the republican Left. The veiled young woman and the sexually violent young man are complementary figures of the Islamic threat, the one as victim, the other as aggressor.[13]

A striking picture made the cover of *L'Express* in the late 1980s: it showed an amphitheater at Tehran University where hundreds of female students identically dressed in chadors received what was signified as political-theological indoctrination, the standardization in ideas mirroring the strict replication of physical appearance. The hallucinating, infinite replication of identical veiled young women represented collectivistic brainwashing by the theocratic educational authorities, the totalitarian nightmare of political Islam as the reverse of the highly individualized, pluralistic ideal of Western democracy. At the same time, the image suggested the possible future of liberal democracies if they were unable to stop the cancer-like proliferation of the Islamist (and Islamic) threat.

The veil-as-main-threat-to-*laïcité* is both a (Freudian) symptom (a displaced *effect* of all the related crises of the modernist project, from education and representative democracy to nation-state, immigration policies, and urban planning) and a *sinthome* (*laïcité*-as-a-response-to-the-veil is the glue that holds the neo-Jacobin worldview together). On the one hand, we have the intense visibility of veiled women (in France and abroad) that adorns the covers of newsmagazines and invades television screens every time the issue of Islamism flares up again; on the other, there is the discursive focalization on *laïcité*

---

13. See, for example, Guénif-Souilamas and Macé, *Les féministes et le garçon arabe*.

as the central component of the resistance to the threat posed by veiled women. The hesitant rhetoric of the Stasi commission's report stems from the ambivalence of the veil itself, as it is both a positive marker of religious freedom and a negative reminder of the impossibility of the national compact.

Difference cuts both ways, as a "good" sign of a healthy democracy and as a "bad" sign of its intolerant negation. At the end of the day, the commission found that the negative uses of the veil (the threat to public order) outweigh its positive meaning (as an expression of individual rights): "The commission, after having heard testimonies, considers that what is at stake today beyond freedom of conscience is public order. . . . Young women need to be protected and, to this end, strong signals need to be sent by public authorities to Islamic groups" (128). The purpose of the commission's recommendation was thus the reassertion of public authority in the face of extremist "political-religious pressure groups" that "are working in our country to test the resistance of the Republic and push some of our youth to reject France and its values. . . . In this context, it is only natural that many of our compatriots [*concitoyens*] wish for the restoration of republican authority, particularly in school" (13).

While the public intellectuals Bourdieu ridiculed as ceaselessly staking a claim as master thinkers waxed lyrical about philosophical betrayal, cultural decline, and the threat of postmodernism, the role of the state as manager of social change and political order was the real issue behind the new law. Teachers and administrators complained that the directives from the Education Ministry and the recommendations of the Constitutional Council were not clear and coherent enough to serve as reliable guidelines to deal with the issue of religious dress in their schools. It was in large part to respond to this disarray that Jacques Chirac decided to appoint an expert commission charged with drafting a proposal for a new law. Beyond the principles of Third Republic educational philosophy, it was the day-to-day administration of the public schools that was undermined by some parents' refusal to let their daughters take part in physical education and swimming classes because wearing shorts or bathing suits is contrary to Islamic law. In the same way, those Muslim men who did not allow their wives, sisters, or daughters to be treated by a male physician seriously impaired the daily management of public health, one of the central missions, with education, of the liberal-democratic state.

Religious prescriptions ran afoul of two types of institutionally sanctioned rationalities linked to the advent of the modern: a pedagogical rationality requiring that no child be dispensed from fulfilling any curricular requirement (in the name of equality), and an instrumental-scientific rationality that looks for best practices in the medical field. What the veil issue brought to the fore was the contradiction, within the state apparatus itself, between *public* interest (i.e., the collective management of social needs) and the *private* rights of the "users" (*usagers*) of the state, as well as the rights of government employees. State workers could also claim, like middle school students, the right to wear religious garments, have their special dietary needs acknowledged in the cafeteria, or be allowed to take a day off for religious observance. This tension between the public and the private, between the legally sanctioned prerogatives of the state, on the one hand, and the ever-expanding field of individual rights on the other, produces a series of paradoxes that underlie the complexity of the *laïcité* issue.

The opponents of the veil see it primarily as a symbol of women's oppression, which it is in many cases, but clearly not in all cases. And yet, as critics were quick to point out, the law only sanctions girls and teenagers who are already dominated as women, as legal minors, and as daughters or granddaughters of immigrants, but does not target the agents of the patriarchal ideology that forces many of them to wear the veil in the first place (i.e., fathers, older brothers, and beyond, the extremist organizations and religious authorities that encourage them to defy the government). A law meant to facilitate the integration of all in the national community ended up excluding its most vulnerable members from the benefits of public education.

The pro- and anti-veil camps oppose each other in the name of the same principles of liberty, equality, and modernity, although they interpret these in opposite terms. For the secularists, the veil is a symbol of the intolerant dogmatism of archaic religions, while for their opponents, it is the banning of the veil that is a manifestation of (secular) intolerance and dogmatism, a sign of the oppression of ethnic minorities by state power. Islamophobes and antiracists clash over the same set of democratic values inherited from the Enlightenment and the French Revolution, but while for some the veil symbolizes cultural freedom (the right to be different), for the others it suppresses political liberty (the right to be different from one's group difference).

The two sides of the democratic coin, its rationalist, absolutist, and universalistic side, and its libertarian, individualistic side, fuel the controversy, pitting once again the centralists against the federalists, the neo-Jacobins against the neo-Girondists. The conflict revives the two-hundred-year-old conundrum of what François Furet called the invention of modern politics by the French revolutionaries. The challenge of democratic politics calls for the creation of a unified political whole out of highly differentiated parts—the making of a cohesive nation out of citizens conceived as abstract individuals emancipated from any premodern "natural" community, parish, guild, caste, linguistic or ethnic group, and so forth. The process of modernity produced the nation-state, whose power rests on the fiction of a homogeneous people. But it also triggered an ever-expanding individualism that has dissolved most of the traditional collective affiliations of the French, from the Catholic Church to the Communist Party, all carriers of a strong identification with the nation-state itself.

In fact, both sides in the battle of *laïcité* have a point, since each position rests on one of the many dynamics that can lead a teenager to visibly manifest her religious affiliation in the public space. Sociological studies have shown that there are many reasons to wear the veil. Familial pressure to conform, which denies freedom of conscience, is undoubtedly one of them, but so are genuine spirituality, respect for the parents' culture of origin, the quest for difference in an increasingly homogeneous society, a protection against the male gaze, or even, for some, a postmodern fashion statement, where the traditional scarf meets blue jeans.

These various modalities can dominate in turn within a single personal trajectory, or even coexist amid one single identitarian project. How are we to draw a line, among the choices we make of dress, job, or belief, between the product of social pressure, familial legacy, class origins, or psychological tendencies, and the autonomous decision of a self-determined subjectivity? As Françoise Gaspard and Farhad Khosrokhavar have argued, "It is worth noting that the young women who choose to wear the veil are often the most successfully integrated [in French society]: as a whole, they do well in school, speak French in a overly correct way, and define themselves as French. Their leitmotiv is often: 'French and Muslim.' What is perceived as antagonistic by a large part of French society, seems to be part of their identity."[14]

The battle of the veil involves neither a neatly drawn opposition between the scarf as constraint and the scarf as free expression, nor a confrontation between the Left and the Right. In fact, it divides all parties (with the exception of the National Front), pitting feminists against multiculturalists, rationalists against relativists, and absolutists against pragmatists within each political group. We have witnessed a struggle for the legitimate definition of *laïcité* in the French context, a context that differs markedly from that of other European countries, such as Britain or Germany, where secularism has taken different historical forms. In France, the question is whether to return

---

14. Gaspard and Khosrokhavar, *Le foulard et la République*, 24.

to the militant views of the anticlerical radical republicans of the late nineteenth century, who wanted to replace Catholicism with a civil religion based on scientific reason and a positivist social philosophy. Another option is to grant Muslims the same historical compromise as was reached with the liberal law of 1905, a compromise that has been quite beneficial to Catholicism once the Church fully accepted the consequences of the law after World War II.[15] Some today go as far as proposing to make adjustments to the separation of church and state, such as allowing the state to finance the building of new mosques, instead of these projects being funded by donors from Arab countries who can exert a determining influence on French Muslim organizations. Tinkering with one of the cornerstones of French republicanism is no easy task: despite his popularity among conservative voters, President Nicolas Sarkozy was recently accused by his own camp of undermining the secular foundations of the Republic by openly advocating such public financing of religious buildings.

The variety of reasons to wear the veil in school and in the street is only matched by the variety of competing definitions of *laïcité* throughout French history, from Bonaparte's Concordat in 1803 to current reformulations of the law of 1905. Part of the unreality of the current controversy comes from the fact that it often takes place in a mythical space, in complete disregard for historical change. Many in the secularist camp dream of reenacting once again the "war between the two Frances" of the beginnings of the Third Republic, with contemporary political Islam playing the role of Catholic traditionalists in the 1880s. But history does not repeat itself. Islam is a minority religion in France, a kind of informal, loose federation of local communities and places of worship, without a centralized hierarchy or a cadre of legitimate representatives clearly mandated to interact with the government. This structure

---

15. The law on the separation of the churches and the state was passed by the French National Assembly on December 9, 1905, under a government led by the Bloc des gauches, a coalition of moderate and radical republicans and socialists. The law affirmed the neutrality of the state, recognized religious freedom, and stated that the Republic does not subsidize any religion. It is one of the major episodes in the struggle between anticlerical republicans and right-wing supporters of Catholicism between 1871 and 1914. The law weakened the Catholic Church by targeting its finances: in addition to removing any funding from the state, it declared churches to be the property of the government. Right-wing governments subsequently found ways to bypass the strict separation of church and state and provide public funding to Catholic schools, for example. The law has remained a symbol of French *laïcité* and of republican principles. It finds itself once again at the center of recent debates on the place of Islam in French society, especially when it comes to government funding of new mosques. Nicolas Sarkozy, then interior minister, was taken to task by the Left for involving the government in the constitution in 2003 of the Conseil français du culte musulman (French Council of the Muslim Faith), a representative structure of French Islam whose secretary's salary was paid by the state, in violation of the law of 1905.

bears little resemblance to the Catholic Church of a century ago. In those days the radical republicans wanted to put an end to the influence of a longstanding *institution*, a fifteen-century-old state religion that had served to legitimate the rule of absolute monarchy.

A Tale of Two Orthodoxies

Today's debate often proceeds as though the philosophical arguments derived from Condorcet and Comte can be used as such in a radically different context, marked not by the triumph of positivism as in the 1880s, but by a concurrent weakening of both traditional religious beliefs *and* rationalist worldviews. These new developments are driven by an increasing privatization of personal belief, a dynamic that Marcel Gauchet has called "exit from religion" (*sortie de la religion*). Individuals do not "lose" faith or religion in our late modernity; rather, they engage in a sort of metaphysical bricolage, cobbling together highly personalized systems of belief, independent of the dogmas of established religions, although these individuals might still retain an affiliation with historical church structures. While a growing number of Europeans "convert" to various forms of Buddhism and Hinduism or to "New Age" gnosticism, American Catholics turn a deaf ear to the pope's admonitions regarding divorce and contraception.

What the late nineteenth-century radical republicans failed to achieve—a substantial weakening of the Church's power over the minds and hearts of the faithful—is being accomplished through the increasing privatization of religious belief in liberal democracies. The problem for the militant secularists is that the tide has swept away rationalist philosophies as well. All creeds, including the freethinkers' belief in the necessary demise of all beliefs, have been profoundly transformed by the surge of individualism. Scientific atheism is now just one option among others in the supermarket of ideas, at a time when many intellectuals and academics question the foundationalist regimes of truth on which the rationalism of the founders of the Republic was based.

What is known as radical Islamism is also a product of our times, in the sense that its followers are affected by the developments I have briefly sketched above. The rise of à la carte religious belief forces fundamentalists to return to dogmas that individualism keeps hollowing out, following the logic of what Eric Hobsbawm, in the context of nationalism, has called the invention of tradition. Just as the friends and foes of the law on *laïcité* confront one another in the name of the same principles of freedom, equality, and individual autonomy, the new defenders of the secular faith resemble their Islamic opponents in that they, too, have to reinvent their own tradition. Hence the return to the founding fathers, from Gambetta and Jaurès to Jules Ferry, and to the sacred texts of republican educational philosophy; the condemnation of heretics, schismatics, and other traitors to the cause; the apocalyptic tone of end-of-the-world prophecies; the refusal to compromise; and the plea to resist the corrupting signs of the times. The new republicans want to fight all forms of communalism in the name of a superior community, the nation as Republic, and so what we really have is the clash of two communitarian traditionalisms, each of them looking through a mythical past for ways to restore the faith of disoriented followers.

The two ideologies are obviously not equivalent in their consequences (nobody gets jailed or killed for disagreeing with republican orthodoxy in France, as is the case with opponents to or transgressors of the sharia in Islamic theocracies), but they share similar cognitive patterns and structures of feeling. Both camps display a common rhetoric of the threatened community, a desire for unity and homogeneity, and a fantasy of the unbroken solidarity of the group. The lost paradise of Islam—before what the Muslim Brothers call the *Jahiliyyah*, the ungodly society born of modernity—corresponds to the golden age of the French Republic, from 1880 to 1914.[16] France in the Belle Epoque was not the reconciled nation dreamed up by today's national-republicans. It was a country profoundly divided by ideology, class struggle, and imperialism, as witnessed by the Dreyfus Affair, the republicans' colonialist agenda, or the way the uprising of impoverished winegrowers in southern France was ruthlessly repressed by Clémenceau's government in 1907.

A similar process of idealization applies to the discourse on state-sponsored education. Thirty years ago, the intellectual Left denounced the elitist nature of a school system founded on republican meritocracy in theory and class-based student selection in reality. Education reproduced the social order by relegating the sons and daughters of the working class to technical training and manual labor. Today, the same school system is hailed by those same critics as the bulwark of democracy against religious obscurantism and "totalitarian" group identification. This profound change in the valuation of public education goes hand in hand with new ways of framing the issue of immigration. In the sixties and seventies, the Left viewed unskilled immigrant workers

16. On the concept of *Jahiliyyah* and the ideology of the influential Muslim Brothers, which provides the ideological basis for much of what is known today as "radical Islamism," see Keppel, *Revenge of God*.

in the automobile industry as the new proletariat from the third world whose emancipation would pave the way to a socialist society. Thirty years later, the children and grandchildren of the sixties' universal class have become "Islamists," victims at best, or at worst accomplices of a reactionary religious ideology bent on destroying the foundations of liberal democracy, as if all Arabs were Muslims, and all Muslims fundamentalists.

Some of the roots of the new law on *laïcité* can be found in this sweeping redirection of public and academic discourse, the substitution of ethnic-cultural categories for the socioeconomic vocabularies of the sixties and seventies. The electoral success of the National Front since 1983 was instrumental in bringing about the racialization of both public discourse and academic research agendas. The eclipse of the revolutionary Left, the rise of unemployment, and the weakening of the national state, both in terms of identification processes and actual decision-making power in the new global economy, have pushed reactive nationalistic and culturalist agendas to the fore. Nowhere is this more evident as in the recent debates about affirmative action.

Communitarianism and Its Discontents

The updating of the republican idea I have examined in previous chapters is a flexible enough ideology that it can serve to address all kinds of challenges to what is perceived as the legitimate functioning of France's political institutions. Prominent among these challenges in recent years is the emergence of new egalitarian claims emanating from social groups (self-)defined in terms of race, gender, and sexuality: Muslim female students insisting on wearing headscarves in public schools, immigrants' advocates pushing for noncitizens to have the right to vote in local elections, feminists and women's rights activists advocating gender parity in the electoral process, gay-rights organizations campaigning for same-sex marriage, and most recently, French blacks asking for public recognition of their contribution to society and for the reassessment of the role of colonialism and racism in the construction of Frenchness.[17] These various forms of identity politics have been deployed within the framework of postmodern conceptions of the self in society, and are increasingly at odds with earlier understandings of individualism, the social

---

17. On sexual politics in France, see Fabre and Fassin, *Liberté, égalité, sexualités*; Fassin, *L'inversion de la question homosexuelle*; Iacub, *L'empire du ventre*; and Tin, *L'invention de la culture hétérosexuelle*. On the recent rise of a "black question" in France, see Ndiaye, *La condition noire*; and Fassin and Fassin, *De la question sociale à la question raciale*.

compact, and national identity. In this context, Régis Debray, one of the most prolific and influential advocates of the return of the "republican idea," has wondered whether national identity would survive the demise of the nation-state.

Neo-republicanism, as a third way between liberalism and populism, has been described by one of Debray's critics as "a nationalism celebrating the French Revolution rather than Joan of Arc," the latter being one of the emblematic figures of the National Front. The use of the prefix "neo" in order to describe the new ideology is justified here, not only because its deployment within the French political space is relatively recent, but also because of the considerable selectivity involved in this particular rewriting of historical republicanism. Many components of that legacy have been distorted or left out in the new version, as historical complexity is sacrificed to political efficiency. Given the equation between the Republic and the nation in this particular example of the invention of tradition, I have also borrowed the term "national-republicanism" to refer to the new ideology. The term was originally coined by critics of that position, but was subsequently taken over by some of its proponents, as is often the case in social or cultural struggles over meaning.

Neo-republicanism operates on the basis of what Pierre Bourdieu called the logic of practice, a loose cognitive and discursive structure of interpretation that is flexible enough to answer all sorts of ideological needs and harbor all manner of contradictory statements. Although demands from dispossessed groups in the past twenty years or so originated from very different sections of the population and concerned vastly different domains of the social (education, law, electoral politics, sexuality, race relations, and the construction of national memory), they were met with a relatively homogeneous set of arguments that lumped them all together under the label "communitarian." But because of the flexible logic inherent in ideological practice, after a setback anti-communitarians often shift their opposition from one issue to the next. For example, having unsuccessfully tried to prevent the establishment of gender parity as sanctioned by law, they turned their attention to issues of racial diversity. Fine, goes the redefined argument, women are not a community, but ethnic groups certainly are, so communitarianism is still rearing its ugly head, so we have to be vigilant, stand firm on the principles, rally behind the threatened Republic, and so forth.

Within the binary logic of this catchall, "big tent" kind of rhetoric, communitarianism or communalism simply, and simplistically, stands as the opposite of the universal individualism associated with the French Revolution. In the standard universalistic view favored by the anti-communitarians, political equality warranted by constitutional law transcends and disregards the particularities, hierarchies, and inequalities constitutive of civil society—hence an almost exclusive focus on abstract philosophical notions of citizenry, and a belief that any talk about "minorities" implies a culturalist agenda. In fact, as Eric Fassin has remarked, the debate about affirmative action need not be couched in terms of essentialized communities, since "you don't have to believe in Jewish identity to combat anti-Semitism, in Arab culture to fight racism," while "to combat homophobia in no way implies homosexual communitarianism."[18]

The insistence on the principle of the indivisibility of the *political* body masks a growing unease with, and in many cases intolerance for, the racial diversity of the *social* body. The philosophical notion that race and religion do not or should not matter as far as political institutions are concerned is transferred to the sphere of social relations—that is, from the state to civil society (hence the constant temptation to use the law to solve cultural issues rooted in social and economic inequalities). In its most extreme versions, neo-republicanism takes the form of an active denial, not only of the legitimacy but even of the *existence* of racial difference as a valid category of analysis. The most often quoted example of this situation is the absence of any statistical data on the ethnic/racial composition of the French population. Surveys aimed at providing an assessment of the management of difference are deemed incompatible with the oneness of "the People." The perverse consequences of this kind of logic have been abundantly documented. Since minorities do not exist in the eyes of the law, one cannot constitute them as such to determine whether they are the targets of exclusionary practices. Color blindness as a political postulate encourages the denial of a racial question in French society. Although France is obviously a multiethnic society, it cannot be conceived in such a way as a nation, which leads to the denial of concrete, empirical inequalities in the name of an abstract political equality.

Indivisibility breeds invisibility. The logic of denial at work in color blindness explains that the memory wars in contemporary France (from the "Vichy syndrome" to the current conflict of interpretations of slavery and colonialism) take the form of the return of the repressed. Recent films such as *Indigènes* from 2006 (about enlisted Arab men in the French Army during World War II) and the 2007 television series *Tropiques amers* ("Bitter tropics," on slavery in the French West Indies at the time of the French Revolution) attempt to make the invisible visible by imaging the unimaginable. The

---

18. Fabre and Fassin, *Liberté, égalité, sexualités*, 92.

ideological invisibility of people of color in the dominant representation of Frenchness flies in the face of everyday social relations saturated with racialized references and racial tensions. The constant public debate about immigration, Islam, and positive discrimination displaces anxieties about the racial diversity of postcolonial France onto an increasingly untenable national consensus regarding institutional arrangements and the rule of law.

A Genealogy of Anti-communitarianism

Up to the end of the 1980s, reference to the Republic was virtually absent of major postwar debates, or served as a mere background, ignored or taken for granted, for political and cultural struggles. In the fifties and sixties, the main conflict of ideas opposed socialism to capitalism, and leftists tended to dismiss the contribution of republicanism to progressive politics. In their view, most republicans had historically shied away from real social and economic transformations. The classic republican conceptions of rights, freedom, and equality were seen as limited to what Marxists had always denounced as mere "bourgeois liberties." The return of the republican idea coincided, as already mentioned, with (at least) two concurrent developments: the delegitimization of revolutionary socialism as a viable alternative to a market economy, and new pressures bearing on national sovereignty in the context of economic competition on a global scale and the rise of transnational institutions such as the European Union. All of a sudden, former internationalist revolutionaries who had rejected the philosophical principles of the bourgeois revolution of 1789 rediscovered the virtues of liberal conceptions of the nation-state.

As in the case of *laïcité*, the debate about affirmative action can be traced back to the first affair of the veil. The basic features of what would become the new dogma regarding the "question of minorities" were outlined in the article published by *Le Nouvel Observateur* I discussed previously. Three of the signatories, Régis Debray, Alain Finkielkraut, and Elisabeth Badinter, were, as we saw, major figures of the intellectual Left, and the other two, Elisabeth de Fontenay and Catherine Kintzler, respected members of the academy. The fact that all the signatories were philosophers accounts for the abstract, almost ahistorical nature of their conception of the republican legacy. Their critique of the government's handling of what was fast becoming the "affair of the veil" rested on the indivisibility of the citizenry (the anti-communitarian argument) and the centrality of a rational education in the establishment and maintenance of democratic liberties (the anti-relativist argument). In a sense, those to whom the article was addressed were asked to resist not only the specific agents of Islamic radicalism, but also the broader developments that threatened the very survival of the French difference (i.e., cosmopolitanism, philosophical relativism, postcolonialism, political correctness, multiculturalism, etc.).

The ideological trajectories of the signatories, before and after the publication of the *Nouvel Observateur* article, illustrate the complex relationship between belated converts to civic humanism and the issue of ethnic pluralism in contemporary France. Debray gained notoriety in the sixties after spending several years in Bolivian jails (1967–71) for his participation in Ernesto Guevara's revolutionary guerrilla operations. He was released by the Bolivian government thanks to de Gaulle's personal intervention. Upon his return to France in 1973, Debray abandoned revolutionary politics, embarked on a successful literary and academic career, and joined the Socialist Party, later serving as foreign affairs adviser to President François Mitterrand. His involvement in the first affair of the veil in 1989 was followed by a series of essays in which he praised his teachers for having instilled in him the principles of a secular and rationalist education, faulted the political class for surrendering those same republican principles to the media-driven, image-conscious demands of the new "seductive state," and rehabilitated the figure of de Gaulle as the quintessential symbol of French civic nationalism.[19]

Cosignatory Alain Finkielkraut was also an important figure on the French intellectual scene. He had played a key role in the debate over postmodernism, defending the Enlightenment tradition against contemporary popular culture in *The Defeat of the Mind*, an influential book published in 1987. In many ways, the postmodern debate had prepared the ground for the subsequent controversies over the republican legacy, by popularizing the notion of a cultural war between the champions of universalism and the supporters of cultural relativism. Elisabeth Badinter—a self-described feminist, and like Catherine Kintzler, a specialist of the Enlightenment—was every bit as outspoken as the first two signatories. Throughout the eighties, she had been engaged in a protracted struggle against difference feminists, arguing for the greater significance of the similarities between the genders. Badinter's feminist connection is important here, as women's rights would figure prominently in the discussion of the Islamic scarf as a symbol of women's oppression in Muslim cultures.

---

19. See Debray, *Contretemps*; *L'Etat séducteur*; and *Charles de Gaulle*.

Beyond their diverse conceptual backgrounds, the three philosophers shared a common outlook, based a strong allergy to major postwar developments in French philosophy and social sciences, from Lévi-Strauss and Foucault to Deleuze and Lyotard. They rejected all forms of post-structuralist thought, perspectivism, anti-foundationalism, and radical constructivism. As a consequence of her ongoing critique of difference feminism, Badinter strongly opposed the gender parity movement of the late 1990s. Finkielkraut, for his part, has consistently linked his critique of communitarianism with his concern for the future of Judaism in France. During a visit to Israel in March 2007, he argued that "there is a future for Jews in France if France is a nation; but there is no future for Jews in a multicultural society, because then the power of anti-Jewish groups is liable to be greater."[20]

The nation form is clearly incompatible, in this view, with a multicultural society, because a multicultural society is always antagonistic, racked by internal divisions, and because without the protection of the state, small minorities fall prey to bigger ones. Finkielkraut's "nation" no longer refers to the classical definition proposed by Ernest Renan at the end of the nineteenth century—that is, a mixture of shared memories and a willingness to live together under the same laws, a position the author of *The Defeat of the Mind* had advocated two decades earlier. For France to remain a nation supposes that the state renounce its previous role as the "neutral" arbiter of the common good, and become instead the protector of one "community" against another, more powerful and dangerous one. The neutrality of the state is no longer possible since the widely accepted pluralism of the postmodernists has undermined the common culture that was at the heart of the republican national project after 1870. Finkielkraut acknowledges the fragmented, tension-filled nature of French civil society, which he describes in terms of antagonistic "groups." In other words, France is already a "multicultural society." The nation-state is no longer an alternative to it, but rather the last bulwark against its disintegration into an anomic space, within which the war of all against all will become endemic.

Beyond the obvious reference to the rise of Muslim anti-Semitism in France as a response to the Israeli-Palestinian conflict, Finkielkraut was most likely thinking of the Balkans, about which he wrote extensively during the Yugoslavian wars, taking up the cause of the Croatians against the Serbs. The specter of ethnic cleansing figured prominently in the debate on multiculturalism in France throughout the 1990s, and Finkielkraut was instrumental,

---

20. Yair Sheleg, "A Racist Attack," *Ha'aretz*, March 28, 2007.

with a number of other "antitotalitarian" intellectuals, as they were called then, in popularizing the notion that fascism was returning to European politics, replacing communism as the major threat to Western democracy. The theme of the return of fascism prefigured the current use of Islamofascism to describe the most radical forms of political Islam.

Given the importance of the Shoah and of Serbian ethnic cleansing in his writings, one possible reading of Finkielkraut's comments in *Ha'aretz* was that any attempt to have the state officially recognize the existence of racial minorities in France would remove the last barrier against ethnic warfare, turning France into the next Yugoslavia. Finkielkraut's ideological trajectory led him from the apology of universalism to anti-communitarian communitarianism, a paradox many of his critics were quick to point out. Like many neo-republicans, Finkielkraut often confuses nation, republic, and democracy. It is true that only democratic institutions, based on the rule of law, can guarantee that no individual or group is threatened by the actions of other groups and individuals. But the nation, even in its republican form, did not always protect Jews from persecution, as the obvious case of the Dreyfus Affair, as well as the inability or unwillingness of the state to curb anti-Semitism in the 1930s, make patently clear.

As demands for recognition from racial minorities became more vocal and more visible, Finkielkraut's position hardened, and less palatable aspects of his civic humanism came to the fore. In November 2005, he had drawn fire for his comments in an interview for *Ha'aretz* on the racial composition of the French national soccer team: "People say the French national team is admired by all because it is black-white-and-*beur* [*beur* is slang for Arab]. Actually, the national team today is black-black-black, which arouses ridicule throughout Europe."[21] The color-blindness imperative of the neo-republican creed has turned into an obsession with color, a heightened sensitivity to the racial nature of the image France projects on the international scene. Since the cat is out of the bag, difference can no longer be denied, but rather must be deplored and denounced as a stain on the country's international image.

In the early 1990s, national-republican intellectuals fulfilled their Gramscian organic function by providing the initial articulation of the new ideology. Their arguments soon found their way into political speeches and media outlets, as befits a country in which philosophers have always enjoyed the respect of the political elites. (As mentioned in an earlier chapter, in one of

---

21. Dror Mishani and Aurelia Smotriez, "What Sort of Frenchmen Are They? Interview with Alain Finkielkraut," *Ha'aretz*, November 18, 2005.

his letters to Sartre, who opposed his government's policy in Algeria, de Gaulle addressed him as "my dear master.") The call to arms directed at the teachers had the trademark of the traditional intervention of the intellectuals in the public arena. It was both a short pamphlet and a small-scale petition, two of the critical intelligentsia's favorite modes of collective mobilization.[22] The warning, as we saw, was clearly directed at the leadership of the Socialist Party, which meant that the struggle needed to be carried all the way to the seat of political power.

Spreading the Word

The anti-communitarian agenda outlined in the fall of 1989 was soon shared by a wide-ranging coalition of politicians, opinion makers, and militant organizations, from the far-right National Front to the Gaullists, and from nationalist socialists to radical feminists. Multiculturalism became a prominent topic in academic writings, and racism was now openly discussed and analyzed by sociologists, political scientists, and philosophers eager to help answer the question that made the headlines of weekly magazines: "Can we all live together?" In the last decade, several websites have been created whose main purpose is to provide readers and bloggers with arguments for the ongoing debate. The Réseau France Républicaine (Republican France Network, http://www.france-republicaine.fr/), for example, founded in 2000 by a Gaullist politician, presents itself as a nonpartisan association whose goal is to inform visitors on the "life of republican movements and to promote the indivisible, secular, democratic, and social Republic" (a direct quote from the 1958 Constitution). The site provides synoptic descriptions of major republican principles, short biographies of leading historical figures, political speeches of significance, and major constitutional documents. Links to several related organizations, from daily newspapers and academic reviews to foundations and politicians' websites, are meant to suggest the existence of a vast network of opinion behind the republican idea. A cursory reading of the news briefs listed on the site of the Observatoire du communautarisme (Observatory of Communitarianism, http://www.communautarisme.net/), founded in 2003, illustrates the diversity, so to speak, of the organization's preferred targets, the litany of Kleinian bad objects that render the mourning of the neo-Jacobin Marianne properly interminable: gay and black activists, pro-Israel lobbies, Muslim and Jewish associations, Basque, Catalan, and Corsican

---

22. See Sirinelli, *Intellectuels et passions françaises*.

nationalists, antiglobalization radicals, politically correct socialists, right-wing multiculturalists, European Union advocates, antiracism groups, free traders, regionalists, ethnic-based electoral politics, leaflets in Arabic, radio stations in Chinese, and so forth.

As an ideological construct, neo-republicanism relies on a highly idealized and highly selective view of France's past and present. It conveniently ignores the discriminatory practices that have plagued the last century and a half of republican rule, both in the metropole and the colonies. Today, the virtues of the theoretical Republic cover up, and often excuse, the sins of the empirical one. Colonial history invalidates most of the current rhetoric, especially as regards the indivisibility of the people, the invisibility of difference, and the strict incompatibility between ethnic particularism and civic universalism. In Algeria, for example, colonized people were given the status of French "subjects," not of "citizens." As a consequence, they did not enjoy equal rights under the protection of French law, but were submitted to the Code de l'indigénat (Indigenous code) that gave extensive discretionary power over their persons and possessions to the governor's office, in flagrant disregard for the basic republican principle of the separation of judiciary and administrative powers.

The legal status of the French subjects was clearly ethnic in character, placing them beyond the scope of the supposedly universal conception of political rights, which were in fact reserved for "French people of metropolitan origin." The category "Muslim" had little to do with religion, since Arabs who had converted to Catholicism were still subject to Islamic law as long as they remained noncitizens. From 1865 to 1962, only seven thousand "Muslims" were granted French citizenship, while Algerian Jews became citizens *as a group* in 1870.[23] Ethnic-based communitarianism remained part and parcel of the legal and organizational basis of the colonial Republic until the 1950s. Today, similar ambiguities and double standards remain, albeit with less drastic consequences.

While race-based (i.e., black) and faith-based (i.e., Muslim) organizations are accused of sowing the seeds of separatism, other associations celebrating ethnic-cultural identities receive the support of public authorities. Former president Jacques Chirac, for example, was extremely active in promoting on the international scene demands from the French Armenian "community" that Turkish authorities publicly acknowledge the Armenian genocide of 1915.

---

23. Figures quoted by Patrick Weil, "Le droit de la nationalité est un combat," *Le Nouvel Observateur*, May 30, 2002. See also, by the same author, *Qu'est-ce qu'un Français?*

The French National Assembly officially did so in January 2001, extending the politics of memory to crimes against humanity committed in other countries (beyond the legacy of French colonialism or the French government's complicity in the Holocaust). Many Armenian organizations mix politics with ethnicity, lobbying for the recognition of the genocide while at the same time celebrating their national origins, without being perceived as threatening France's national unity and cultural identity. For example, one such organization, created in 1976 in southern France, aims at "uniting all French people of Armenian origin around the cultural, religious, and historical values of their ancestors." These ancestors, obviously, are neither the Gauls nor the Franks. And yet to pay homage to them or celebrate their memory does not call into question the national loyalty of the association's members. As Louis-George Tin, one of the leaders of the Representative Council of Black Organizations, has said, "The anti-community rhetoric is not against communities, it is against certain communities."[24]

Not only do neo-republicans conveniently ignore the close connection between communalism and colonial policy during the Third and Fourth Republics, but they also oppose minority politics in the name of a larger, legitimate "community of affections" (a phrase coined during the French Revolution by the Jacobin Saint-Just), whose boundaries coincide with that of the nation. Historically, the attachment to republican principles was never entirely based on rational principles, but always included a large dose of political passion and emotional investment. As a consequence, the republican imagination has been informed by a variety of exclusivist structures of feeling, from sentimentalism and patriotic fervor to chauvinistic jingoism and outright xenophobia.

In *Le code et le glaive* (The code and the sword), Régis Debray explored this tension between the Republic of the heart and the Republic of the mind. The book's title refers to the figure of the soldier-citizen as the historical embodiment of the double-sided nature of the republican project, which associates the Kantian peaceful reign of universal reason with war, conquest, and assimilation in the name of freedom, equality, and a civilizing mission. In the course of his demonstration, Debray points to the source of anti-communitarian communitarianism in Renan's already mentioned conception of civic identity as bringing together the past and the present, as being both a legacy

24. "Louis-George Tin, porte-parole du CRAN: 'La rhétorique anti-communautaire n'est pas contre les communautés, elle est contre certaines communautés,'" *Observatoire du Communautarisme*, March 17, 2006, http://www.communautarisme.net/.

of shared memories and a willful, conscious desire to live together (as opposed to the passive, organic, racial belonging associated with German nationalism after the Franco-Prussian War of 1870). "This composite addition," Debray writes, "hides in its depth a strange paradox: the republican nation as a barrier against [group] identification is itself the expression of an identity."[25] With his characteristic rhetorical flourish, Debray goes on to argue that the philosophical republic was not so much the child of the eighteenth century as it was the creature of the nineteenth. Born of the Enlightenment, it matured in the age of romantic culturalism, Bonapartist militarism, repeated wars with Britain and Germany, and colonial conquests. Borrowing from Lacanian theory, Debray anchors the dual nature of national identification in the tension between the symbolic (the law, the father, language) and the imaginary (the flag, the mother, the body). The power of the imaginary drives the mythic conception of the nation today, just as it did in the past.

French-Style Affirmative Action

Anti-communitarian rhetoric in France often conflates policies addressing patterns of exclusion with multiculturalist agendas, discredited as "Anglo-Saxon" and "politically correct," code words for made in America. This conflation makes it more difficult to address structural exclusion, and to recognize the racial motivations behind a lot of discriminatory practices. Anti-communitarians often hold together two contradictory arguments: (1) the imperative of diversity based on group identity is about to destroy the very fabric of French society by making the politics of victimization the main engine of public policy, although (2) the imperative of diversity does not change anything, as it is merely a cosmetic procedure ("the Benetton effect") aimed at giving progressive institutional leaders and cultural elites a good conscience at a small price. In many instances, these two lines of argumentation reinforce one another: a progressive rhetoric based on the legacy of the French Revolution and of the post–World War II welfare state is used to maintain the status quo. As Gwénaële Calvès has argued, the threat of "political correctness" remains pure fantasy, since French law prevents anyone from giving the slightest positive content to the notion of "origin."[26]

The confusion between diversity as a symbolic weapon in the French culture wars, on the one hand, and concrete affirmative action policies in specific

---

25. Debray, *Le code et le glaive*, 82.
26. Calvès, "Pour une analyse (vraiment) critique," 166.

areas of public administration or the economy, on the other, is characteristic of the debate on social inclusion in France, which is plagued by a mixture of ideological distortions, politically motivated agendas, ignorance or misrepresentation of the history of foreign and domestic positive action policies, the collapse of analytically distinct objects and levels of discussion, and a general lack of conceptual rigor. Some denounce affirmative action as undermining the principle of indifference to "race, belief, and national origin," while others argue that it is the only way to achieve a color-blind and faith-blind society. In this latter view, the only way to overcome ethnic-cultural differences is first to acknowledge them. Opposite conclusions are drawn from the dialectics of difference and visibility, or indifference and invisibility. While for some the recognition of racial minorities contradicts the principle of indifference, and multicultural agendas produce the visibility of difference, for their opponents this very visibility is not the cause but rather the consequence of discrimination.

The polemic use of communalism leads to the systematic distortion of the historical goals of affirmative action, as they were put forward in the United States and elsewhere from the 1960s on. The objective of addressing structural inequalities through state voluntarism in order to ensure that individuals from certain groups are not discriminated against *despite their competence* becomes, in the eyes of its critics, an attempt to promote entire groups *despite their incompetence*. Actions aimed at insuring that indifference to difference prevails in hiring practices are redescribed as an effort to legitimize differences. The promotion of underprivileged individuals *despite* their origin is reinterpreted as the promotion of underprivileged groups *because of* their origin.

The argument that some groups are unduly "privileged" by public policy is nothing new in France. The traditional conservative critique of the welfare state throughout the postwar period relied in part on the notion that public sector workers and civil servants were given unfair advantages by the state, since they usually enjoyed guaranteed employment and were able to retire five to ten years before their private sector counterparts. More generally, any kind of public policy based on income redistribution through taxation or legislation can be discredited as fostering inequality by favorably targeting specific segments of the population.

Several affirmative action policies have been put in place since the 1980s without being considered incompatible with republican civic principles, in large part because they were based on residential and economic criteria rather than on religious, cultural, or ethnic attributes. The creation of the ZEP (zones d'education prioritaire, or priority educational zones) in 1981 provided increased state funding to schools with "underprivileged" students, mainly to hire additional staff and reduce class size. The law of November 14, 1996, extended the notion of "positive territorial discrimination" from schools within a particular geographical entity to entire "sensitive urban zones" and "zones of urban redynamization." A variety of fiscal measures were aimed at encouraging economic activity, reducing unemployment, and promoting "urban mixing" (*mixité urbaine*) in depressed areas of the country. More surprising is the case of the 1987 legislative act reserving 6 percent of jobs to disabled workers. The law was passed although it included a specific target number, presumably because physical disabilities, like economic and spatial disparities, cut across racial, gender, and cultural differences and can affect anyone as the outcome of a disease or an accident.

The hegemonic nature of the republicanist orthodoxy throughout the 1990s forced partisans of equity policies to both use strategies of accommodation and come up with compromise formations acceptable to the dominant political culture. For example, in order to make the principle of equal representation of men and women on electoral lists more attractive to the (overwhelmingly male) representatives in the French National Assembly, the supporters of gender parity argued that it did not undermine the Republic, since women were not a specific community but represented "one half of humankind." The new measure was presented as based on abstract principles and not on empirical considerations, and its proponents stressed the fact that they did not advocate the establishment of a quota, since numerically women in fact represented more than half the population. Wishful thinking also led them to assure the political class, and the philosophical guardians of the faith, that parity would not lead the country down a slippery slope. Since women were not a minority and were not given preferential treatment on any kind of numerical basis, real statistical minorities, whether based on race, religion, or sexual orientation, would not feel empowered to use parity to advance their own multicultural agendas (a prediction that proved incorrect).

The history of "positive discrimination," as positive action is usually called in France, offers numerous instances of similar strategies of accommodation. In order to respect the sacred principle of an undifferentiated citizenry, affirmative action policies based on geographical criteria used categories such as "ZEP students" or "youth from the projects" (*jeunes des quartiers*) to avoid referring explicitly to these individuals' racial/ethnic origin. This hypocritical "logic of the palimpsest," to borrow a phrase from Gwénaële Calvès, allows public discourse, both in the political sphere and in the media, to name a specific kind of citizen the law forbids to name in any other way. Supporters of positive discrimination often play fast and loose with the taboo of racial difference and the specter of racial violence, arguing that preferential treatment based on socioeconomic criteria is in fact the only way to prevent the rise of ethnic separatism.

Nicolas Sarkozy used a similar argument in November 2003, when he was still minister of the interior, in a series of remarks (widely available online) on French television that immediately sparked yet another heated controversy over the merits of compensatory differentiation. His views and the reaction they prompted are symptomatic of the ambiguities generated by the appeal to universalistic principles in matters of social inclusion. Sarkozy framed his support for targeted interventions within the larger context of the "failure of the French model of integration," illustrated by the cliché of the "stalled social elevator." "When the state is strong," he declared, "when the state enacts policies based on fairness, when there is equity, when everyone thinks, 'I can also have a chance,' when the social elevator is for everyone, one does not need to be defended by one's community." Equality of opportunity, a major component of the republican tradition, serves here to justify a political voluntarism that supersedes the abstract notion of formal equality in the name of Rawlsian "equity," while at the same time eliminating the threat of ethnic strife, thereby killing two birds with one stone. Concrete equality of opportunity versus abstract, formal juridical equality: the distinction points to the complexity of the republican reference, and beyond, to the tensions that have informed the republican project in the course of its historical application (liberal republicans vs. socialists, idealists vs. positivists, moderates vs. radicals, agnostics vs. social Christians, etc.).

In the first part of his remarks, Sarkozy remained within the boundaries of a color-blind ideology, following the logic of the palimpsest, granting needs and agency not to groups or individuals but to geographical areas ("There are territories that have so many more handicaps that if they are not given more than the others, they won't be able to make it"). The rest of his statement, however, got him into a lot of trouble. Following a plea for going beyond purely symbolic correctives to social inequalities ("Zinedine Zidane and soccer, that's wonderful, but that is not enough"), Sarkozy suddenly shifted his focus from territory to religion, venturing onto dangerous ground. Suggesting a possible ethnicization of public policy, he argued that "French Muslims are also capable of having high civil servants, researchers, doctors, professors," and proceeded to announce the impending appointment of "a Muslim" to a high-ranking position in the government.[27]

The proposal, which implied in passing that many of his compatriots were not convinced that "Muslims" could become professionals, was immediately criticized from the Right and the Left as substituting group affiliation for individual merit. The first secretary of the Socialist Party, François Hollande, denounced in Sarkozy's formulation "a very liberal, Anglo-Saxon conception," while Malek Boutih, a member of the party's national leadership, equated the proposal to appoint high-level state functionaries on the basis on religious affiliation with "a project of French-style communitarianism" (*communautarisme à la française*).[28] In addition to being a euphemistic stand-in for "Arab" (as in the days of colonial rule), the word "Muslim" used as a criterion for promotion within the civil service reinforced the suspicion that neoliberals such as Sarkozy were about to undermine the century-old separation of church and state, another pillar of the republican legacy, and a prominent feature of the successive "affairs of the Islamic veil" that inflamed ideological passions throughout the 1990s.

This example shows to what extent anti-communalism works in a variety of contexts to address a variety of controversial issues, from the Islamic veil to parity and affirmative action, and from the crisis of the public schools to memorial laws and historical revisionism. Neo-republicanism is a kind of catchall ideology that enables its proponents to react defensively to the totality of the challenges faced by French society in the era of globalization and international migrations. The double nationalization of the issue of positive discrimination as the (dangerous) French version of a (bad) American idea is typical of the ritualistic, and for that reason highly predictable, content of the debate. The American reference, via the negative connotations it carries, helps to discredit any attempt to acknowledge that discriminatory practices in hiring and housing are overwhelmingly directed at racial minorities. Affirmative action is said to be wrong for (at least) three reasons: it does not work, it is incompatible with the homegrown political tradition, and, last but not least, it comes from the United States. The efficient mobilization of endemic French anti-Americanism through a series of controversial issues is

27. See Sylvie Kaufmann, "Les avantages de la discrimination positive," *Le Monde*, January 5, 2004.

28. See "Malek Boutih: La discrimination positive est 'dangereuse' pour la République," November 22, 2003, http://www.kabyle.com/archives/Malek-Boutih-la-discrimination.html; François Hollande is quoted in Kaufmann, "Les avantages de la discrimination positive" (see above).

based, in the case of affirmative action, on a willful ignorance of American politics. For example, the association of American-style affirmative action with the establishment of numerical targets flies in the face of repeated rulings by the U.S. Supreme Court that quotas are unconstitutional.

Despite the repeated nationalization of issues of social integration in public discourse, dominant representations, and patterns of collective self-identification ("the French model," "the French exception," etc.), there is no more French exceptionalism in these matters than in many others, as ongoing tensions over positive action all over the world clearly demonstrate. Arguments against the compensatory treatment of group-based inequality are well known and strikingly consistent, regardless of the specificities of political culture and legal tradition born of particular national histories. Whether in the Indian, Brazilian, or South African contexts, affirmative action policies are deemed unable to combat poverty, exclusion, and discrimination. Their critics claim that they end up stigmatizing the very people they aim to help by raising doubts regarding their competence, since they unfairly advantage certain groups by lowering in their favor the standards required of the majority in accessing jobs and diplomas.

The struggles over positive action have more to do with the unequal competition of various groups for limited economic chances and welfare state benefits, legal rights, and public recognition than with philosophical considerations about the nature of the French Enlightenment's metaphysical subject. While it is true that the conflict takes on a particular form in the French context due to the dominance of Jacobinism in the country's political history, the structural mechanisms that lead to systematic discrimination and the ideological paradigms that legitimize it are comparable to those that prevail in other national contexts. The Brazilian case, for example, is a particularly useful point of comparison, since a similar color-blind ideology based on republican principles (borrowed from Europe, and especially France, in the latter part of the nineteenth century) has been used to obfuscate issues of race-based injustice.

In the case of France, the issue of positive action is ultimately about the nature of Frenchness as the contested signifier of an imagined community, even though, at the same time, the notion of a French exception regarding the resistance to affirmative action is highly questionable. The current crisis of the accepted notion of a collective "being French" is all the more striking because it was the product of a systematic process of cultural work performed by the state and the schools for the past one hundred and fifty years. In this sense, the current struggles are about the symbolic limits of *francité*, about who is included and who does not make the cut, and about what is being lost in this redrawing of the boundaries of identity. But principles of inclusion and exclusion are not always based on race and ethnicity. Revered literary figures such as the Senegalese poet and statesman Leopold Senghor (who became a French citizen, was elected to the prestigious Académie française, and whose work is taught in high school "French literature" courses) or internationally acclaimed Moroccan novelist Tahar Ben Jelloun (who lives in Paris and was awarded the most prestigious French literary prize, the Prix Goncourt, in 1987) are in, but Senegalese street sweepers and Moroccan autoworkers are out, as are many second- or third-generation Arab or black citizens, eternally considered as "descended from immigration." In their case, citizenship and nationality, the latter being broadly defined in cultural rather than simply legal terms, do not coincide. The reference to their immigrant parents, and increasingly, grandparents, remains the most important component of their identity for journalists, experts, and politicians who write and talk about them.

The constant reminder of some citizens' ancestry is hardly an expression of enlightened universalism. On the contrary, it manifests the communitarianism of the dominant, as Christine Delphy has called the new republicanism. The repeated reference to the origin of those who are eternally "descended from immigration" functions as a marker of their externality, a constant reminder, to them and to the rest of their compatriots, that they are still standing outside looking in. Positive action policies encounter so much resistance because they are designed to address patterns of exclusion from the idea of Frenchness, which are manifest in housing segregation, job discrimination, and beyond, in symbolic representations, as in the recurrent anxious wondering whether the national soccer team has enough white players to adequately represent the country's image abroad and comfort the national imagination at home. The current conflicts that divide public opinion in France around issues of diversity, the instrumentalization of history, the memorialization of the Shoah, of the Vichy regime, of slavery, of the Algerian War, or the emergence of a black movement all have one thing in common: the contestation, displacement, and maintenance of the ever-shifting boundaries of Frenchness, and the refusal by many to come to terms with the wrenching cultural loss involved in such a process.

CONCLUSION

Barack Obama's election to the presidency of the United States in 2008 was hailed at home and abroad as a new dawn for the United States and the world. Commentators stressed the world-historical nature of the event, and many presented it as the sign of a generational sea change in American culture, especially as regards race relations. Voters under forty years of age were said to have made all the difference by showing that they had fewer misgivings than their elders, on the whole, about electing a black man to the highest office in the land. The French reaction was mixed. The media loudly congratulated the American people for putting an end to a long history of bigotry and bringing American idealism back to center stage. Amid the slightly condescending consensus about the fact that the Americans finally had got it right, a few, more penetrating, voices arose, remarking that what had just taken place in the United States would be impossible in France, and most likely for quite a while. This book has addressed many of the issues raised by the immediate reaction to the recent U.S. presidential elections, from national narrative and generational change to the capacity of a liberal democracy to offer symbolic as well as institutional responses to a less than adequate past.

Nicolas Sarkozy's election to the French presidency the previous year had also prompted talk of change (the Sarkozy campaign called it *rupture*) and of a new generation coming to power. A number of the newly appointed cabinet members were born in 1965, and the fifty-two-year-old president was said to be introducing a new style of political leadership. Much was made of his predilection for jeans, bomber jackets, and aviator sunglasses, and of his daily jogging routine in the neighborhood of the Elysée Palace. These were all taken as signs of a major break with the more solemn protocol of his predecessors raised in pre–World War II France (Mitterrand was born in 1916, Giscard d'Estaing in 1926, and Chirac in 1932). Daniel Cohn-Bendit, the former 1968 student radical, once quipped that for all his avowed hostility toward May 1968 as having started France on a downward spiral, Sarkozy was the perfect child of the sixties, sharing with many baby boomers the desire to "have it all, right now." In many ways, Sarkozy's election represented a generational changing of the guard, both in terms of the political personnel and in terms of the ideologies this new generation would champion.

A large part of this book has been about the profound disenchantment of the preceding intellectual generation, those who came of age in the decade following World War II. The late Richard Rorty, himself a member of that demographic cohort, proposed in the afterword of his *Philosophy and Social Hope* that one of the main features of "postmodernism" (a word he did not have much use for) has been a perceived loss of unity. In Rorty's words, "This sense of loss results from the confluence of a philosophical movement which is now a century old with the realization that the institutions of liberal democracy might not endure. The sense that everything has recently fallen to pieces results from combining a renunciation of the traditional theologico-metaphysical belief that Reality and Truth are One—that there is One True Account of How Things Really Are—with the inability to believe that things are going to get better" (263).

The French context provides ample evidence of this confluence of philosophical anxiety and historical pessimism among the fin-de-siècle intelligentsia. But the same was not true of the rest of the population. Interestingly enough, opinion polls taken between 1980 and 2000 showed that many in France did not share the despondency of the country's cultural elites. Despite the dramatic rise in the rate of electoral abstentions throughout the 1980s, by the end of the decade confidence in political institutions remained quite high among a people known for their chronic distrust of institutional power. Sixty percent of respondents still had a positive opinion of the "workings of democracy" (slightly up from 1985) and 61 percent of them thought that politics was "an honorable activity," even though they remained critical of the political class (more than half considered career politicians "distant" and "not conscientious"). Eight respondents out of ten considered the National Assembly as a "useful" institution.¹ There was certainly no sign of a crisis in political representations among the professional classes or among left-wing voters: three-quarters of those in upper-management positions (*cadres supérieurs*) and 70 percent of Socialist voters held a high opinion of French democracy.

A January 1989 poll dedicated to "the image of public services" showed comparable results. Three out of five respondents declared that public services "worked well" (including 71 percent of the elderly): so much for the collapse of the nation-state. Eighty-two percent of Corsicans opposed independence: so much for the erosion of the centralist Jacobin ideology. Ninety-four percent of teenagers said they got along fine with their parents, and 75 percent of them said that their elders had taught them the value of hard work: so much for the dissolution of the family and the decline of the work ethic. Three-quarters of Muslim respondents were satisfied with the "conditions of the practice of Islam," and 71 percent of them favored the public school system over the creation of private religious schools: so much for the immigrants' inability to express their cultural and religious specificity (the view from the Left) or unwillingness to accept national secular values (the argument from the Right). As for the crisis of the public schools, a recurrent theme in the media and among doom-and-gloom essayists, 81 percent of respondents to a summer 2001 poll financed by the major teachers' union (Syndicat national des enseignements de second degré) were satisfied with their children's junior high schools, while more than 90 percent of those polled remained confident that the upcoming back-to-school period would happen without a hitch. Less than a quarter of the respondents declared that the school system worked poorly or very poorly.²

A comparative study of public opinion conducted in December 1985 and February 1993 showed remarkable stability across time. Confidence in the family and education were up one point during the period (93 percent and 86 percent, respectively, in 1993),³ while the public's confidence in schoolteachers had been steadily increasing since 1981. A majority of those surveyed still viewed the institutions of the Fifth Republic and the state administration positively (58 percent and 53 percent in 1993, 56 percent and 52 percent in

---

1. SOFRES, *L'état de l'opinion*, 1990, 163, 165, 167, 166.
2. SOFRES, *L'état de l'opinion*, 2002, 185, 200, 205, 200, 138, 183, 184, 139. In a *Nouvel Observateur* survey published in June 1993, 88 percent of the respondents said they were personally happy, while 72 percent believed other people to be less happy than they were. Satisfaction with one's situation went hand in hand with a more sanguine view of French society as a whole. The reference to the level of happiness among French people is in SOFRES, *L'état de l'opinion*, 1994, 242–43.
3. SOFRES, *L'état de l'opinion*, 1994, 221.

1985).⁴ In 1993, 71 percent had faith in the military, 70 percent in the police, 73 percent in the elementary and secondary schools, 72 percent in the universities, and 78 percent in the elite *grandes écoles*.⁵ Support of the state implies both high expectations of its performance and a willingness to defend it against neoliberal threats. Eight of ten individuals polled in a survey published in *La Croix* in 1992 found it "normal that the state should contribute to finance culture."⁶ At the same time, a plurality of respondents to public polls seemed to share with critical intellectuals a distrust of globalization and big business (only 29 percent of the respondents in 1993 had confidence in multinational corporations, and 30 percent in the stock exchange).⁷ The French attachment to state institutions explains the recurring mobilization (in 1981, 1995, and 2006) against attempts to dismantle the welfare state. In July 2001, a large majority said that "there were not enough rules to protect citizens" (76 percent) and the environment (85 percent overall, 93 percent among the young) against globalization.⁸

While "ordinary" French citizens seemed to share with many intellectuals and politicians a desire to preserve the best of the national culture of solidarity, they often were more willing than the elites to tailor the country's historical legacy to new social demands and expectations, as the public support for *la parité* (gender parity on electoral lists) clearly showed in 2000. Media pundits and television philosophers warned that parity would amount to introducing "Anglo-Saxon" quotas in the electoral process, thereby undermining the national understanding of the democratic principle of equality before the law, interpreted as excluding gender (or any other specific, "nonuniversal" individual characteristic) as a distinctive criterion for political eligibility. Antiparity advocates hoped the supposedly conservative bent of public opinion would reject what they portrayed as a quasi-apocalyptic blow to the national psyche. And yet several surveys indicated that ordinary citizens were more ready for the change than opinion makers had expected them to be. To everyone's surprise, parity became law in a matter of months (which does not mean there is no longer any resistance to its implementation).

Younger educators' views of their social role illustrate the extent to which the culture of self-expression and individual rights has transformed expectations of public education. In this respect, they continuously part company

---

4. Ibid., 236.
5. Ibid., 221.
6. Ibid., 244.
7. Ibid., 226.
8. SOFRES, *L'état de l'opinion*, 2002, 119–20.

with the orthodox supporters of the republican model of rationalist pedagogy as the basis for the formation of the citizenry's moral character. While 54 percent of all teachers declared it was impossible to ensure the success of every student, half of their junior colleagues put the "blossoming out" of the child as the main goal of schooling. Only 23 percent of young educators said their priority was to create citizens, and only 19 percent of them saw their main role as the transmission of knowledge, the two foundational principles of Third Republic pedagogical ideology. Opinions regarding the ethical dimension of education also showed a marked difference between the population at large and the younger generations. Sixty-one percent of all respondents to a 1999 poll declared that the main goal of the school system should be to promote discipline and effort, but only 20 percent of teachers, and 8 percent of the younger ones, agreed. Eighty-seven percent of the younger educators viewed their primary function as teaching students to think critically.[9]

The cultural gap between the youth and those among their elders who have been shaping public opinion in France for more than a quarter century came to the fore once again during the *banlieue* uprisings of 2005. While the usual establishment commentators insisted on ascribing the violence to society's inability to disseminate the much-vaunted "French model of integration" among the "youth born of immigration," a new generation of social scientists and journalists reassessed the past history of assimilation, immigration policies, and race relations, examined the country's current failure to ensure justice and equality for all, and searched for ways of imagining a national culture of inclusion. The debates among the political class over the distinction between "affirmative action" and "positive discrimination" discussed in the previous chapter, and the need to borrow models, ideas, and vocabularies from Britain, the United States, and other countries to deal more satisfactorily with multiculturalism and racial discrimination, are signs that a profound reevaluation is underway.

Sarkozy's iconoclastic presidential habitus is more than just image, style, and spin—it does represent a significant cultural change. The cadre of young technocrats who make up his administration are more intent on "reforming" the French economic and political institutions and "modernizing" the country, and perhaps are closer to achieving these goals, despite the current financial and economic crisis, than their predecessors in previous right-wing administrations. In contrast, most of the scholars and public intellectuals, who

---

9. "Les priorités de l'école," SOFRES, *L'état de l'opinion*, 2002, 190–91.

for the last thirty years have been on the forefront of the French culture wars, were born between 1930 and 1945. They grew up in a world in which progressive rationalism was under attack from a coalition of reactionary, religious, antimodernist forces, from monarchist Catholicism (*pétainisme*) to fascism, all intent on turning back the clock, erasing the memory of the French Revolution and its institutional incarnation in the secular Republic. The generation who dominated the world of ideas after 1945 shared a political culture inherited from the Résistance movement, in both its Gaullist and communist versions, a culture that combined national pride with a strong transformative agenda, whether reformist or revolutionary.

The transference of the spirit of the Résistance to postwar issues colored the new generation's response to the geopolitical configurations of the fifties and sixties, from the cold war and decolonization to Vietnam and the counterculture. When the specter of postmodernism was raised, many participants in the national debate naturally went back to the ideological framework of their youth. Those who had grown up in left-leaning households read the new developments with lenses borrowed from their parents' experience of, and in some cases struggle against, totalitarianism in the thirties and forties. They treated postmodernism as the return of antimodernism, as another mixture of irrationalism, relativism, and defeatism in the face of an increasingly consumerist capitalism. But the challenge to the Enlightenment worldview that came to be identified with both the Republic and the nation was of a different order, and proved to be much harder to overcome. The new France was not looking to the past, as *la vieille France* of *pétainists*, collaborators, and imperialists had done, but at a rapidly changing present and a frighteningly uncertain future.

The modernist resistance mistook one opponent (postmodernism) for another (antimodernism). In retrospect, the sixties could not be read only as another episode in the revolutionary saga or, on the other hand, as pure collaboration with reactionary forces. The critique of rationalism put forth by Foucault, Deleuze, or Derrida was not simply a throwback to the antirationalism of Barrès and Maurras. Appealing to the spirits of the Résistance and the République to protect against Benjamin's storm of history did not do the trick, because the birth pangs of the new France have not been about erasing the democratic past, as in the days of the great secular religions of fascism and Stalinism, but about demanding *more* democracy, more rights, more equality, more civic liberties, more tolerance, more respect, more security, more government accountability, and, yes, at times in ridiculous, over-the-top, misguided, and self-defeating ways. One of the goals of this book was to document this generational misapprehension of the nature of cultural and political change in post-1968 France, and its consequences for the life of ideas. It is too early to tell how much the current economic crisis will shift the conversation from the apologetics of the free market back to the need for more government intervention. As those who have initiated and policed the public debates since the end of the sixties leave the stage, other actors and other ideas will come to the fore, and the intellectual landscape will change accordingly.

As I noted previously, Julia Kristeva argued in 1998 that France had fallen prey to a serious case of national depression. Interestingly enough, she had remarked a decade earlier that French culture is not prone to melancholia. "Melancholia is not French," she had written in *Black Sun*, because a strong secular and libertine tendency, born in the Renaissance and affirmed with Enlightenment materialism, countered the deep pessimism of Augustinian Christianity. "The rigor of Protestantism or the matriarchal weight of Christian orthodoxy," Kristeva went on, "admits more readily to complicity with the grieving person when it does not beckon him or her into *delectatio morosa*. While it is true that the French Middle Ages rendered sadness by means of delicate tropes, the Gallic, renascent, enlightened tone tended toward levity, eroticism, and rhetoric rather than nihilism. Pascal, Rousseau, and Nerval cut a sorry figure—and they stand as exceptions" (6) when compared, say, to Rabelais, Sade, or Bataille.[10]

If Kristeva is right, then the French may find in themselves the resources to recover from the national depression, and its attendant symptoms, from withdrawal into the self to feelings of insecurity and persecution. In a lecture given at New York University in 1997, Kristeva revisited the theme of "psychoanalysis as antidepressant" she had developed in *Black Sun*. "It is important," she told her American audience, "to restore national confidence as one restores the narcissism or ego ideal of a depressed patient before embarking

---

10. For Kristeva, melancholia affects both atheists and mystics, and the combination of both modalities in the French literary tradition gives rise to the atheistic mysticism she calls "secular sacredness [*sacré laïc*], a kind of radical atheism that might be the only non-vulgar and non-dogmatic form of atheism. . . . I'm thinking less of Fourier than Georges Bataille" (*Dépression nationale*, 49). In *Black Sun*, she wrote that "my depression points to my not knowing how to lose—I have perhaps been unable to find a valid compensation for the loss? It follows that any loss entails the loss of my being—and of Being itself. The depressed person is a radical, sullen atheist" (5). See also, in the same work: "I have assumed depressed persons to be atheistic—deprived of meaning, deprived of values. For them, to fear or to ignore the Beyond would be self-deprecating. Nevertheless, and although atheistic, those in despair are mystics—adhering to the preobject, not believing in Thou, but mute and steadfast devotees of their own inexpressible container" (14).

on the genuine analysis of her resistances and defenses."[11] She picked up again the motif of the return of confidence in *Contre la dépression nationale*, listing her own reasons for trusting the ability of her compatriots to overcome melancholy: "I trust the respect of the public space; the deculpabilization of misery and the solidarity that welcomes it; pride in the cultural heritage; the cultivation of 'enjoyment' and freedom. I distrust the attraction exerted by archaism, nationalism (which is not the nation), and sexism" (71).

Despite their divergent political views on many subjects, Kristeva seemed to share in this particular instance Marcel Gauchet's hope in the regenerative power of civil society as a way out of the repetitive deadlock of melancholy mourning. I quoted in the introduction Gauchet's "long-term optimism" in the ability of ordinary citizens ("farmers, teachers, middle-level managers, railroad workers, and small business owners") to find solutions to the predicament of late modern democracy. Kristeva similarly puts a lot of faith (at least in her 1998 dialogue with Philippe Petit) in the life of associations, which could be "a new version of the nation: both as unifying public space, which provides identity markers and fulfills its role of memory and ideal, i.e., of antidepressant, and as a multiplication of singular contacts, of specific instances of care adapted to a diversity of needs" (70). The failure of what she calls *les idéologies de la promesse* make it all the more urgent to hear, "beyond the national depression, the demand for another civilization" (112).

This "demand for another civilization" has many facets, and though the diagnosis is clear enough (volumes have been devoted to it), the path to recovery is far from obvious. For all the talk about the *refondation* of this and that in the media and in political circles, announcing the dawn of a new morning remains in that sense more descriptive than ascriptive, more diagnostic than programmatic, since it is difficult to find any convincing redefinition of the republican legacy that could really move the debate forward at this point. Another France has come to be in the last two decades, that is beyond dispute, but the language to describe what it is all about, the categories with which to analyze it, have not coalesced yet in any significant and coherent manner. The depressive state is often described as one of *asymbolia*, a lack of words to express the long-suffering grief and the extent of the loss it responds to. Kristeva, who is a practicing psychoanalyst, provides an example of the *asymbolia* of contemporary French culture: during the political unrest of December 1995, one of her patients remarked to her that "it was a good strike, but we did not find the words."[12]

11. Kristeva, *Dépression nationale*, 70.
12. Ibid., 106.

The social movements that have rocked the country, questioned the Republic's complicity with racism, sexism, and colonialism, and further destabilized the already shaky foundations of a wounded collective identity, have been loud enough to be heard, but are they being listened to? Regarding the issue of ethnic diversity, for example, public authorities have made symbolic gestures, such as appointing minority anchors on news television programs (the symbolic, of course, is a key factor of cultural change in a media-run society), but the socioeconomic roots of racial inequalities remain largely unaddressed, no doubt because of their complexity, and because of the cost (both symbolic and material) involved in the successive, and unsuccessful, *plans pour les banlieues* that have been proposed by various administrations for the past twenty years.

Here and there, new signifiers have appeared to name the deadlock and offer ways of going beyond it, words such as "minority" and "diversity" that, a decade ago, were unable to find a semantic niche within the political repertory of republican discourse. A new generation of scholars has been addressing the challenges faced by French society, and I have referred to several of them in this book. A recent book by the sociologist Florence Weber illustrates the way many scholars in France today approach the daunting intellectual task of rearticulating collective representations and practices. Weber ascribes the renewed interest in ethnography in recent years to the large-scale transformations faced by the contemporary world since the end of the cold war. As a consequence, the categories in use since the 1950s to make sense of the relationship between work and social position, national belonging, mass consumption, the welfare state, even the belief in the stability of individual identity, have lost their ability to help people understand and change the social world: "After triumphant modernity, after the postmodern reign of the individual, new collective entities are emerging, new articulations between personal relations and anonymous institutions, new forms of domination as well. The ethnographer, closer to social interactions, to the material world and indigenous perceptions, is well situated to analyze what is moving in the shadows and to help construct new analytical categories that will make it possible, once they are stabilized, to rebuild ways of understanding and acting."[13] In Weber's description, the task of forging new analytical instruments is a work in progress, as long as these interpretive notions remain tentative, experimental, "unstable."

The point is not to do away with the republican tradition. It is too deeply embedded in the French national psyche to be recklessly ignored or radically

13. F. Weber, *Manuel de l'ethnographe*, 15.

displaced. The Republic as conceptual form and cultural norm remains, to paraphrase one of Sartre's best-known phrases (regarding Marxism in the twentieth century), the "unsurpassable horizon" of current French debates. It should, however, be reformulated to fit the new times. The history of the republican idea in France shows that its forms and contents have evolved over time, from the Enlightenment philosophes' recovery of ancient democracy to the *radical-socialistes'* compromise with capitalism and modernity more than a hundred years ago. Unreconstructed institutions are headed for the dustbin of history, but the void that would be left at the heart of French society should the current ideological crisis remain unresolved for too long is a risk nobody should want to take.

The necessity to move on beyond fossilized notions of cultural identity is bound up with the intersubjective dispositions I have described as being part of a required, if painful, work of remembrance. Melanie Klein believed that the successful completion of the mourning work and the attendant overcoming of the depressive position reactivated by the loss of a loved one entailed "regaining trust in external objects and values of various kinds." In her writings on the relation between mourning and depression, she described this process as one of integration, reparation, restoration, and restitution, all words that entail making amends for the past through a work of anamnesis that rescues the "good" object from the damages done to it by the "bad" objects that still haunt the patient's psyche, fueling bouts of guilt and anxiety. Freud's remarked in "Mourning and Melancholia" that it is only "when the work of mourning is completed [that] the ego becomes free and uninhibited again" (245).

France's reckoning with its own past implies that the positive and negative aspects of the republican heritage (as a stand-in for the national psyche as a whole) be remembered together. The cost of remembrance is the price to be paid for being free from the melancholy politics that have held the country in its grasp for more than three decades. The idealization of the glorious past of the nation, from the revolutionary saga to the educational accomplishments of the Third Republic, can no longer obfuscate the dark side of the regime, including its repression of working-class and peasant uprisings, its colonial and postcolonial legacy, and its inability to reverse in recent years the gradual weakening of the social-democratic project that has stood at its core since 1848. The memory wars discussed in chapter 6 are a prime example of this return of the republican repressed and an illustration of the need for the French to collectively face the "bad" objects of the national legacy together with the "good" ones. Renan's description of France's identity as a "daily plebiscite" was based on the desirable forgetting of the violent origins of the nation, whether it meant the revolutionary Terror of 1793–94, or further yet in time, the unspeakable (and, for Renan, better left unspoken) horrors that presided over the gradual unification of the territory, from the Albigensian "crusade" to the religious wars of the sixteenth and seventeenth centuries. Walter Benjamin claimed the opposite, namely, that redemption could only come from the substitution of another memory, that of the oppressed, for the official narratives of those who ruled over them.

Benjamin's melancholy dialectics might be useful to a more balanced assessment of the current "crisis of the future." Drawing on the politically progressive uses of historical memory in Benjamin's "Theses on the Philosophy of History," some recent readings of historical loss complicate Freudian views of melancholia as the failure of the mourning work to reach its healthy, normal conclusion by withdrawing the libido from the lost object. Rather than a uniquely destructive pathological condition, melancholia, as distinguished from nostalgia, could provide an opportunity to rewrite the past and reimagine the future. In the words of David Eng and David Kazanjian, "Benjamin proffers a continuous double take on loss—one version moves and creates, the other slackens and lingers. . . . Indeed, the politics of mourning might be described as that creative process mediating a hopeful or hopeless relationship between loss and history."[14] The response to the dialectics of loss and history in the French context has been complex and contradictory. The tension between loss as creation and loss as paralysis is still unresolved, and the way forward remains unclear. As Pierre Nora has remarked, in a somewhat prophetic tone, there might be a time when "the French have settled on another way of living together, . . . settled on the contours of what will no longer be called identity." When this time comes, "the era of commemoration will be over for good. The tyranny of memory will have endured for only a moment—but it was our moment."[15] Although change is inevitable, and taking place before our very eyes, it is too early to say whether viable alternatives to the current ideological deadlock will emerge or solidify. This is indeed our moment. I have examined some of the ways in which the present predicament came about. Its resolution belongs to the future.

---

14. Eng and Kazanjian, "Introduction," 2. On Benjamin's view of melancholy, see also Butler's "Afterword" in the same volume.

15. Nora, *Realms of Memory*, 3:637.

Bibliography

Abraham, Karl. "Melancholia and Obsessional Neurosis." In *Selected Papers of Karl Abraham, M.D.*, translated by Douglas Bryan and Alex Strachey, 422–32. London: Hogarth, 1927.
Alford, C. Fred. *Melanie Klein and Critical Social Theory: An Account of Politics, Art, and Reason Based on Her Psychoanalytic Theory.* New Haven: Yale University Press, 1989.
Anderson, Perry. "Dégringolade." *London Review of Books*, September 2, 2004.
———. *La pensée tiède: Un regard sur la culture française.* Paris: Seuil, 2005.
———. "Union sucrée." *London Review of Books*, September 23, 2004.
Aron, Raymond. *The Elusive Revolution: Anatomy of a Student Revolt.* Translated by Gordon Clough. New York, Praeger, 1969.
Aubrac, Lucie. *La Résistance expliquée à mes petits-enfants.* Paris: Seuil, 2000.
Audier, Serge. *La pensée anti-68.* Paris: La Découverte, 2009.
Badiou, Alain. *Being and Event.* Translated by Oliver Feltham. London: Continuum, 2007.
———. *Peut-on penser la politique?* Paris: Seuil, 1985.
Balbure, Brigitte. "La mélancolie." *Le Discours psychanalytique* 1 (February 1989): 135–62.
Balbus, Isaac D. *Mourning and Modernity: Essays in the Psychoanalysis of Contemporary Society.* New York: Other Press, 2005.
Balibar, Etienne. *L'Europe, l'Amérique, la guerre: Réflexion sur la médiation européenne.* Paris: La Découverte, 2003.
———. *Les frontières de la démocratie.* Paris: La Découverte, 1992.
Baudrillard, Jean. *The Anti-aesthetic: Essays on Postmodern Culture.* Edited by Hal Foster. Seattle: Bay Press, 1983.
———. *Fatal Strategies.* Edited by Jim Fleming. Translated by Philip Beitchman and W. G. J. Niesluchowski. London: Pluto, 1990.
———. *La gauche divine: Chronique des années 1977–1984.* Paris: Grasset, 1984.
———. *Seduction.* Translated by Brian Singer. New York: St Martin's Press, 1990.
———. *Simulacra and Simulations.* Translated by Sheila Faria Glaser. Ann Arbor: University of Michigan Press, 1996.
Bauman, Zygmunt. *Intimations of Postmodernity.* London: Routledge, 1992.
Baverez, Nicolas. *La France qui tombe: Un constat clinique du déclin français.* Paris: Perrin, 2003.
Baynac, Jacques, Hervé Le Bras, Henri Weber, and Paul Yonnet. "Le mystère '68." *Le Débat* 50 (May–August 1988): 61–78.
Bénéton, Philippe, and Jean Touchard. "Les interprétations de la crise de Mai–Juin 1968." *Revue Française de Science Politique* 20, no. 3 (1970): 503–44.
Benjamin, Walter. *Illuminations: Essays and Reflections.* Edited by Hannah Arendt. Translated by Harry Zohn. New York: Schocken, 1969.

———. "Left-Wing Melancholy." In *Selected Writings*, vol. 2 (1927–1934), edited by Michael W. Jennings, Howard Eiland, and Gary Smith, translated by Rodney Livingstone and others, 423–27. Cambridge: Harvard University Press, 1999.

———. *The Origin of German Tragic Drama*. Translated by John Osborne. London: Verso, 1977.

———. "Theses on the Philosophy of History." In *Illuminations: Essays and Reflections*, edited by Hannah Arendt, translated by Harry Zohn, 253–64. New York: Schocken, 1969.

Bensoussan, Georges. *Histoire de la Shoah*. Paris: PUF, 1997.

Blanchard, Pascal, and Isabelle Veyrat-Masson, eds. *Les guerres de mémoires: La France et son histoire, enjeux politiques, controverses historiques, stratégies médiatiques*. Paris: La Découverte, 2008.

Blanchot, Maurice. "La fin de la philosophie." *Nouvelle Revue Française* 81 (1959): 286–98.

Bourdieu, Pierre. *Acts of Resistance: Against the New Myths of Our Time*. Translated by Richard Nice. Cambridge, U.K.: Polity Press, 1998.

———. *Contre-feux: Propos pour servir à la résistance contre l'invasion néo-libérale*. Paris: Liber-Raisons d'agir, 1998.

———. *Leçon sur la leçon*. Paris: Minuit, 1982.

———. *Pascalian Meditations*. Translated by Richard Nice. Stanford: Stanford University Press, 2000.

———. *Political Interventions: Social Science and Political Action*. Translated by David Fernbach. London: Verso, 2008.

———. *Practical Reason: On the Theory of Action*. Translated by Randal Johnson. Stanford: Stanford University Press, 1998.

———. *The Rules of Art: Genesis and Structure of the Literary Field*. Translated by Susan Emanuel. Stanford: Stanford University Press, 1996.

———. *Sur la télévision*. Paris: Liber-Raisons d'agir, 1996.

Bourdieu, Pierre, and Jean-Claude Passeron. *The Inheritors: French Students and Their Relation to Culture*. Translated by Richard Nice. Chicago: University of Chicago Press, 1979.

Bourdieu, Pierre, and others. *The Weight of the World: Social Suffering in Contemporary Society*. Translated by Priscilla Parkhurst Ferguson and others. Stanford: Stanford University Press, 1999.

Bourg, Julian. *From Revolution to Ethics: May 1968 and Contemporary French Thought*. Montreal: McGill–Queen's University Press, 2007.

Brown, Wendy. "Resisting Left Melancholia." In *Loss: The Politics of Mourning*, edited by David L. Eng and David Kazanjian, 458–65. Berkeley and Los Angeles: University of California Press, 2003.

Bruckner, Pascal. *La mélancolie démocratique*. Paris: Seuil, 1990.

Burrin, Philippe. *Ressentiment et apocalypse: Essai sur l'antisémitisme nazi*. Paris: Seuil, 2004.

Butler, Judith. "After Loss, What Then?" In *Loss: The Politics of Mourning*, edited by David L. Eng and David Kazanjian, 467–73. Berkeley and Los Angeles: University of California Press, 2003.

Calvès, Gwenaële. "Color-Blindness at a Crossroads in Contemporary France." In *Race in France: Interdisciplinary Perspectives on the Politics of Difference*, edited by Herrick Chapman and Laura Levin Frader, 219–26. London: Bergahn Books, 2004.

———. "Pour une analyse (vraiment) critique de la discrimination positive." *Le Débat* 117 (November–December 2001): 163–74.

Castoriadis, Cornelius. "The Anticipated Revolution." In *Political and Social Writings*, edited by David Ames Curtis, vol. 3 (1961–1979), 124–56. Minneapolis: University of Minnesota Press, 1988.

———. "The Crisis of Western Societies." In *The Castoriadis Reader*, edited by David Ames Curtis, 253–66. London: Blackwell, 1997.

———. "Culture in a Democratic Society." In *The Castoriadis Reader*, edited by David Ames Curtis, 338–48. London: Blackwell, 1997.

———. "The Greek *Polis* and the Creation of Democracy." In *Philosophy, Politics, Autonomy*, edited by David Ames Curtis, 81–123. New York: Oxford University Press, 1991.

———. *The Imaginary Institution of Society*. Translated by Kathleen Blamey. Cambridge: MIT Press, 1987.

———. "The Retreat from Autonomy: Post-modernism as Generalized Conformity." *Thesis Eleven* 31, no. 1 (1992): 14–23.

———. *The Rising Tide of Insignificancy*. Translated anonymously. Available online at http://www.notbored.org/RTI.pdf.

Castoriadis, Cornelius, and Edgar Morin. *Mai '68: La brèche*. Paris: Fayard, 1968; rev. ed., Paris: Editions Complexe, 1988.

Charle, Christophe. *Naissance des "intellectuels," 1880–1900*. Paris: Minuit, 1990.

Christofferson, Michael Scott. *French Intellectuals Against the Left: The Antitotalitarian Moment of the 1970s*. New York: Berghahn Books, 2004.

Cohn-Bendit, Daniel. "Allemagne: La jeunesse et le passé." *Le Débat* 51 (September–November 1988): 161–63.

Colombani, Jean-Marie. *Les infortunes de la République*. Paris: Grasset, 2000.

Comte, Bernard. *Une utopie combattante: L'Ecole des cadres d'Uriage, 1940–1942*. Paris: Fayard, 1991.

Conan, Eric, and Henri Rousso. *Vichy: An Ever-Present Past*. Translated by Nathan Bracher. Hanover: University Press of New England, 1998.

Crozier, Michel. "Révolution libérale ou révolte petite bourgeoise?" *Communications* 12, no. 12 (1968): 38–45.

Cusset, François. *Contre-discours de Mai: Ce qu'embaumeurs et fossoyeurs de '68 ne disent pas à leurs héritiers*. Arles: Actes Sud, 2008.

———. *La décennie: Le grand cauchemar des années 1980*. Paris: La Découverte, 2006.

Debray, Régis. *Charles de Gaulle: Futurist of the Nation*. Translated by John Howe. London: Verso, 1994.

———. *Le code et le glaive: Après l'Europe, la nation?* Paris: Albin Michel, 1999.

———. *Contretemps: Eloge des idéaux perdus*. Paris: Gallimard, 1992.

———. *L'Etat séducteur*. Paris: Gallimard, 1993.

———. *Modeste contribution aux discours et cérémonies officielles du dixième anniversaire*. Paris: Maspéro, 1978.

———. *La République expliquée à ma fille*. Paris: Seuil, 1998.

de Certeau, Michel. *The Writing of History*. Translated by Tom Conley. New York: Columbia University Press, 1988.

Delestre, Antoine. *Uriage, une communauté, et une école dans la tourmente, 1940–1945*. Nancy: Presses universitaires de Nancy, 1989.

Deleuze, Gilles, and Michel Foucault. "Les intellectuels et le pouvoir." *L'Arc* 49 (1972): 3–10.

Derrida, Jacques. *Specters of Marx: The State of the Debt, the Work of Mourning, and the New International*. Translated by Peggy Kamuf. London: Routledge, 1994.

Dosse, François. *History of Structuralism*. Translated by Deborah Glassman. 2 vols. Minneapolis: University of Minnesota Press, 1997.
Duval, Julien, and others. *Le "Décembre" des intellectuels français*. Paris: Liber, 1998.
Eco, Umberto. *Apocalypse Postponed*. Edited by Robert Lumley. Bloomington: Indiana University Press, 1994.
Eng, David L., and David Kazanjian. "Introduction: Mourning Remains." In *Loss: The Politics of Mourning*, edited by Eng and Kazanjian, 1–28. Berkeley and Los Angeles: University of California Press, 2003.
Escobedo, Andrew. *Nationalism and Historical Loss in Renaissance England: Foxe, Dee, Spenser, Milton*. Ithaca: Cornell University Press, 2004.
Fabiani, Jean-Louis. *Les philosophes de la République*. Paris: Minuit, 1988.
Fabre, Clarisse, and Eric Fassin. *Liberté, égalité, sexualités: Actualité politique des questions sexuelles*. Paris: Belfond, 2003.
Fassin, Didier, and Eric Fassin, eds. *De la question sociale à la question raciale*. Paris: La Découverte, 2006.
Fassin, Eric. *L'inversion de la question homosexuelle*. Paris: Editions Amsterdam, 2008.
Ferry, Luc, and Alain Renault. *French Philosophy of the Sixties: An Essay on Antihumanism*. Translated by Mary Cattani. Amherst: University of Massachusetts Press, 1990.
Finkielkraut, Alain. *The Defeat of the Mind*. Translated by Judith Friedlander. New York: Columbia University Press, 1995.
Foucault, Michel. *The Essential Foucault*. Edited by Paul Rabinow. New York: New Press, 2003.
——— . *Madness and Civilization: A History of Insanity in the Age of Reason*. Translated by Richard Howard. New York: Vintage, 1988.
——— . "Vérité et pouvoir." *L'Arc* 70 (1977): 22.
Freud, Sigmund. "Mourning and Melancholia." In *The Standard Edition of the Complete Psychological Works of Sigmund Freud*, edited by James Strachey, translated by Joan Riviere, 14:239–60. London: Hogarth Press, 1953–74.
Friedländer, Saul. *Les années de persécution, 1933–1939*. Vol. 1 of *L'Allemagne nazie et les juifs*. Paris: Seuil, 1997.
Fukuyama, Francis. *The End of History and the Last Man*. New York: Free Press, 1992.
Furet, François. "Editorial: Le XIXe siècle et l'intelligence du politique." *Le Débat* 1 (May 1980): 120–25.
——— . *The Passing of an Illusion: The Idea of Communism in the Twentieth Century*. Translated by Deborah Furet. Chicago: University of Chicago Press, 1999.
Furet, François, Jacques Julliard, and Pierre Rosanvallon. *La République du centre: La fin de l'exception française*. Paris: Calmann-Lévy, 1988.
Gallo, Max. *L'amour de la France expliqué à mon fils*. Paris: Seuil, 1999.
Gaspard, Françoise, and Farhad Khosrokhavar. *Le foulard et la République*. Paris: La Découverte, 1995.
Gauchet, Marcel. *La condition historique*. Paris: Stock, 2003.
——— . *La démocratie contre elle-même*. Paris: Gallimard, 2002.
Glazer, Nathan, and Daniel Moynihan. *Beyond the Melting Pot: The Negroes, Puerto Ricans, Jews, Italians, and Irish of New York City*. Cambridge: MIT Press, 1970.
Guénif-Souilamas, Nacira, and Eric Macé. *Les féministes et le garçon arabe*. Paris: Editions de l'Aube, 2004.
Guillebaud, Jean-Claude. *Les années orphelines, 1968–1978*. Paris: Seuil, 1978.
Hall, Stuart. *The Hard Road to Renewal: Thatcherism and the Crisis of the Left*. London: Verso, 1988.

Hartog, François. *Régimes d'historicité: Présentisme et expériences du temps*. Paris: Seuil, 2003.
Hazareesingh, Sudhir. *Intellectuals and the French Communist Party: Disillusion and Decline*. Oxford, U.K.: Clarendon Press, 1991.
Hewlett, Nick. *Badiou, Balibar, Rancière: Re-thinking Emancipation*. London: Continuum, 2007.
Hilberg, Raul. *La destruction des juifs d'Europe*. Paris: Fayard, 1985.
Huyssen, Andreas. *After the Great Divide: Modernism, Mass Culture, Postmodernism*. Bloomington: Indiana University Press, 1986.
Iacub, Marcela. *L'empire du ventre: Pour une autre histoire de la maternité*. Paris: Fayard, 2004.
Jameson, Fredric. *Postmodernism, or the Cultural Logic of Late Capitalism*. London: Verso, 1991.
Judt, Tony. *The Burden of Responsibility: Blum, Camus, Aron, and the French Twentieth Century*. Chicago: University of Chicago Press, 2007.
———. *Past Imperfect: French Intellectuals, 1944–1956*. Berkeley and Los Angeles: University of California Press, 1994.
Keppel, Gilles. *The Revenge of God: The Resurgence of Islam, Christianity, and Judaism in the Modern World*. Translated by Alan Braley. Cambridge, U.K.: Polity Press, 1994.
Kergoat, Jacques. "La fin de la Fondation Saint-Simon." *L'Humanité*, June 30, 1999.
Klein, Melanie. "A Contribution to the Psychogenesis of Manic-Depressive States (1934)." In *Contributions to Psycho-Analysis, 1921–1945*. London: Hogarth Press, 1965.
———. "Mourning and Its Relation to Manic-Depressive States (1940)." In *Contributions to Psycho-Analysis, 1921–1945*. London: Hogarth Press, 1965.
Kriegel, Blandine. *Philosophie de la République*. Paris: Plon, 1998.
Kristeva, Julia. *Black Sun: Depression and Melancholia*. Translated by Leon S. Roudiez. New York: Columbia University Press, 1989.
———. *Contre la dépression nationale*. Paris: Textuel, 1998.
Kuisel, Richard F. "The France We Have Lost: Social, Economic, and Cultural Discontinuities." In *Remaking the Hexagon: The New France in the New Europe*, edited by Gregory Flynn, 31–48. Boulder, Colo.: Westview Press, 1995.
Laclau, Ernesto. "The Time Is Out of Joint." In *Emancipation(s)*. London: Verso, 1996.
Laclau, Ernesto, and Chantal Mouffe. *Hegemony and Socialist Strategy: Toward a Radical Democratic Politics*. London: Verso, 1996.
Lanzmann, Claude. *Shoah*. Paris: Gallimard, 1997.
Laurent, Vincent. "Enquête sur la Fondation Saint-Simon." *Le Monde Diplomatique*, September 1998.
Lepenies, Wolf. *Melancholy and Society*. Translated by Jeremy Gaines and Doris Jones. Cambridge: Harvard University Press, 1992.
Liauzu, Claude. "Non à la loi scélérate!" *L'Histoire* 302 (2005): 52–53.
Lilla, Marc. "The Legitimacy of the Liberal Age." In *New French Thought: Political Philosophy*, edited by Marc Lilla, 3–34. Princeton: Princeton University Press, 1994.
Lindenberg, Daniel. *Le rappel à l'ordre: Enquête sur les nouveaux réactionnaires*. Paris: Seuil, 2002.
Lipovetsky, Gilles. *L'empire de l'éphémère: La mode et son destin dans les sociétés modernes*. Paris: Gallimard, 1987.
———. *L'ère du vide: Essais sur l'individualisme contemporain*. Paris: Gallimard, 1983.
———. "Tout est hyper." *Télérama*, March 13, 2004.
Lipovetsky, Gilles, and Sébastien Charle. *Hypermodern Times*. Translated by Andrew Brown. Cambridge, U.K.: Polity Press, 2005.

Lyotard, Jean-François. *The Postmodern Condition: A Report on Knowledge.* Translated by Brian Massumi. Minneapolis: University of Minnesota Press, 1993.

———. *Tombeau pour l'intellectuel et autres papiers.* Paris: Galilée, 1984.

Mathy, Jean-Philippe. *French Resistance: The French-American Culture Wars.* Minneapolis: University of Minnesota Press, 2000.

Mendras, Henri. *La seconde révolution française 1965–1984.* Paris: Gallimard, 1989.

———. *Social Change in Modern France: Towards a Cultural Anthropology of the Fifth Republic.* Translated by Alistair Cole. Cambridge: Cambridge University Press, 1991.

Mongin, Olivier. *Face au scepticisme: Les mutations du paysage intellectuel ou l'invention de l'intellectuel démocratique.* Paris: La Découverte, 1994.

Montrémy, Jean-Maurice de. "Marcel Gauchet, le franc-tireur des Hautes Etudes." *L'Histoire* 130 (1990): 64–67.

Nachmani, Amikam. *Europe and Its Muslim Minorities: Aspects of Conflict, Attempts at Accord.* Eastbourne, U.K.: Sussex Academic Press, 2009.

Narot, Jean-Franklin. "Mai '68 raconté aux enfants." *Le Débat* 51 (September–November 1988): 179–92.

Ndiaye, Pap. *La condition noire: Essai sur une minorité française.* Paris: Calmann-Lévy, 2007.

Nicolet, Claude. *La République en France: Etat des lieux.* Paris: Seuil, 1992.

Nietzsche, Friedrich. *Basic Writings of Nietzsche.* Translated by Walter Kaufmann. New York: Modern Library, 2000.

Nora, Pierre. "Dix ans de *Débat.*" *Le Débat* 60 (May–August 1990): 3–11.

———. "Que peuvent les intellectuels?" *Le Débat* 1 (May 1980): 3–19.

———, ed. *Realms of Memory.* English-language version edited by Lawrence D. Kritzman. Translated by Arthur Goldhammer. 3 vols. New York: Columbia University Press, 1998.

———. *Rethinking France: Les Lieux de Mémoire.* English-language version edited by David P. Jordan. Translated by Mary Seidman Trouille. 2 vols. Chicago: University of Chicago Press, 1999.

Novak, Michael. *The Rise of the Unmeltable Ethnics: Politics and Culture in the Seventies.* New York: Macmillan, 1972.

Ory, Pascal, and Jean-François Sirinelli. *Les intellectuels en France: De l'affaire Dreyfus à nos jours.* Paris: Armand Colin, 1986.

Pechanski, Denis. *La France des camps, 1938–1946.* Paris: Gallimard, 2002.

Pensky, Max. *Melancholy Dialectics: Walter Benjamin and the Play of Mourning.* Amherst: University of Massachusetts Press, 2001.

Pervillié, Guy. "La confrontation mémoire-histoire en France depuis un an." Colloquium on Results and Perspectives in the History of the Present, Toulouse, France, April 5–6, 2006.

Pétré-Grenouilleau, Olivier. *Les traites négrières: Essai d'histoire globale.* Paris: Gallimard, 2006.

Poliakov, Léon. *Histoire de l'antisémitisme.* 4 vols. Paris: Calmann-Lévy, 1955–77.

Pomian, Krzysztof. "Les avatars de l'identité historique." *Le Débat* 3 (July–August 1980): 114–18.

———. "La crise de l'avenir." In *Sur l'histoire.* Paris: Gallimard, 1999.

Pressac, Jean-Claude. *Les crématoires d'Auschwitz: La machinerie du meurtre de masse.* Paris: CNRS Editions, 1993.

Prochasson, Christophe. *L'empire des émotions: Les historiens dans la mêlée.* Paris: Démopolis, 2008.

Rancière, Jacques. *Dis-agreement: Philosophy and Politics*. Translated by Julie Rose. Minneapolis: University of Minnesota Press, 1998.
Ribbe, Claude. *Napoleon's Crimes: A Blueprint for Hitler*. Oxford, U.K.: Oneworld, 2007.
Ricoeur, Paul. *Memory, History, Forgetting*. Translated by Kathleen Blamey and David Pellauer. Chicago: University of Chicago Press, 2004.
Rieffel, Rémy. *La tribu des clercs: Les intellectuels sous la Vème République*. Paris: Calmann-Lévy, 1993.
Rorty, Richard. *Philosophy and Social Hope*. London: Penguin, 1999.
Rosanvallon, Pierre. "Oublier les modes." *Le Débat* 4 (September 1980): 80–84.
Ross, Kristin. *May 1968 and Its Afterlives*. Chicago: University of Chicago Press, 2002.
Rothberg, Michael. *Multidirectional Memory: Remembering the Holocaust in the Age of Decolonization*. Stanford: Stanford University Press, 2009.
Rouart, Jean-Marie. *Adieu à la France qui s'en va*. Paris: LGF, 2005.
Roudinesco, Elisabeth. *Jacques Lacan: Esquisse d'une vie, histoire d'un système de pensée*. Paris: Fayard, 1993.
Rousso, Henri. *Le syndrome de Vichy: De 1944 à nos jours*. 2nd ed. Paris: Seuil, 1990.
———. *The Vichy Syndrome: History and Memory in France Since 1944*. Translated by Arthur Goldhammer. Cambridge: Harvard University Press, 1991.
Santner, Eric L. *On the Psychotheology of Everyday Life: Reflections on Freud and Rosenzweig*. Chicago: University of Chicago Press, 2001.
———. *Stranded Objects: Mourning, Memory, and Film in Postwar Germany*. Ithaca: Cornell University Press, 1990.
Sartre, Jean-Paul. "L'ami du peuple." In *Situations VIII*. Paris: Gallimard, 1972.
Scott, Joan W. *The Politics of the Veil*. Princeton: Princeton University Press, 2007.
Scribner, Charity. "Left Melancholy." In *Loss: The Politics of Mourning*, edited by David L. Eng and David Kazanjian, 300–319. Berkeley and Los Angeles: University of California Press, 2003.
Silverman, Max. *Facing Postmodernity: Contemporary French Thought on Culture and Society*. London: Routledge, 1999.
Sirinelli, Jean-François. *Intellectuels et passions françaises: Manifestes et pétitions au XXe siècle*. Paris: Fayard, 1990.
SOFRES. *L'état de l'opinion, 1990*. Paris: Seuil, 1990.
———. *L'état de l'opinion, 1994*. Paris: Seuil, 1994.
———. *L'état de l'opinion, 2002*. Paris: Seuil, 2002.
Starr, Peter. *Logic of Failed Revolt: French Theory After May '68*. Stanford: Stanford University Press, 1995.
Stasi, Bernard, ed. *Laïcité et République: Rapport au président de la République*. Paris: La Documentation française, 2004.
Stavrakakis, Yannis. *Lacan and the Political*. London: Routledge, 1999.
Steinberg, Steven. *The Ethnic Myth: Race, Ethnicity, and Class in America*. New York: Scribner, 1981.
Taylor, Charles. *The Ethics of Authenticity*. Cambridge: Harvard University Press, 1991.
Tin, Louis-George. *L'invention de la culture hétérosexuelle*. Paris: Autrement, 2008.
Todd, Emmanuel. *The Making of Modern France: Ideology, Politics, and Culture*. Translated by Anthony and Betty Forster. Oxford, U.K.: Blackwell, 1991.
Todorov, Tzvetan. *L'esprit des Lumières*. Paris: Laffont, 2006.
Toubiana, Eric. *L'héritage et sa psychopathologie*. Paris: PUF, 1988.
Vaisman, Sima. *Parmi les cris, un chant s'élève: Le témoignage exceptionnel d'une femme médecin déportée à Auschwitz*. Paris: Laffont, 2002.

Vattimo, Gianni. *The End of Modernity: Nihilism and Hermeneutics in Post-modern Culture.* Translated by John R. Snyder. Cambridge, U.K.: Polity Press, 1991.
Virilio, Paul. *The Aesthetics of Disappearance.* Translated by Philip Beitchman. New York: Semiotext(e), 1991.
———. *Speed and Politics: An Essay on Dromology.* Translated by Mark Polizzotti. New York: Columbia University Press, 1986.
Weber, Florence. *Manuel de l'ethnographe.* Paris: PUF, 2009.
Weber, Henri. *Que reste-t-il de Mai '68? Essai sur les interprétations des "événements."* Paris: Seuil, 1998.
Weber, Max. "The Prophet." In *The Sociology of Religion*, translated by Ephraim Fischoff. Boston: Beacon Press, 1993.
Weil, Patrick. *Qu'est-ce qu'un Français? Histoire de la nationalité française depuis la révolution.* Paris: Grasset, 2002.
Winock, Michel. "Les affaires Dreyfus." *Vingtième Siècle* 5 (January–March 1985): 19–37.
Yonnet, Paul. *Jeux, modes, et masses: La société française et le moderne, 1945–1985.* Paris: Gallimard, 1985.
Žizek, Slavoj. *The Sublime Object of Ideology.* London: Verso, 1989.
———. *The Ticklish Subject: The Absent Centre of Political Ontology.* London: Verso, 1999.
Zola, Emile. *L'affaire Dreyfus: La vérité en marche.* Paris: Editions Flammarion, 1969.
———. *L'assommoir.* Translated by Leonard Tancock. London: Penguin, 1970.

Index

Abraham, Karl, 45, 227
affirmative action, 18, 202, 210–12, 213, 214, 220
Agulhon, Maurice, 145, 147
Algerian War, 17, 96, 102, 103, 110, 113, 128, 143, 150, 154–55, 157, 215
altermondialistes, 34, 55, 93, 132
anamnesis, 8, 100, 117
Anderson, Perry, 13–14, 227
anti-communitarianism, 124, 162 n. 26, 183, 200, 202–15
anti-totalitarian movement, 31–32, 90, 93, 94 n. 27, 133 n. 6, 164, 205
Aragon, Louis, 171
Aron, Raymond, 27, 88, 227
Aubrac, Lucie, 168, 170–71, 172, 175, 227

Badinter, Elizabeth, 181 n. 2, 202, 203
Badiou, Alain, 35, 36, 37, 43, 141, 227
Balbus, Isaac, 6, 21–24, 227
Balibar, Etienne, 35, 36, 43, 96, 105, 125 n. 53, 227
banlieues, 158, 177 n. 37, 220, 224
Baudrillard, Jean, 66, 67, 136, 227
Bauman, Zygmunt, 52–56, 66, 68, 227
Benjamin, Walter, 2, 14, 22, 23, 38, 40, 44, 221, 226, 227
Ben Jelloun, Tahar, 167 n. 33, 215
Blanchot, Maurice, 38, 42–43, 228
Bonaparte, Napoleon, 41, 160, 175, 196
Bourdieu, Pierre, 3, 15–16, 33, 34, 67, 70, 73, 82, 83, 93, 96–126, 185, 193, 200, 228
Bourg, Julian, 28, 80, 228
Brown, Wendy, 40, 41, 44, 45, 228
Bruckner, Pascal, 3, 85, 86, 228

Calvès, Gwénaële, 209, 211, 228
Castoriadis, Cornelius, 19–20, 26, 27, 37, 45, 57, 58, 75, 229
Catholicism, 2, 32, 59, 60, 61, 89, 93, 116, 190, 195, 196, 197, 207, 220, 221
Charle, Christophe, 102, 108, 229
Chevènement, Jean-Pierre, 131–32, 139, 169

Chirac, Jacques, 16, 103, 127–29, 131, 135, 158, 161, 186, 193, 207, 217
churches and the state, separation of the, 17, 41, 101, 181, 196
Claudel, Paul, 171, 173
Cochin, Augustin, 145
Cohn-Bendit, Daniel, 21, 26, 229
colonialism, 8, 110, 149, 155, 164, 198, 201, 207, 208, 224
communism, 45, 59, 60, 72, 79, 150 n. 12, 195, 221
Corneille, Pierre, 174

Debray, Régis, 26, 27, 36, 66, 76, 115, 133, 134, 136, 137, 139, 169, 170, 172, 176–77, 181 n. 2, 202, 203, 208–9, 229
de Certeau, Michel, 5, 88, 229
déclinisme, 3, 13
de Gaulle, Charles, 41, 42, 47, 55, 135, 144, 152, 175, 203, 206
Deleuze, Gilles, 96–97, 134, 204, 221, 229
Derrida, Jacques, 14, 15, 37–44, 67, 80, 221, 229
de Tocqueville, Alexis, 26, 57, 63, 66, 79 n. 10, 87, 136, 145
deuxième gauche, 94
discrimination positive. See affirmative action
Dreyfus Affair, 100–103, 108, 109, 111, 150, 198, 205
Dumas, Alexandre, 138 n. 10, 174 n. 36

Eluard, Paul, 171
Enlightenment, 2, 17, 38, 41, 51, 57, 76, 109, 116, 118, 120, 123 n. 50, 124, 181, 190 n. 10, 194, 203, 214, 225

Fassin, Eric, 199 n. 17, 201, 230
Ferré, Léo, 171
Ferry, Jules, 198
Ferry, Luc, 26, 67, 72, 92, 230
Fifth Republic, 13, 109, 186, 218
Finkielkraut, Alain, 55, 72, 85, 86, 105, 124, 133, 137, 160, 170, 181 n. 2, 202–5, 230
Fondation Saint-Simon, 47, 92
Foucault, Michel, 28, 67, 72, 80, 85, 96–97, 98, 116, 117, 118–20, 165, 204, 221, 230

236 INDEX

Fourth Republic, 18, 109, 135, 208
French exceptionalism, 55, 111, 133, 137, 172, 186, 214
French Resistance, 167, 168, 172, 175, 221
French Revolution, bicentennial of the, 16, 29, 31, 136, 165
Freud, Sigmund, 8–9, 11–12, 20, 23, 38, 39, 40, 45, 87, 140, 147, 225, 230
Front national, 47, 59, 60, 102, 128, 130–32, 140, 141 n. 15, 153, 176, 195, 199, 200, 206
Fukuyama, Francis, 38, 42, 230
fundamentalism, 7, 125, 183, 198, 199
Furet, François, 29, 46–48, 53, 76, 78, 79, 85, 145, 194, 230

Gallo, Max, 133, 136, 167–70, 172–79, 230
Gauchet, Marcel, 15, 19, 62–65, 66, 67, 69, 78, 79, 81–83, 87, 89, 91, 94, 133, 197, 223, 230
Gaullism, Gaullists, 6, 26, 27, 47, 59, 133, 155, 206, 221
Glucksmann, André, 75
Guillebaud, Jean-Claude, 30, 85 n. 18, 221, 230

Hall, Stuart, 45, 230
Heidegger, Martin, 27, 42, 57
harkis, 150, 151, 155, 156
Holocaust, 103, 143, 144, 146, 147, 148, 149, 160, 163, 168, 205, 208, 215
Hugo, Victor, 138 n. 10, 171, 178
human rights, politics of, 65, 82, 102, 111
hypermodernity, 2, 63, 68, 69

individualism, 15, 64, 66, 68, 93, 197
Islam, 139, 185, 192, 197, 198, 202, 205, 218

Jaurès, Jean, 138 n. 10, 170, 178, 198
Joan of Arc, 176, 200
Jospin, Lionel, 16, 127, 128, 133, 140, 181

Klein, Melanie, 7, 9, 23, 45, 183, 225, 231
Kojève, Alexandre, 42, 43, 45
Kriegel, Blandine, 72, 85, 133, 135, 190 n. 10, 231
Kristeva, Julia, 10, 22, 137–38, 182, 22–23, 231

Lacan, Jacques, 10, 36, 67, 80, 140, 191
laïcité, 17, 133, 136, 139, 156, 167, 169, 172, 177, 181–99
Le Débat, 15, 16, 70, 71–95
Lefort, Claude, 63, 87
left melancholy, 22, 40, 45, 100
Le Pen, Jean-Marie, 16, 93, 127–31, 139, 176
Lévinas, Emmanuel, 38
Lévy, Bernard-Henri, 14, 31, 56, 81, 93, 147
Liauzu, Claude, 157–58, 231

Lindenberg, Daniel, 42, 94, 133, 231
Lipovetsky, Gilles, 26, 32, 66–70, 79 n. 10, 231
loi Taubira, 149, 151, 158, 159, 161
lois mémorielles, 148–51
Lyotard, Jean-François, 8, 15, 48, 50–51, 53, 56, 64, 66, 67, 204, 232

Malraux, André, 138, 178
Maoists, 46, 135, 189
Marx, Karl, 38, 39, 40, 41, 44, 87, 117
Marxism, 15, 26, 38, 41, 42, 44, 54, 63, 64, 79, 80, 91, 202, 225
Michelet, Jules, 141, 142, 145
Mitterrand, François, 46, 71, 72, 113, 138, 203, 217
Morin, Edgar, 26, 27, 28, 37
Moulin, Jean, 138, 138 n. 10, 175, 178
mourning work, 8–9, 23, 38, 39, 69
multiculturalism, 85, 132, 156, 183, 203, 206, 210, 220
Muslims in France, 17, 41, 180, 193, 195–96, 199, 203, 207, 212–13, 218

Nancy, Jean-Luc, 140–41
national-republicans, 6, 93, 124, 134
neo-Jacobins, 16, 46, 56, 122, 123, 192, 194, 200, 205, 213
neoliberalism, 16, 46, 55, 93, 100, 108, 110, 119, 123, 124, 132, 219
Nicolet, Claude, 169, 232
Nietzsche, Friedrich, 2, 42, 44, 57, 87, 118, 171, 232
Noiriel, Gérard, 164–65
Nora, Pierre, 15, 26, 31, 76–81, 89, 92, 145–46, 147–48, 160–61, 168, 226, 232
nostalgia, 6, 7, 8 n. 11, 10, 21, 24, 25, 32, 42, 54, 94, 134
nouveaux philosophes, 49, 80

Obama, Barack, 216

Panthéon, 138, 138 n. 10, 171, 178
parité, 200, 219
Parti Communiste Français. *See* communism
Péguy, Charles, 100, 102, 109, 114, 171, 178
Pétré-Grenouilleau, Olivier, 158–59, 162, 232
pieds-noirs, 150, 151, 155
Pomian, Krzysztof, 74, 84, 103, 232
postmodernism, 2, 7, 8, 15, 26, 46, 49–70, 85, 119, 156, 169, 193, 203, 217, 221, 224

Rancière, Jacques, 35, 37, 43, 125 n. 53, 142, 233
Rémond, René, 161, 162 n. 26, 163
Renan, Ernest, 4, 170, 204, 208, 225, 226
Ribbe, Claude, 159–61, 233
Ricoeur, Paul, 8, 12, 20, 105, 147, 165, 233

Rorty, Richard, 217, 233
Rosanvallon, Pierre, 72, 75, 79 n. 10, 90–92, 94, 233
Rousseau, Jean-Jacques, 66, 80, 138 n. 10, 139, 222
Rousso, Henri, 11–12, 103, 146, 233

Santner, Eric, 6, 7, 13, 140, 233
Sarkozy, Nicolas, 166, 196, 212–13, 216–17, 220
Sartre, Jean-Paul, 15, 28, 55, 64, 71, 72, 80, 84 n. 16, 85, 96, 98, 100, 112, 117, 120, 206, 225
Senghor, Léopold Sédar, 215
Shoa. *See* Holocaust
Silverman, Max, 52, 54, 55, 233
Socialist Party, 49, 61, 72, 93, 94, 110, 113, 136, 155, 203, 206
Stasi Commission, 186–90, 193

Third Republic, 6, 41, 46, 51, 123 n. 50, 135, 166, 190, 193, 208, 225

Todd, Emmanuel, 19, 59–61, 64, 66, 86, 133, 177 n. 37, 233

universalism, 56, 57, 112, 120, 121, 124–25, 134, 135, 136, 156, 207

veil, affairs of the, 17, 137, 180–81, 186, 192, 195, 213
Verlaine, Paul, 171
Vichy France, 6, 11, 17, 22, 93, 101 n. 9, 103, 135, 146, 154, 156, 201, 215
Voltaire, 116, 134, 138 n. 10

Weber, Florence, 224, 234
Weber, Max, 4, 64, 97 n. 4, 116, 117, 164, 234
Winock, Michel, 101–2, 109, 234

Zizek, Slavoj, 10, 190–92, 234
Zola, Emile, 15–16, 73 n. 5, 96, 98–100, 110–17, 119, 120, 126, 134, 138 n. 10

www.ingramcontent.com/pod-product-compliance
Lightning Source LLC
Chambersburg PA
CBHW021401290426
44108CB00010B/333